Martin Butler, Jens Martin Gurr, Olaf Kaltmeier (Eds.)

EthniCities

Metropolitan Cultures and Ethnic Identities in the Americas

 Wissenschaftlicher Verlag Trier

Copublished by

Bilingual Press / Editorial Bilingüe

EthniCities
Metropolitan Cultures and Ethnic Identities in the Americas /
Martin Butler, Jens Martin Gurr, Olaf Kaltmeier (Eds.). -
(Inter-American Studies | Estudios Interamericanos; 3)
Trier : WVT Wissenschaftlicher Verlag Trier, 2011
    ISBN 978-3-86821-310-2
Tempe, AZ : Bilingual Press / Editorial Bilingüe
    ISBN 978-1-931010-81-8

Cover Artwork: Daniel Bläser
Cover Photographs: Elisabeth Hagopian and Marc Simon Rodriguez
Cover Design: Brigitta Disseldorf

Library of Congress Cataloging-in-Publication Data

Ethnicities : metropolitan cultures and ethnic identities in the Americas /
Martin Butler, Jens Martin Gurr, Olaf Kaltmeier (eds.).
    p. cm. -- (Inter-American studies : cultures, societies, history =
Estudios Interamericanos : culturas, sociedades, historia)
    Includes bibliographical references and index.
    ISBN 978-1-931010-81-8 (alk. paper) -- ISBN 978-3-86821-310-2 (alk. paper)
    1. Urbanization--Social aspects--America. 2. Ethnicity--America. 3. America--
Civilization--21st century. I. Butler, Martin, Dr. II. Gurr, Jens Martin, 1974- III.
Kaltmeier, Olaf, 1970-
    HT384.A45E84 2011
    305.80097--dc23

                                            2011019078

© WVT Wissenschaftlicher Verlag Trier, 2011

WVT Wissenschaftlicher Verlag Trier   Copublisher:
Postfach 4005, 54230 Trier   Bilingual Press / Editorial Bilingüe
Bergstraße 27, 54295 Trier   Hispanic Research Center
Tel. 0049 651 41503, Fax 41504   Arizona State University
http://www.wvttrier.de   PO Box 875303
wvt@wvttrier.de   Tempe, AZ 85287-5303
                                             http://www.asu.edu/brp
                                             brp@asu.edu

Martin Butler, Jens Martin Gurr, Olaf Kaltmeier (Eds.)

EthniCities

Metropolitan Cultures and Ethnic Identities in the Americas

INTER-AMERICAN STUDIES
Cultures – Societies – History

ESTUDIOS INTERAMERICANOS
Culturas – Sociedades – Historia

Volume 3

v

CONTENTS

vi

III. PRECARIOUS IDENTITIES: ETHNIC SELVES & COMMUNITIES AND THE CHALLENGE OF THE CITY

* * * * *

Acknowledgments

This volume is based on selected papers delivered during the international and interdisciplinary conference *EthniCities: Ethnicity and Metropolitan Cultures in the Americas* held at the Zentrum für interdisziplinäre Forschung (ZiF) at the University of Bielefeld in March 2009. The conference took place in the context of the year-long ZiF research group *E Pluribus Unum? Ethnic Identities in Transnational Integration Processes in the Americas* organized by Olaf Kaltmeier, Josef Raab, and Sebastian Thies and generously funded by the ZiF. We are very grateful to the ZiF, particularly to Sue Fizell, for so effectively organizing the conference, and to the organizers of the research group for allowing this conference to be part of their stimulating program. Further thanks are due to the Fritz Thyssen Stiftung for most generously funding the conference and for supporting the editorial work on this volume. We would also like to acknowledge the support provided by the University of Duisburg-Essen's Main Research Area "Urban Systems" and the Rector's office as well as by the Department of Anglophone Studies. We are grateful to Erwin Otto from WVT for his support during the editing process and to Josef Raab and Sebastian Thies for including this volume in their series *Inter-American Studies/Estudios Interamericanos*. Particular thanks are due to our research assistants Verena Warda, Katharina Bieloch, Stefanie Albers, and Gregor Pudzich for their professional editorial assistance in formatting and proofreading the volume. We are grateful to Daniel Bläser for the cover artwork and to Elisabeth Hagopian and Marc Simon Rodriguez for providing the photographs used in the cover collage. Thanks also to Ines Fricke-Groenewold and Ulrich Bauer for their help with the formatting of graphics. Finally, we would like to express our gratitude to our contributors for their essays, for their commitment to the venture, and for the pleasant and smooth cooperation in the editing process.

February 2011

Martin Butler, Jens Martin Gurr, and Olaf Kaltmeier

Introduction: On the Intersection between Urban Environments and Ethnic Identities in the Americas

MARTIN BUTLER, JENS MARTIN GURR, AND OLAF KALTMEIER

Over the last decades, processes of urbanization in the Americas and elsewhere have accelerated at an unprecedented pace.[1] Both in the northern and the southern hemisphere, the metropolis has assumed a crucial position, continuously shaping and challenging the living together of literally billions of people. According to the UN-HABITAT Report of the year 2000, almost 80% of the Latin American population, for instance, live in urban regions such as Mexico City, São Paulo, Buenos Aires, Rio de Janeiro, Lima, Bogotá, or Santiago de Chile. Such trends of urbanization can also be observed in the United States, where cities such as Los Angeles, New York, Chicago, or Dallas have been growing at an accelerated pace. Besides these dramatic developments, the recent past has witnessed the emergence of transnational cities in the U.S.-Mexican borderlands, where border towns such as San Diego and Tijuana, or Ciudad Juarez and El Paso, seem to merge in spite of ongoing border patrols.

Yet, as highly complex and dynamic systems, cities in the Americas not only serve as habitats for the majority of people, but also work as economic and political centers both linking peripheral regions with globalizing markets and providing grounds for the emergence of so-called 'global cities' (cf. Sassen). Moreover, taking into consideration the colonial, or postcolonial, condition of the American societies as well as the sharp demarcation line between 'First World' and 'Third World' that characterizes the continent, urban areas have been functioning as nuclei for the negotiation and hybridization of identities, as 'laboratories,' so to speak, for the formation, reformation, and transformation of individuals and communities. Thus, in a globalizing context, urban agglomerations in particular provide spaces for transgressing national and cultural boundaries and for redefining ethnic identities. Moreover, as Brian J. Godfrey observes, along with these dynamics of ethnic encounter in cities, we are witnessing a continuously growing variety of forms of representing urban ethnicity in the media, which underlines the intricate relationship between the shaping of ethnic identities and the metropolis. "Modern technologies of communication and entertainment," as he argues,

---

[1] 2007 is said to have been the year in which, statistically, the number of people living in cities globally surpassed the number of people living in non-urban environments. The annual growth rate of urban populations is currently estimated at 5% (cf. Faßler 12, as well as numerous statistics by the UN and other international organizations readily available on the internet).

only strengthen the roles of urban districts as cultural seedbeds of ethnicity. Television, film, and news media rely on urban landscape images—too often stereotypes—to depict ethnic groups, while advantages in transportation, telecommunication, and money transfer encourage transnational linkages. In short, ethnic representations continue to emerge, now as in the past, in urban America. (331)

It is the examination of this intricate relationship between urban spaces and ethnic identities which all the contributions to this collection are concerned with. From a number of different disciplinary perspectives—ranging from literary and cultural studies via history and sociology to urban geography—they deal with this complex interface in order to come to a closer understanding of how the infrastructural, economic, political, social, and cultural parameters constituting urban environments contribute to shaping, or reshaping, ethnic identities. Scholars both from Europe and from the Americas entered this interdisciplinary dialogue and provide both theoretical approaches towards the relationship between urban culture and ethnic identity as well as case studies from a variety of urban regions in the Americas.

What might suggest itself as a guiding heuristic framework for such an endeavor (due to its particular emphasis on the processual quality of both identity formation and urbanization), and what indeed connects the essays gathered in this collection, is an understanding of the city as an extremely complex and dynamic cybernetic (eco-) system—or 'urban metabolism'[2]—, as something which is subject to constant change and development. This understanding of the city as a 'complex adaptive system' in the sense of the Santa Fe Institute's complexity theory (cf. Miller/Page)[3] not only does justice to the complexity of urban dynamics and interaction,[4] but also satisfies the need expressed by a number of 'second-wave' ecocritics (cf. Buell 23) to apply the theories and findings of earlier ecocritical scholarship to the metropolis, which would help approach the complex interdependence of urban environments and their inhabitants.[5]

---

[2] Organicist conceptions of the city as a single living super-organism have of course been a recurring idea; cf., e.g., the work of the Japanese 'Metabolists' Noboru Kawazoe, Masato Otaka, Kiyonori Kikutakek, and others, who first presented their ideas during the 1960 World Design Conference in Japan (cf. also Alison et al. 126-39; Vanderbeke).

[3] This might also, of course, be conceptualized from other systems-theoretical perspectives.

[4] For the foundations of such an understanding we are indebted to Allen et al. For literary and other medial representations of urban complexity, cf. Gurr/Raussert.

[5] It would seem that, given the strong interest in ecocritical approaches and in urban studies in recent years or even decades, an application of ecocritical paradigms to the study of the metropolis lies close at hand. However, while some forays into this domain have been made (cf. esp. Bennett; Bennett/Teague), most studies in ecocriticism—both classics in the field and more recent work—have remarkably little to say about urban cultures. We therefore propose to heed Bennett's still pertinent warning that "ecocriticism will continue to be a relatively pale and undertheorized field unless and until it more freely ventures into urban environments" ("Urban Challenge" 304). For an attempt at integrating ecocritical approaches into urban cultural studies, cf. Gurr/Butler.

It is important, however, to note that a view of the city as an '(eco)system' does not imply a functionalist or organicist bias. As García Canclini, Martín-Barbero, and others have conclusively demonstrated, some of the problem-laden megacities can no longer be regarded as functional entities and are not perceived as such by their inhabitants. Rather, they frequently disintegrate into chaotic, self-organizing sub-systems largely out of anyone's control. Nor should a view of the city as a system suggest a normative, top-down understanding of urban governance, according to which central control is desirable and 'inorganic' growth and uncontrollable forms of self-organization are inherently problematic. The 'system of the city' is thus neither regarded as a fixed entity nor as an abstract 'container,' but as part of a translocal network of relationships, connections, and interdependencies.

Against this backdrop, emerging urban cultural practices and forms of expression as well as individual and collective identities are necessarily results of processes of hybridization, of *mélange*, of *bricolage*, as they are constantly in flux due to a rapidly changing environment to which they have to adjust. Thus considering both the city as well as urban cultures and identities as dynamic, at times highly unstable and slippery entities, our attention is drawn to the relational, to the in-between, to processes of change and transformation, aspects which are also highlighted in a number of performative and post-structuralist approaches such as *Estudios Culturales Latinoamericanos* (cf., e.g., García Canclini, Martín-Barbero; Yúdice; Navia/Zimmermann; Moraña; Reguillo/Godoy-Anativia), Actor-Network-Theory (cf. Latour), Non-Representational Theory (cf. Thrift), cultural ecology or ecocriticism, and sociological studies on over-complex systems (cf. Urry).

Once we acknowledge the ever-changing nature of urban environments and the processual quality of ethnic identities—and all contributions in this volume explicitly or implicitly do so—, we arrive at a set of guiding questions that is at the very heart of our interdisciplinary dialogue about the interface between cities and ethnicities:

1.) How can we, on a theoretical level, adequately conceptualize the relationship between urban cultural practices and urban ethnic identities?

2.) What are the connections between globalization, migration, and urban ethnicities both historically and in present-day developments?

3.) Which forms and functions of urban cultural practices that contribute to shaping ethnic identities are *specifically* American/Latin American/U.S.-American/Mexican-American...?

4.) Do we witness the emergence of 'new ethnicities' in urban agglomerations in the Americas? If so, how do they come into being and how do they affect urban social interaction and communication?

5.) How do urban actors come to terms with the local, the regional, and the global dimensions of the city, and how do they communicate 'across' different social milieus via different forms of cultural practices?

6.)   How is urban ethnicity represented in literature and the media? And by whom?
      And for what purposes?

Ultimately, all essays in this volume address one (or more) of these questions and set
out to give answers from a particular disciplinary perspective and for a particular
urban region in the Americas, thus providing a range of intriguing insights into the
relationship between ethnic identities and urbanity, while at the same time mapping
the terrain for further research. In this vein, some of the contributions focus on very
specific cultural practices employed by individual or collective actors in processes of
ethnic identity formation in the city, starting from the assumption that these practices
are by no means detached from their urban environment, but, in a number of intricate
ways, are shaped by and tied to a range of infrastructural, architectural, and technological parameters that constitute this environment. At the same time, as these contributions show, individual or collective actors, who are confronted with the restrictions of
a particular metropolitan setting, constantly try to (re-)appropriate, (re-)define, (re-)
arrange, (re-)semioticize this environment for their own ends and purposes, both in
everyday life as well as in different media.[6]

Other contributions in this volume give substance to the above observation that
urban systems are not necessarily self-regulatory, are not necessarily functioning in a
way satisfying the needs and demands of all social, cultural, religious, or ethnic communities. More often than not, as they convincingly illustrate, the metropolis indeed
does not work as an organic whole, but is characterized by processes of exclusion, by
disintegration and the falling apart into a set of urban sub-systems. Thus, what Les
Back, with reference to European cities, describes as the "metropolitan paradox," may
also hold true for the metropolis in the Americas, i.e., that "complex and exhilarating
forms of transcultural production exist simultaneously with the most extreme forms of
violence and racism" (7). Against this backdrop, these contributions are particularly
concerned with the continuous struggles over social, cultural, and economic resources,
thus providing insights into how the city 'works' (or can be made 'workable'), how the
dynamics of the metropolis affect ethnic communities, and how, in turn, ethnic diversity
may contribute to changing social, political, and economic developments within urban
systems.

What is also at stake in a number of essays is the role of the metropolis in processes of globalization (or the role of globalization in the development of cities

---

[6]   Already in 1974, Ulf Hannerz pointed to this (at times highly conflict-laden) interdepen-
      dence between urban environment and ethnic identities: "The study of ethnicity in urban
      communities has as its focus the strains and the congruences between two principles of
      organization. On the one hand there are the cultural, historical, and geographical groupings
      of people who have come to regard themselves or to be regarded by others as being of the
      same kind, irrespective of the roles they play in urban social systems. On the other hand
      there is the functional differentiation of that system itself, with its distribution of tasks and
      resources, with slots to which personnel must be recruited in one way or other, which will
      determine the interests of that personnel to a considerable extent" (37).

respectively). Of course, urban environments are not hermetically sealed entities, but are—socially, culturally, politically, economically, religiously, as well as ethnically—tied to and shaped by dynamics of migration, transfer, and exchange within a globalizing world. Urban agglomerations, as these essays highlight, are embedded in global networks and constitute sites for inter-American, transnational negotiations, for the emergence of cosmopolitan cultures and identities. Nowhere else do we encounter cultural difference, overlap, fusion, and hybridization in such a dense form.[7] The metropolis thus becomes 'cross-cultural,' and it is one of the aims of these essays to describe and examine the role of the city within global contexts.

Due to these different foci, and certainly due to the generally known but hardly ever solved difficulties of interdisciplinary research, it remained a challenge to systematize the manifold perspectives gathered in this volume. To be sure, a 'spatial scale' (including the micro-level of urban actors in their concrete environments, the meso-level of the city as a system, and the macro-level of the city as a node in a global network), though conceptually and heuristically fruitful, did not really turn out to be an adequate device to structure this volume, especially due to the manifold 'overlaps' between the levels; in other words: To clearly separate the 'local' from the 'global,' or the actor from the network, turned out to be close to impossible. Rather, the contributions to this volume can be arranged into three thematic clusters, which, we believe, both represent the scope of this collection and help identify the most important concerns in our project of analyzing and describing the interaction between urban environments and the formation of ethnic identities.

The first part of our collection, "Useable Pasts & Indigenous Identities: Ethnic Heritage, Urban Renewal, and the Politics of Cultural Memory," deals with the manifold strategies of 'using' the (often indigenous) past of ethnic communities to foster collective identities in urban environments, which, more often than not, are thus turned into battlegrounds for conflicting interests and ideologies. Juliana Ströbele-Gregor, for instance, sheds light on the mechanisms of re-incorporating the indigenous in processes of creating and shaping an "Aymara urbanity" in the city of El Alto in Bolivia. She traces the various practices the city's inhabitants make use of to rediscover and revitalize the past and, eventually, to contribute to "a 're-founding' of Bolivia and for politically giving the country an indigenous face."

That indigenous cultures can also be used for urban marketing is shown in Olaf Kaltmeier's contribution, which examines the relationship between cultural heritage and urban cultural economies, particularly focusing on the forms and functions of reconstructing and thus redefining historic city centers. According to Kaltmeier, cities frequently rely on these historic centers as distinguishing features and, as such, as a particular form of cultural capital, which can be used (or rather: abused) in processes of cultural commodification.

---

[7] For a case study focusing on urban popular music, cf. Butler.

Eva Marsch's contribution sheds light on the potential functions of street art in the construction of ethnic identities. After a number of theoretical considerations on the relationship between street art, ethnicity, and urban space, she examines a number of classic as well as contemporary examples from different urban contexts—ranging from the mural tradition to recent graffiti—and explores the visual and textual strategies these forms of urban cultural expression employ to express and (re)negotiate ethnic identities.

Marc Simon Rodriguez's essay is also concerned with street art, focusing on the significance of Latino urban murals for processes of identity formation in ethnic communities; he argues that the mural cityscape works as a 'seismograph' tracking demographic as well as architectural changes in the city; moreover, Latino murals also promote alternative versions of history and, embedded in diverse social movements, contribute to articulating resistance. For a case study, he focuses on Chicago "as a birthplace of Latino art, cross-ethnic, cross-racial muralist movements" and claims that social and art historiography should include these movements and their cultural production "as they attempt to present a national history of Chicano and Latino art in the United States."

From a literary and cultural studies perspective, Cerstin Bauer-Funke also explores the workings of cultural memory and the politics of representation through a close analysis of both the architectonic design of the Plaza de las tres Culturas in Mexico City as well as of a variety of literary renderings of that monument and the historical events associated with it. Conceptualizing the Plaza as a *lieux de mémoire* (*sensu* Nora), Bauer-Funke argues that it indeed bears a particular trans-epochal significance in acts of ethnic identity formation and, as a point of crystallization of collective memories, "has been transformed into an aesthetic *memento mori*" sustaining processes of creating a 'useable past.'

The second part of our collection, "Ethnicities on the Move: Migrations, Mobilities, and the Metropolis," focuses on the multiple forms of ethnic mobility and migration in urban centers in the Americas. Indeed, big cities such as New York, São Paulo, Los Angeles, or Santiago de Chile are shaped by flows of people who come and go, either bringing new cultural practices with them, or leaving parts of their cultural baggage behind. These ethnic and cultural flows, often stimulated by economic and/or political factors, result in a particularly vibrant, but nonetheless conflictual ethnic *mélange*, in which both individuals and collectives seek and claim their very territories. This second part is introduced by Axel Borsdorf and Aloisia Gómez Segovia's contribution, which portrays and explains the patterns of Peruvian immigration to Santiago de Chile by outlining both the reasons for and the consequences of this form of transnational mobility. Providing an impressive range of empirical data, their contribution both makes evident how this migration has been affecting the social, cultural, as well as economic dynamics within urban environments and—via a number of maps—makes visible forms of ethnic (as well as gender) segregation and discrimination that still determine the lives of many Peruvian immigrants and that, unfortunately, seem to be fostered by the Chilean mass media.

In his essay on "Urban Ethnification of Mapuche in Santiago de Chile," Walter Alejandro Imilan is also concerned with Santiago de Chile, as he draws a comprehensive picture of the history and social organization of the Mapuche and sheds light on the consequences of their migration to the city of Santiago, which accelerated in the 1960s. He elaborates on the strategies of ethnic community formation among the migrant Mapuche and, through an ethnographic 'thick description' of a musical performance at the Centro Cultural La Barraca in Santiago, illustrates that the Mapuche identity is particularly hybrid, being based on both traditional cultural practices and specifically urban forms of cultural expression and articulation.

Filmic representations of ethnicity in urban environments are the subject of the essays by Alexandra Ganser and Karin Höpker. Their contributions can be seen as complementary pieces, as they share a theoretical perspective particularly informed by Michel de Certeau and his heuristically useful analytical (and ideological) categories of 'strategies' and 'tactics.' While Höpker examines Jim Jarmusch's *Night on Earth*, focusing on the film's staging of "practices of motion and interaction as a part of everyday itineraries" and illustrating the significance of the cab as a cultural and ethnic 'contact zone,' Ganser's contribution analyzes "the enactment of ethnic (im)mobility" and the representation of the 'ethnic enclave' in Martin Scorsese's *Mean Streets*. Through their dense and highly stimulating readings, the two contributions highlight both the potential of film to render the complex relationship between cityscapes and ethnicity as well as the potential of a Certalian approach to urban cultural practices and forms of expression.

Rüdiger Kunow's contribution sets out to analyze the city as a 'contact zone' of a special kind, i.e., he sheds light on the mobility of germs and their socio-cultural impact on urban dwellers, particularly illustrating how the spreading of communicable diseases affects the representation of the ethnic Other in urban environments. Considering urban landscapes as ecosystems, Kunow unfolds his argument by drawing on two historical case studies—Philadelphia and Kolkata—and convincingly demonstrates how texts from the late 18th to the late 20th century discursively construct diseases, try to make sense of their often incomprehensible causes and consequences, and, at the same time, function as urban imaginaries creating a specific vision of the city as both a cultural and a biological realm.

Finally, the third part of our collection focuses on "Precarious Identities: Ethnic Selves & Communities, and the Challenge of the City," including essays which are particularly concerned with the fragility of ethnic identities in urban agglomerations as well as with the cultural practices which might help overcome the at times highly precarious state of individual as well as communal selves. Paulo Barrera Rivera is concerned with the role of Pentecostal churches in processes of identity formation in the urban periphery of São Paulo. Drawing on empirical data from a field research project, he persuasively shows that these institutions indeed provide social and cultural resources, which may help foster a feeling of shared identity in a region usually characterized by poverty and social disintegration.

Yvonne Riaño also deals with ways of stabilizing fragile communities, examining forms of urban governance in Bogotá since the early 1990s. She particularly focuses on the so-called 'Culture of Citizenship' approach, which was initially developed and implemented by the city's mayor Antanas Mockus. This approach, as Riaño shows, puts special emphasis on the collective well-being of the city's inhabitants and, as a comprehensive and integrated attempt at tackling problems of violence and fear in the Colombian capital, relies both on the responsibility of the individual citizen as well as on forms of decentralized cooperation, thus turning from a rather traditional, economically driven approach to urban governance to an approach predominantly based on social and cultural education.

That the fragility of urban ethnic identities can also be highlighted in medial representations of urban scenarios is illustrated in Rainer Winter and Sebastian Nestler's essay. Their analysis of Alejandro González Iñárritu's celebrated *Amores Perros* is guided by the theoretical assumption that watching a film is a highly active endeavor during which the recipient constantly (re)negotiates her or his identity through processes of appropriation. Winter and Nestler thus argue that film analysis "also offers pedagogic opportunities for intervention." Incorporating ideas from critical media pedagogy into their approach, they develop an innovative perspective from which they set out to analyze the representation of ethnic identities in the film, arguing that its drawing on ethnic stereotypes has to be understood not as a perpetuation of these stereotypes in the first place, but as "a performative subversion of current ethnic clichés, because it confuses rather than confirms certain ideas of ethnicity" and thus portrays ethnic identities as highly fragile and ever-changing constructs.

The three thematic clusters are framed by two contributions which particularly focus on urban ethnicity in processes of globalization—one with a historical, the other with a contemporary perspective—and thus provide the broader context for the phenomena discussed in the other essays: The opening contribution by Christoph Marx meticulously reconstructs the emergence of a particular type of city during a first wave of globalization in the 19th century. Marx argues that cities of this type, such as Chicago, Calgary, Rio, or Melbourne, "were the result and at the same time the motor of globalization" and exclusively appeared in settler colonies. Through a close analysis of two examples—Vancouver and Johannesburg—he shows that globalizing cities, very much in contrast to 'global cities' (*sensu* Sassen), can be regarded as "enclaves of cosmopolitanism within a newly emerging nation state" and were thus sites for cultural and ethnic contact, but also for conflict and racist exclusion. With a particular focus on the effects of globalization on urban ethnic identities in the 21st century, Lawrence A. Herzog closes the volume with an analysis of the history and development of what he calls a "transnational place identity" in the U.S.-Mexico border region, considering this region as a site of economic, social, and cultural exchange and integration, but also as a highly precarious and slippery ground, on which the formation of an identity resembles "a dance between two realities, often contradictory—one old … the other new … one modern, the other post-modern, one planned, the other spontaneous, one rich, the other poor." Focusing on the dynamics in the so-called 'transfrontier metropolis,' he demonstrates that the border region can indeed be characterized as a "connector," a site of creative entrepreneurship and cultural hybridization, while moments of redrawing social, cultural, and economic boundaries seem to prevail at the same time.

Incorporating these manifold perspectives on the relationship between urban environments and both individual and collective identities, this volume has two goals. First, it sets out to emphasize that both an accelerating urbanization and a subsequent increase in ethnic encounters of all kinds, now and then fostered by ever-changing social, political, and economic parameters in a globalizing context, can lead to a highly creative, fruitful, and productive exchange of individuals and communities. The same conditions, however, may also contribute to ethnic exclusion and disintegration, turning the city from a liberating space into an oppressive realm characterized by ethnic segregation and discrimination. Against this backdrop, this volume aims to draw attention to some of the most important factors that will determine the living together of people in the 21st century, not only in the urban centers in the Americas, but worldwide. Second, this book aims to demonstrate the benefits, or rather the necessity, of an interdisciplinary dialogue when it comes to designing a holistic approach to the interface between city and ethnicity. Without neglecting the difficulties inherent in such an interdisciplinary endeavor (which the contributors, time and again, became aware of while exchanging and discussing their perspectives), we very much hope that this dialogue will continue—may this book contribute to it.

Works Cited

Alison, Jane, Marie-Ange Brayer, Frederic Migayrou, and Neil Spiller, eds. *Future City: Experiment and Utopia in Architecture*. London: Thames & Hudson, 2006.

Allen, Peter, Mark Strathern, and James Baldwin. "Complexity: The Integrating Framework for Models of Urban and Regional Systems." *The Dynamics of Complex Urban Systems: An Interdisciplinary Approach*. Ed. Sergio Albeverio, Denise Andrei, Paolo Giordano, and Alberto Cancheri. Heidelberg: Physica, 2008. 21-41.

Back, Les. *New Ethnicities and Urban Culture: Racism and Multiculture in Young Lives*. London: Routledge, 1996.

Bennett, Michael. "From Wide Open Spaces to Metropolitan Places: The Urban Challenge to Ecocriticism." *ISLE: Interdisciplinary Studies in Literature and Environment* 8.1 (2001): 31-52.

———, and David Teague. *The Nature of Cities: Ecocriticism and Urban Environments*. Tucson: U of Arizona P, 1999.

Buell, Lawrence. *The Future of Environmental Criticism: Environmental Crisis and Literary Imagination*. Malden: Blackwell, 2005.

Butler, Martin. "Towards a Topograpy of Hybridization in U.S. Urban Popular Music."
   *"Cornbread and Cuchifritos": Ethnic Identity Politics, Transnationalization, and
   Transculturation in American Urban Popular Music.* Ed. Wilfried Raussert and Michelle
   Habell-Pallán. Inter-American Studies/Estudios Interamericanos 2. Trier and Tempe:
   WVT and Bilingual P, 2011. 105-16.

Faßler, Manfred. "Vorwort: Umbrüche des Städtischen." Faßler. *Die Zukunft des Städtischen:
   Urban Fictions.* München: Fink, 2006. 9-35.

García Canclini, Néstor. "Mexico: Cultural Globalization in a Disintegrating City." *American
   Ethnologist* 22.4 (1995): 743-55.

———. *Hybrid Cultures: Strategies for Entering and Leaving Modernity.* Trans. Christopher
   L. Chiappari and Silvia L. López. Minneapolis: U of Minnesota P, 1995.

———, ed. *Culturas en globalización: América Latina—Europa—Estados Unidos: Libre
   comercio e integración.* Caracas: Nueva Sociedad/CLACSO, 1996.

———. *La globalización imaginada.* Buenos Aires: Paidós Ibérica, 1999.

———. *Consumers and Citizens: Globalization and Multicultural Conflicts.* Trans. George
   Yúdice. Minneapolis: U of Minnesota P, 2001.

———. *Diferentes, desiguales y desconectados: Mapas de la interculturalidad.* Barcelona:
   Gedisa Editorial, 2004.

Godfrey, Brian J. "New Urban Ethnic Landscapes." *Contemporary Ethnic Geographies in
   America.* Ed. Ines M. Miyares and Christopher A. Airriess. Lanham: Rowman &
   Littlefield, 2007. 331-54.

Gurr, Jens Martin, and Martin Butler. "Against the 'Erasure of Memory' in Los Angeles City
   Planning: Strategies of Re-Ethnicizing L.A. in Digital Fiction." *Selling EthniCity: Urban
   Cultural Politics in the Americas.* Ed. Olaf Kaltmeier. London: Ashgate, 2011. 145-63
   (forthcoming).

Gurr, Jens Martin, and Wilfried Raussert, eds. *Cityscapes in the Americas and Beyond: Representations of Urban Complexity in Literature and Film.* Inter-American Studies/
   Estudios Interamericanos 4. Trier and Tempe: WVT and Bilingual P, 2011 (forthcoming).

Hannerz, Ulf. "Ethnicity and Opportunity in Urban America." *Urban Ethnicity.* Ed. Abner
   Cohen. London: Routledge, 1974. Rpt. 2004. 37-76.

Latour, Bruno. *Reassembling the Social: An Introduction to Actor-Network-Theory.* Oxford:
   Oxford UP, 2007.

Martín-Barbero, Jesús. *De los medios a las mediaciones: Comunicación, cultura y hege-
   monía.* Naucalpan: Gili, 1987.

———. *Contemporaneidad latinoamericana y analisis cultural: Conversaciones al
   encuentro de Walter Benjamin.* Princeton: Markus Wiener Publishers, 2003.

Miller, John H., and Scott E. Page. *Complex Adaptive Systems: An Introduction to Compu-
   tational Models of Social Life.* Princeton: Princeton UP, 2007.

Moraña, Mabel, ed. *Espacio urbano, comunicación y violencia en América Latina.* Pittsburgh:
   Instituto Internacional de Literatura Iberoamericana, 2002.

Navia, Patricio, and Marc Zimmerman, eds. *Las ciudades latinoamericanas en el nuevo
   (des)orden mundial.* Mexico: Siglo XXI, 2004.

Reguillo, Rossana, and Marcial Godoy-Anativia, eds. *Ciudades translocales: Espacios, flujos, representación: Perspectivas desde las Américas*. Guadalajara: ITESO, 2005.

Sassen, Saskia. *The Global City: New York, London, Tokyo*. Princeton: Princeton UP, [2]2001.

Thrift, Nigel. *Non-Representational Theories: Space, Politics, Affect*. London: Taylor & Francis, 2007.

Urry, John. *Global Complexity*. Cambridge: Polity P, 2003.

Vanderbeke, Dirk. "The City as a Superorganism." *"The Mighty Heart" or "The Desert in Disguise": The Metropolis between Realism and the Fantastic*. Ed. Anne Hegerfeld, James Fanning, Jürgen Klein, and Dirk Vanderbeke. Tübingen: Stauffenburg Verlag, 2007. 162-83.

Yúdice, George. *The Expediency of Culture: Uses of Culture in the Global Era*. Durham: Duke UP, 2004.

Globalizing Cities: Ethnicity and Racism in Vancouver and Johannesburg in the First Wave of Globalization

CHRISTOPH MARX

The term 'globalization' became common currency only during the 1990s, but the phenomenon itself is much older, of course. The second half of the 19th century was probably the high-tide of globalization. Economic historians emphasize that the world before the First World War was much more global and the world economy much more integrated than between 1914 and the 1960s (cf. James 10-13). World economic production grew by 2.7% on average each year between 1870 and the beginning of the First World War, but foreign trade during the same time increased by 3.5%. This difference is evidence that external trade and economic contacts grew dispropor-tionately (cf. Borchardt 6). This dynamic development was stabilized by the fact that currencies were linked to the gold standard. Technologically, globalization was driven by a number of crucial innovations of the 19th century like the telegraph and the tele-phone, railways, and steam ships. These innovations in turn led to an increasing mobil-ity of people (cf. Belich; Wendt 266ff.; Osterhammel 235ff.). Between 1850 and 1915 about 70 million migrants left their home countries; labor migrants who periodically went back to their countries of origin are not even included in this number (cf. Fischer 36-48, esp. 46). It is not possible to give an exact date when this first wave of global-ization ended, but with the outbreak of the First World War at the latest, a phase of national segmentation and confrontation began, linked to strong efforts towards eco-nomic autarchy. It was only since 1945 that a new phase of increasing integration fol-lowed which gained sustainability during the next decades. From the 1980s onwards, through the digital revolution it accelerated to an extent unheard of before. This intense experience with a completely new situation of interlinkage, of international ex-change, and of growing interdependencies results in the conviction that a new and adequate name for this phenomenon is needed. This is why we call it globalization.

During the last decades of the 19th century, a growing number of states reacted with nationalism to the increasing mobility of capital and migrancy. Economic global-ization and colonial expansion generated ever more cheap labor and encouraged labor migrancy, whereas the governments of nation states came under pressure from their citizens who feared for competition on the job market.[1] Power elites began to im-plement restrictions wherever they could, and the easiest and most popular way to do this was by limiting migrancy.

---

[1] For a good overview, cf. O'Rourke/Williamson, esp. 185-206; on immigration restrictions in Canada, cf. 203; Zolberg, esp. 285ff.

The tremendous economic expansion fostered the growth of big cities, some of which developed into global cities like London, Paris, New York, and later also Tokyo. But there was also a dramatic increase in urban population in many other regions in Europe and elsewhere during the second half of the 19th century: Chicago, Birmingham, Berlin, the Ruhr, Calgary, Shanghai, Singapore, Rio de Janeiro, or Melbourne are just a few examples of a world-wide phenomenon.

In this article I will attempt to identify a special type of city, which is closely connected to this first wave of globalization and which I want to describe as a globalizing city. Cities of this type emerged at about the end of the 19th century, sometimes literally out of nowhere, and they were the result and at the same time the motor of globalization. The historical context of their founding was the creation of nation states, the frightening extent of globalization being defused through nationalism. These cities are a phenomenon restricted to settler colonies. Settler colonies are those countries to which Europeans migrated in order to stay there and which they dominated politically. I want to present and compare two such cities, both of them results and motors of globalization at the same time. One of them came into existence through a mobilizer—the railway—, the other through a stabilizer—gold-mining. In spite of the different impulses which led to their founding, both cities display remarkable parallels in their further development. At the end of my paper, I want to summarize what they have in common, and from there I want to develop some kind of ideal type of a globalizing city.

1.   Vancouver

Native Americans on the west coast trapped sea otters, whose furs brought a good price in China. Members of the Chinese upper class had their winter coats furnished with sea otter furs. During the early 19th century, American traders, mostly from Boston, sold sea otter skins in Guangshou until after a few decades the number of otters was drastically reduced by over-hunting (cf. Gibson ch. 3; Clayton 74). The American traders pulled out of this business and shortly afterwards the United States began to settle the northern part of their west coast, called Oregon territory. This brought them increasingly into conflict with the British to the north of them. The energetic governor of the Hudson's Bay Company, Sir James Douglas, succeeded in securing first Vancouver Island and later, in 1858, annexed as a British colony the territory which was to become British Columbia. British Columbia as a mountainous region was of little use for agriculture, and for this reason the number of settlers remained very small, so that British rule remained precarious. The region was even in danger of being swamped by American immigrants, when gold was found in the Fraser River valley. Because of the constant threat by the expansionist U.S.A., a solution offered itself when the confederation movement in the British colonies in the east opened the possibility of integrating British Columbia into an emergent continental state of Canada. British Columbia joined the Federation of British North America in

1871, although the large prairie and plains regions between the west coast and Manitoba remained under the control of the Hudson's Bay Company. Canada's first Prime Minister John A. Macdonald realized that the building of a transcontinental railway was the best way to create a nation-state out of the different colonial territories in northern North America. Constructing the Canadian Pacific Railway was not only an impressive engineering feat, but also part of nation-building (cf. Creighton 291f.; Glazebrook 45ff.). For this reason the Canadian government spent enormous amounts of capital and considerable political efforts to build the railway from Toronto to the west coast in only five years. The railway company chose as the western terminal a small peninsula at Burrard Inlet, close to which a number of small settlements already existed. When this became public, a wave of land speculation started and a new settlement quickly came into existence. Only three years after its founding this town became incorporated as the city of Vancouver. It grew further to become the metropolis of British Columbia, which in 1891 was already the most urbanized Canadian province with 43% of the population living in cities, by far the most of them in Vancouver with its more than 100,000 inhabitants in 1911 (cf. Barman 189).

The growth of Vancouver was due to the concentration of the lumber industry at Burrard Inlet, because timber was floated and assembled there from all the river mouths and fiords in the region. Timber was processed in Vancouver, then either transported by rail to the east or shipped to Japan in the west. Vancouver became the base of a salmon-processing and canning industry as well, but as the terminal of the railway, it also developed into a service center and an early tourist attraction. Later it grew into an important *entrepôt* and recreation center for the gold diggers who in large numbers went from there to the Yukon in the far north of Canada. The city at the mouth of the Fraser River became a crucial factor for the integration of the far west into the Canadian confederation and was its gateway to the Pacific.

Over a number of decades, the city center slowly shifted to the west; this is the reason why there is still an 'old town' left over from the foundation period, which opens the opportunity to read the founding history of the city in the present town. In the early years, the city had to be secured against flooding by major earth works, and a period of frenetic building started. At the beginning of the 20th century, Vancouver could boast to have the highest building in the British Empire. The city was attractive for immigrants because people from the backyards of London and other industrial cities in the Old World could afford to buy a home with a garden (cf. Holdsworth 11-32).[2] Vancouver during the early years was advertised as a garden city and nourished expectations for a healthy lifestyle combined with social mobility.

The Asian connection still existed from the old days of the fur trade. Its trajectory was turned the other way round, when Indians, Japanese, and Chinese started to migrate to Vancouver.[3] The Japanese were in a position of relative strength because

---

[2] Upper-class immigrants from England were much more drawn to Vancouver Island. For this reason it made a very British impression on visitors (cf. Bosher).

[3] For a general overview on Asian immigration into western Canada, cf. Kalbach.

Japan was an emerging international power and was able to bear diplomatic pressure to protect its citizens. The Indian Sikhs received at least a limited measure of protection as British subjects, migrating from one British colony to another. But the Chinese were the most vulnerable and the prime target for racists and exclusionist politicians, especially because the Chinese empire was obviously a declining power and could not support its citizens overseas.

Conservative groups, influenced by the contemporary fear of the "yellow peril," (Li, *Chinese* 31f.) found common ground with the white working class and formed a xenophobic alliance. Politicians from the city, from the province, and even from the Canadian confederation dramatized the extent of Asian immigration and initiated exclusionary measures. This alliance worked for the exclusion of Chinese immigrants and at the same time built the ideological foundation for a national integration of whites, irrespective of class or ethnicity. The marginalization of the Chinese was aggravated by legal measures, when Canadian citizens of Chinese origin were deprived of their voting rights at the municipal as well as at the national level. Using political depowerment as a pretense, a number of ordinances banned Chinese from public service and from a number of professions, like lawyer or pharmacist, and even from becoming skilled workers in the coal mines (cf. Li, *Chinese* 32f.). From 1885 onwards, only Chinese had to pay a head tax, which was increased several times with the intent to keep immigrants away from Canadian shores (Li, "Reconciling" 127ff.).

Because of the long-established contacts to Guangshou, most Chinese immigrants came from the rural areas close to the Chinese harbor city, the majority from the district of Taishan (cf. Ng 14f.; Gibson 52ff.). The increasingly violent interventions of Europeans and Americans in China led to the destabilization of Chinese agriculture (cf. Li, *Chinese* 17ff.). Many peasants lost their land and could escape starvation only by emigration. Most Chinese immigrants to Canada arrived as indentured laborers, so-called 'coolies.' They sold their labor power for a number of years to a Chinese entrepreneur who in turn financed their passage to America. When they arrived there, they were forced to work as cheap laborers on the railways, in the lumber camps, or in the mines. This traffic in people was intended by the Western powers, who forced China to allow the emigration of its citizens in order to provide industrialized countries and plantation colonies with cheap labor (cf. Zolberg, esp. 289f.). Once there, the Chinese were confronted with a massive hostility from white workers, who identified them as dangerous competitors, because they earned much less than whites (cf. McDonald, esp. 40f., 67). Exclusion sometimes escalated into violent action.

A number of ugly scenes occurred in the mining areas around Vancouver, because the Chinese were abused by their employers as scabs and for reducing white workers' wages. As unfree laborers, they had no influence on these machinations. Fear for their incomes instilled in whites ethnic hatred for people who could easily be identified and who had neither support nor protection from the state authorities. The rabidly xenophobic Californian trade unions sent their agitators to Vancouver, and in 1887 and 1907 tempers rose when a white mob attacked the city's Chinatown, looted shops and put them to the torch (cf. Ormsby 351).[4] In 1887, the provincial government was forced to intervene and to suspend the mayor and the municipal administration, because they had not only tolerated the excesses, but things went so out of hand that the rule of law could no longer be upheld (cf. Anderson 67f.). The politically radical trade union movement accused employers of deliberately introducing Chinese labor in order to draw white workers down to the same low level of incomes. There was no attempt at all to establish co-operation with Chinese workers and to integrate them into a common class-struggle against capitalism.[5] This was in striking contrast to the international outlook of Canadian trade unions and their outspoken advocacy of the rights of other minorities like blacks and even First Nation Canadians. When they spoke about Chinese in particular and about Asians generally, trade union officials used racist language without any restraint, playing on popular prejudices of Chinese being drug addicts, sexually lascivious, and a danger to white women, of being docile workers with a degraded culture, lacking hygiene, and being content with starvation wages. The supposed docility of the Chinese drew the scorn of a labor movement that underlined its aggressive antagonism towards employers as a manly stance, whereas Chinese behavior was denounced as effeminate. Perceptions of white masculinity were constructed in contrast to the supposedly decadent and degenerate 'Asians.' White men were presented and addressed as protectors of white women against the lecherous Asians and at the same time as manly fighters for the rights of the working class (cf. Goutor 549-76).

In the new city of Vancouver, Chinese made their appearance not merely as cheap laborers, but also as business people who were active in the retail trade, as craftsmen and washermen, but they were also doing business on a larger scale in the import-export-trade (cf. Vee, esp. 72ff., 95). A small number of resourceful merchants gave credits to poorer Chinese, so that the Chinese community became integrated through a web of clientelistic relationships. In the founding period of the city, Chinese merchants and business people were active all over the city, usually living in apartments above their business premises. But soon they were forced by the municipal bureaucracy and the mob on the streets to move into one small area south of the city center, so-called Chinatown.

This area of a small number of blocks along Pender Street, just south of what was at the time the city center, became the stage for the simultaneity of globalization and its rejection in the form of the construction of the national through difference. Urban geographer Kay Anderson, who did pathbreaking research on Vancouver's Chinatown,

---

[4] On the cross-border co-operation of anti-Asian agitators, cf. Jensen 43-51; Buchignani/ Indra/Srivastiva 22. Significantly, much of racist-motivated violence against Chinese was not reported in the English language press, whereas the Chinese developed their own public sphere with their own magazines and newspapers (cf. Stanley 218). For a useful overview on Chinese media in western Canada, cf. Sciban.

[5] Working-class radicalism in Canada was nowhere as pronounced as in British Columbia, cf. McDonald, esp. 33, 57.

has pointed to the asymmetry in the naming: There was a 'Chinatown' and a 'Little Tokyo' adjacent to it, but there was no 'Englishtown,' nor a 'Scottishtown' in Vancouver (cf. 80).[6] Anglophone people were the 'normal' Canadians, whereas the Chinese represented the non-national Others. Chinatown was obviously not some nice place where exotic people huddled together; it was rather a monument for the exclusion of foreigners from the emergent nation. "Chinatown remained an Oriental mystique and novelty in urban Canada" (Li, "Reconciling" 130). This was true not only of Vancouver but of most Chinatowns in North America. The irony lies in the fact that today, they are displayed as showpieces of multiculturalism and tolerance, but a few decades ago, Chinatown's inhabitants were subjected to a multitude of petty bureaucratic restrictions and harassment.[7]

After the First World War, the scale of anti-Asian hysteria was on the rise again. Politicians from all political parties poured oil into the flames and even succeeded with their agitation insofar as the federal parliament in Ottawa put the alleged problem of Asian immigration on the agenda. In a carefully arranged and orchestrated debate, politicians from British Columbia piloted the Chinese Immigration Act of 1923 through parliament, which put a complete stop on Chinese immigration for more than 20 years. As Canadian historian Patricia Roy commented: "Every politician who expected electoral success in British Columbia seemed to think it necessary to have an anti-Oriental statement in his record" (249).

The ban on immigration had consequences for Vancouver's Chinatown, of course. Over the years, the demographic imbalance between men and women became critical, because men were not allowed to bring wives or brides from China into Canada. As a result, the birth rate was very low and the Chinese population quickly became over-aged; its numbers declined considerably.[8] These restrictions on immigration were connected with the global downturn of globalization. Statistics on Canada's demographic development reveal that the immigration curve mirrors the sequence of globalizing integration, nationalist disintegration, and a new wave of globalization, as I have sketched it at the beginning of this paper. A couple of years after Chinese immigration was stopped, the last settlement of Native Americans disappeared from the city, too (cf. Stanger-Ross). Politicians and the dominant white population could deceive themselves that they were living in a white city and in a white nation-state. During the Second World War the 8,000 Canadians of Japanese origin living in Vancouver were summarily accused of being a 'fifth column' of the enemy. They were deported and interned in the interior of British Columbia and their properties and belongings were confiscated (cf. Kluckner 29ff.). This included even those persons who had fought in the Canadian army during the First World War (cf. Neary 423-50).

---

[6]   For the link between the construction of race and Chinatown, cf. ch. 3.

[7]   For the influence of racism on daily life in Chinatown, cf. Yee ch. 3.

[8]   On the threat of extinction, cf. Ng 16.

2.   Johannesburg

My second example is a city that came into existence because of gold, which can be regarded as an economically stabilizing factor in the process of globalization. When mineable gold deposits were discovered in South Africa in 1886 south of a chain of hills called the Witwatersrand, a rush of immigration ensued. The city of Johannesburg was built on top of the gold fields and became the economic power-house of southern Africa. Since the gold could not be mined by individual diggers like in California, from the beginning huge investment in machinery and equipment was necessary for industrialized mining. The founding of Johannesburg was marked by the intrusion of fully developed industrial capitalism into a region which hitherto had not been much integrated into market structures and remained a thinly populated country with a predominantly rural economy (cf. Keegan 158ff.).

Johannesburg mushroomed where no settlement had existed before. Only ten years after its founding, 100,000 people lived in the city; the black inhabitants of the mining compounds are not even included in this number. Besides many white immigrants from abroad, there were a number of Indians and a handful of Chinese coming to the emergent metropolis; many black and white migrants came from other parts of southern Africa, but also Jewish refugees, mostly from the Russian Empire, North American, German, and British adventurers and fortune seekers as well as skilled mine workers from Wales and Cornwall. After Johannesburg had been connected with the rapidly expanding railway network, it became a consumer market for agricultural produce, drawing regions from ever greater distances into its orbit of commercialization. The impact of the labor market could be felt even further away, because migrant labor came from the whole sub-continent even as far away as Tanganyika. Whereas black mine-workers were housed in compounds on the mines and were not very visible in early Johannesburg, it was rather different with all those who looked for jobs in the growing service sector (cf. van Onselen). Many of these were Africans, who became the prime target of city planners and segregationist politicians in the years to come.

Black people living in their neighborhoods were not compatible with many whites' conceptions of respectability. So they tried to push them out and forcibly resettled them. In the early years of the 20th century, Africans who did not work in the mining sector usually dwelled in the city itself. They were successively removed first from the city center and later also from the surrounding areas. When the city's boundaries were extended in 1902, with its 212 square kilometers it became the world's second largest city in terms of space, surpassed only by Tokyo at the time. Through this process, new suburbs came under the administrative authority of the city council. The city fathers used their chance to extend segregationist measures to the newly acquired parts.

Even before the war, the conservative government of Paul Kruger excluded white, mainly English-speaking immigrants from the franchise but at the same time supported them in their endeavors to discriminate against Indians and Africans. But it was the much stronger British colonial state that took it upon itself to start measures of restructuring and planning on a scale that anticipated the hubris of city planners in Europe during later decades. This included attempts to restructure the cityscape by resettling Africans, Indians, and Coloreds. As in the old Boer Republics, measures against Indians under British colonial rule were economically motivated and aimed at pushing them out of business and getting rid of competitors to white shop-owners.[9]

Johannesburg was an enclave of cosmopolitanism within a largely rural environment, whose inhabitants perceived the city as alien and as a place of dangerous cultural mixture and racial 'miscegenation.' Contemporary observers and later-day historians frequently compared Johannesburg to Babylon. Johannesburg surpassed Vancouver in the perception of the rural population as a theater of frightening developments. Even the first stirrings of exclusive nationalism could be witnessed at the time among the rural white populace.

The basic structures of later developments were laid during the early days of Johannesburg, the result of contingencies that nevertheless can still be seen in the social geography of the metropolis today. South African urban geographer Keith Beavon in his excellent account of the city's history shows that the original settlement of 1886, today's Central Business District, can be divided into four quadrants. From the very beginning the northwestern quadrant was fraught with problems, at least in the perspective of the municipal government. When the properties were parceled out and auctioned off, a number of Indian businessmen succeeded in getting hold of some of the properties, which they used as stands for their businesses. This led to a falling of prices for properties in the whole quadrant, not because of the lack of capital on the side of the Indians, but because of sheer racism. In the late 19th and early 20th centuries, racism targeted especially so-called 'Asiatics.' This category encompassed the Indians, the tiny Chinese minority, and initially even Jews (cf. Marx 482; Shain 117). Because of the lower real-estate prices, the northwest of Johannesburg became that part of the city where poor whites, Indians, and blacks found a refuge, whereas the other quadrants were used by affluent whites for homes and businesses. This structure of four quadrants expanded with the growth of the city into the adjoining suburbs. Almost all the resettlements within the framework of racial segregation took place in the northwestern regions of Johannesburg. Especially blacks were pushed out ever further from the city center. In 1903 parts of the city center were cleared when an outbreak of plague induced the government to burn down the so-called 'Coolie Location.' The inhabitants, about 1,600 Indians and 1,400 Africans, were dumped 6 kilometers outside the municipal boundaries without any provision for shelter (cf. Beavon 75ff.; Potgieter). Sanitary reasons were used to enforce so-called 'slum clearance' in other

---

[9]   The urban origin of segregationism and apartheid is widely accepted in the literature now; especially Durban was a pioneer in anti-Indian legislation, whereas Kimberley was the laboratory of compound housing for Africans. On Durban, cf. Grest; Swanson. On Kimberley, cf. Turrell. In Johannesburg these developments culminated due to the speed of the city's growth and its economic prominence.

northwestern suburbs where blacks and Indians lived. Whites obviously could only be imagined as victims of epidemics but never as their source. Exclusion and resettlement culminated in the 1950s, when the apartheid government destroyed a number of suburbs, which were completely depopulated, flattened, rebuilt, and then settled with whites. Among them was Sophiatown, a freehold area for blacks, the cradle of South African jazz and of a new urban literature during the 1950s. The government made it a showpiece of its apartheid policy and aptly named the region 'Triomf' after it was resettled with poor whites in the early 1960s (cf. Lodge).

In a parallel movement to this bureaucratic restructuring of black living spaces, an ethnification of the white northern suburbs of Johannesburg took place. One can roughly speak of three major population groups that tended to settle in different urban regions according to their ethnic background, namely Afrikaners, Jews, and English-speaking Christian whites. These ethnic settlement patterns were further subdivided according to social class. Poor Jewish immigrants, for instance, used to stay in the city center at first. As soon as they succeeded in becoming part of the middle-class income groups, they moved north into Yeoville, and yet further north into Houghton or later Sandton in case they became wealthy.

Although antisemitism was rife amongst Christian whites, Jews as white people were safe from any forcible measures, while the xenophobic fears were directed mainly against Indians. Although they were British subjects, the British conquest of the Boer republics including the city of Johannesburg led to a substantial deterioration of their situation. They became the target of high-handed bureaucratic chicanery to push them out of business and if possible even out of South Africa altogether. After the end of the Boer war, the colonial government under pressure from the mine owners resolved to use indentured laborers from China to work the mines. In this way black wages were reduced successfully and for such a long time that real wages only started to increase from the early 1970s. Interestingly, the Afrikaners or Boers, who had been defeated in the Anglo-Boer War only a few years before, started to organize politically when the mine owners introduced Chinese indentured laborers to overcome a shortage of unskilled labor after the war. Resistance was formidable enough to force the government to abandon its policies and to repatriate all Chinese miners to China once their contracts expired. Afrikaner nationalism was built on the perception of cultural differences of people living in the same country. In the case of the Indians, it took the government until the early 1960s to finally acknowledge that they were part of South African society and that a policy of repatriation was an illusion.

Exclusionism motivated by racism was by no means restricted to conservative Afrikaners, but it was wide-spread within the working class, especially after labor became politically organized through the socialist-inclined Labour Party in 1910. Repeated attempts by mine owners to replace expensive white with cheap black labor led to militant resistance. The confrontations escalated in the so-called Rand Revolt in 1922, when the government sent the army in to quell a general strike that had almost escalated into a civil war (cf. Krikler). During the strike, a banner was displayed, which represented a remarkable mixture of left-wing internationalism and racial exclusionism: "Workers of all Countries unite and fight for a White South Africa." The involvement of trade unions and the working class in racist exclusionism in South Africa as well as in Canada did not come about by coincidence. Rather, it was part of a communication network within the British Empire (cf. Huttenback 195; Tinker). Colonial governments as well as working class leaders observed the exclusionary measures applied in other settler colonies and copied them in their own countries. There is obviously a dark side of working-class internationalism which has not yet been sufficiently researched.

After 1924, a new government integrated the working class into the racist power alliance by legalizing their privileged status in the workplace (cf. Yudelman). In this way working-class solidarity across the color line was prevented and class confrontation within the white community was overcome by installing a system of racial privilege. Until the 1950s, Johannesburg developed into the most segregated city in South Africa (cf. Beavon 127). The municipal administration channeled funds into the upgrading of white suburbs and at the same time grossly neglected the black 'townships.' Africans actually subsidized white suburbs with their taxes and fees. When space was needed, it was Africans and Indians who were forcibly resettled ever further from the city center. Most of them landed 20 kilometers outside Johannesburg, where they had to live in a huge conglomeration of settlements without any infrastructure, without any cultural institutions, a city which today counts more than two million inhabitants and which is called Soweto (cf. Bonner/Segal). The Indians and Chinese also became segregated and resettled under the infamous Group Areas Act during the apartheid years. They were excluded from the central business districts and had to live far outside Johannesburg in their own living quarters like Lenasia close to Soweto.

3.   Conclusion

Is it possible to carve out something like an ideal type of the globalizing city? This can only be a first attempt and it must be left for further research to find out if these results are valid for other cities. It is for good reasons that I use the term 'globalizing city' and not 'global cities,' a term Saskia Sassen has coined. She reserves the dignity of 'global city' for those cities like New York, London, or Tokyo which control processes of globalization (cf. Sassen, esp. 72, 76). In contrast to global cities, globalizing cities are enclaves of cosmopolitanism within a newly emerging nation state. They are the driving forces of globalization within a country and at the same time they are the result of globalizing forces. The concept of 'globalizing city' seems to apply almost exclusively to settlement colonies; it could therefore be tested by comparing Johannesburg and Vancouver with other fast-growing cities in settlement colonies and countries of immigration like Brazil, Siberia, or Israel. This makes them a category separate from other cities like Los Angeles, Chicago, or Mexico City, because those cities experienced their decisive growth process when the nation state had already been established. 'Globalizing city' therefore does not signify the global economic function of such a city, but it points at their impact on the self-perception of a settler colony. What did Vancouver and Johannesburg have in common and what distinguished them from other cities? Both were newly founded cities whose most dynamic growth period was right at the beginning of their existence. Within a decade, they achieved the status of a metropolis, although their actual size was not that decisive; what made a difference, however, was their modern outlook in contrast to their rural hinterland.

Both were the yeast of capitalist penetration and—because of their cosmopolitan outlook—they evoked distrust and fear. The reaction came in the form of an exclusionary nationalism which was directed mainly against defenseless and visible minorities like the Indians in South Africa and the Chinese, Japanese, and Sikhs in Vancouver. Africans in Johannesburg were needed as cheap labor, but they became segregated in separate living quarters. White South Africans imagined their country and their cities to be 'white.' What a nation is can be defined only through difference, by distinguishing the self from the Other, so that Indians and Chinese were necessary for the self-assessment of white settler communities as newly emergent, racially and culturally defined nations.

Both cities made enormous efforts to segregate their populations and both failed after a few decades. Not even the tremendous financial and bureaucratic effort by the apartheid state could subordinate the globalizing Johannesburg to the nationalist project of a white nation state. Since the 1990s, Johannesburg has been more cosmopolitan than ever, with the number of African immigrants surpassing that of newcomers from Europe, America, or Asia. Events in 2008 showed that the fears this evoked are still similar, but now it was the African population reacting violently against immigrants they perceived as a threat and as alien (cf. Bonner/Nieftagodien 416ff.). Vancouver nowadays presents its Chinatown as a tourist attraction, advertising the city as a tolerant, cosmopolitan gate to the Pacific. When in 1971 the Canadian nation became redefined as a multicultural instead of a British nation, Vancouver once more became the focal point of an emerging Canadian nationalism (cf. Wickberg, esp. 188).[10] This time, nationalism presented its friendly face and Vancouver was proud of being the pioneer of multiculturalism, the center of national dynamics shifting from the east of Canada to the west. The city is indeed very much influenced by the growing Chinese population and it became part of a Chinese Pacific rim just like Los Angeles, Honolulu, Singapore, or Jakarta. Nevertheless, multicultural Canada is an ambiguous enterprise, because there are still a 'white' majority and 'visible minorities' like the Chinese—their 'visibility' representing a deficiency as seen against the normative Canadianism of the 'white' majority (cf. Wickberg 187ff.).[11]

---

[10] On today's much larger Chinese community in Vancouver as well as in Canada, cf. Deng; on the Sikh community, cf. Nayar.

[11] For a very instructive contribution in this context, cf. Demel.

In these cities of the early 20th century, we can already observe a phenomenon which is often emphasized to be a significant feature only of the present globalization: glocalization. This neologism signifies the dialectics of globalization and local traditions, the simultaneousness of transcending borders and excluding people. It can be understood also in such a way that the global is to be found in the local, with Chinatown in Vancouver and the northwestern part of Johannesburg being not just miniature versions of globalization in the local space. Rather, these cities are the focal points where international connectiveness manifested itself and led to sometimes violent reactions not just in the cities themselves but also in their large rural hinterlands. The contrast between the rural, ethnically much more homogeneous hinterland and the cities mirrors a dichotomy of land and countryside charged with ethnicity. Globalizing cities are interesting case studies, because they allow us to study many conflicts which we might unfortunately see again in the near future, because the latest wave of globalization is presently coming to an end.

Works Cited

Anderson, Kay J. *Vancouver's Chinatown: Racial Discourse in Canada, 1875-1980.* Montreal and Kingston: McGill-Queen's UP, 1991.

Barman, Jean. *The West Beyond the West: A History of British Columbia.* Rev. ed. Toronto, Buffalo, and London: U of Toronto P, 2004.

Beavon, Keith. *Johannesburg: The Making and Shaping of the City.* Pretoria and Leiden: Unisa P and Brill, 2004.

Belich, James. *Replenishing the Earth: The Settler Revolution and the Rise of the Anglo-World, 1783-1939.* Oxford: Oxford UP, 2009.

Bonner, Philip, and Lauren Segal. *Soweto: A History.* Cape Town: Maskew Miller Longman, 1998.

Bonner, Philip, and Noor Nieftagodien. *Alexandra: A History.* Johannesburg: Wits UP, 2008.

Borchardt, Knut. *Globalisierung in historischer Perspektive.* Bayerische Akademie der Wissenschaften, Philosophisch-Historische Klasse, Sitzungsberichte. München: C.H. Beck, 2001.

Bosher, J.F. "Vancouver Island in the Empire." *Journal of Imperial and Commonwealth History* 33.3 (2005): 349-68.

Buchignani, Norman, Doreen M. Indra, and Ram Srivastiva. *Continuous Journey: A Social History of South Asians in Canada.* Toronto: McClelland and Stewart, 1985.

Clayton, Daniel W. *Islands of Truth: The Imperial Fashioning of Vancouver Island.* Vancouver: U of British Columbia P, 2000.

Creighton, Donald. *John A. Macdonald: The Old Chieftain.* Toronto: Macmillan, 1965.

Demel, Walter. "Wie die Chinesen gelb wurden: Ein Beitrag zur Frühgeschichte der Rassentheorien." *Historische Zeitschrift* 255 (1992): 625-66.

Deng, Jinyang, and Gordon J. Walker. "Chinese Acculturation Measurement." *Canadian Ethnic Studies* 3.1 (2007): 187-217.

Fischer, Wolfram. "Dimension und Struktur der Weltwirtschaft im 19. Jahrhundert." Fischer. *Expansion, Integration, Globalisierung: Studien zur Geschichte der Weltwirtschaft.* Göttingen: Vandenhoeck & Ruprecht, 1998.

Gibson, James R. *Otter Skins, Boston Ships, and China Goods: The Maritime Fur Trade of the Northwest Coast, 1785-1841.* Seattle, Montreal, and Kingston: U of Washington P and McGill-Queen's UP, 1992.

Glazebrook, George Parkin de Twenebroker. *A History of Transportation in Canada.* Vol. 2. Toronto and Montreal: McClelland and Stewart, 1970.

Goutor, David. "Constructing the 'Great Menace': Canadian Labour's Opposition to Asian Immigration, 1880-1914." *Canadian Historical Review* 88.4 (2007): 549-76.

Grest, Jeremy. "The Durban City Council and the 'Indian Problem': Local Politics in the 1940s." *The Societies of Southern Africa.* Vol. 14 (Collected Seminar Papers No. 37). London: Institute of Commonwealth Studies, U of London, 1988. 88-95.

Holdsworth, Derick W. "Cottages and Castles for Vancouver Home-Seekers." *Vancouver Past: Essays in Social History.* Ed. Robert A. J. McDonald and Jean Barman. Vancouver: U of British Columbia P, 1986.

Huttenback, Robert. *Racism and Empire: White Settlers and Colored Immigrants in the British Self-Governing Colonies 1830-1931.* Ithaca: Cornell UP, 1976.

James, Harold. *The End of Globalization: Lessons from the Great Depression.* Cambridge, MA: Harvard UP, 2001.

Jensen, Joan M. *Passage from India: Asian Indian Immigrants in North America.* New Haven: Yale UP, 1988.

Kalbach, Madeline A. "Asian Immigration to Western Canada." *Challenging Frontiers: The Canadian West.* Ed. Lory Felske and Beverly Rasporich. Calgary: U of Calgary P, 2004. 251-68.

Keegan, Timothy. *Colonial South Africa and the Origins of the Racial Order.* Cape Town and Johannesburg: David Philip, 1996.

Kluckner, Michael. *Vancouver: The Way It Was.* Vancouver: Whitecap Books, 1984.

Krikler, Jeremy. *The Rand Revolt: The 1922 Insurrection and Racial Killing in South Africa.* Johannesburg: Jonathan Ball, 2005.

Lodge, Tom. "The Destruction of Sophiatown." *Town and Countryside in the Transvaal: Capitalist Penetration and Popular Response.* Ed. Belinda Bozzoli. Johannesburg: Ravan, 1983. 337-64.

Li, Peter S. *Chinese in Canada.* Toronto: Oxford UP, [2]1998.

———. "Reconciling with History: The Chinese Canadian Head Tax Redress." *Journal of Chinese Overseas* 4.1 (2008): 127-40.

Marx, Christoph. *Oxwagon Sentinel: Radical Afrikaner Nationalism and the History of the Ossewabrandwag.* Pretoria and Münster: Unisa P and LIT, 2008.

McDonald, Robert A.J. "Working Class Vancouver, 1886-1914: Urbanism and Class in British Columbia." *Vancouver Past: Essays in Social History*. Ed. McDonald and Jean Barman. Vancouver: U of British Columbia P, 1986. 33-69.

Nayar, Kamala Elizabeth. *The Sikh Diaspora in Vancouver: Three Generations Amid Tradition, Modernity, and Multiculturalism*. Toronto: U of Toronto P, 2004.

Neary, Peter. "Zennosuke Inouye's Land: A Canadian Veterans Affairs Dilemma." *Canadian Historical Review* 85.3 (2004): 423-50.

Ng, Wing Chung. *The Chinese in Vancouver, 1945-80: The Pursuit of Identity and Power*. Vancouver: U of British Columbia P, 1999.

Ormsby, Margaret A. *British Columbia: A History*. Toronto: Macmillan, 1958.

O'Rourke, Kevin H., and Jeffrey G. Williamson. *Globalization and History: The Evolution of a Nineteenth-Century Atlantic Economy*. Cambridge, MA and London: MIT P, 2000.

Osterhammel, Jürgen. *Die Verwandlung der Welt: Eine Geschichte des 19. Jahrhunderts*. München: C.H. Beck, 2009.

Potgieter, A.J. "Die Johannesburgse Stadsraad en die Indiërs en ander Gekleurdes van die Goudstad, 1900-1910." *South African Historical Journal* 12 (1980): 29-47.

Roy, Patricia E. "The Oriental 'Menace' in British Columbia." *Historical Essays on British Columbia*. Ed. J. Friesen and H.K. Ralston. Toronto: McClelland and Stewart, 1976. 243-55.

Sassen, Saskia. "Global City: Internationale Verflechtungen und ihre innerstädtischen Effekte." *New York: Strukturen einer Metropole*. Ed. Hartmut Häußermann and Walter Siebel. Frankfurt/M.: Suhrkamp, 1993. 71-90.

Shain, Milton. *The Roots of Antisemitism in South Africa*. Johannesburg: Wits UP, 1994.

Stanley, Timothy J. "Schooling, White Supremacy, and the Formation of a Chinese Merchant Public in British Columbia." *Making Western Canada: Essays on European Colonization and Settlement*. Ed. Catherine Cavanaugh and Jeremy Mouat. Toronto: Garamond P, 1996. 215-43.

Stanger-Ross, Jordan. "Municipal Colonialism in Vancouver: City Planning and the Conflict over Indian Reserves, 1928-1950s." *Canadian Historical Review* 89.4 (2008): 541-80.

Swanson, Maynard, W. "'The Durban System': Roots of Urban Apartheid in Colonial Natal." *African Studies* 35.3-4 (1976): 159-76.

Tinker, Hugh. *The Banyan Tree: Overseas Emigrants from India, Pakistan, and Bangladesh*. Oxford: Oxford UP, 1977.

Turrell, Rob. "Kimberley's Model Compounds." *Journal of African History* 25 (1984): 59-75.

van Onselen, Charles. *Studies in the Social and Economic History of the Witwatersrand*. 2 vols. Johannesburg: Ravan, 1982.

Vee, Paul. "Sam Kee: A Chinese Business in Early Vancouver." *Vancouver Past: Essays in Social History*. Ed. Robert A.J. McDonald and Jean Barman. Vancouver: U of British Columbia P, 1986. 70-96.

Wendt, Reinhard. *Vom Kolonialismus zur Globalisierung: Europa und die Welt seit 1500*. Paderborn: Schöningh, 2007.

Wickberg, Edgar. "Global Chinese Migrants and Performing Chineseness." *Journal of Chinese Overseas* 3.2 (2007): 177-93.

Yee, Paul. *Saltwater City: An Illustrated History of the Chinese in Vancouver*. Vancouver and Seattle: Douglas & McIntyre and U of Washington P, 1988.

Yudelman, David. *The Emergence of Modern South Africa: State, Capital, and the Incorporation of Organized Labour on the South African Gold Fields, 1902-1939*. Cape Town: David Philip, 1984.

Zolberg, Aristide R. "Global Movements, Global Walls: Responses to Migration, 1885-1925." *Global History and Migrations*. Ed. Wang Gungwu. Boulder: Westview P, 1997. 279-307.

I. USEABLE PASTS & INDIGENOUS IDENTITIES

ETHNIC HERITAGE, URBAN RENEWAL,
AND THE POLITICS OF CULTURAL MEMORY

The Construction of an Indigenous Culture and Identity in El Alto and Its Impact on Everyday Life and in the Political Arena

JULIANA STRÖBELE-GREGOR

1. Introduction: El Alto and the Power of Social Organizations

El Alto—this city situated at a height of 4,000 m above sea level on the scant Bolivian *altiplano* is considered an indigenous and a rebellious city. 61.35% of its residents (15 years or older) self-identified as indigenous in the National Census 2001, most of them as Aymara, the second largest indigenous group in Bolivia.[1] It was from here that in October 2003 the rebellion began which drove the elected president Sanchez de Lozada to resignation and into exile in the United States. Social organizations in La Paz and Cochabamba joined the rebellion. The protagonists included diverse social movements and anti-capitalist interest groups—but above all the indigenous population. They demanded the renunciation of the neoliberal economic model, the re-nationalization of the natural gas and oil sector, and that fundamental services such as water supply and social security be state-owned. Further demands included the convocation of a constituent assembly involving the participation of the indigenous peoples to devise a new constitution with strong participatory rights of the population on all levels. In January 2005, ongoing strikes and demonstrations of El Alto's neighborhood organizations against the privatized water supply of the city forced the subsequent government under the presidency of Carlos D. Mesa to promise the cancellation of the contract with the international water company. The protest activities continued, however, as the controversial points of the water supply and the nationalization of the gas sector had not been solved in accordance with the demands of El Alto and the nation-wide anti-neoliberal movement. In March 2005 President Mesa threatened to resign, arguing that the oppositional social movements rendered the country ungovernable. Despite the threat of resignation, the protest activities, in which El Alto was decisively involved, continued. Consequentially, President Mesa resigned in June 2005. In December 2005 Evo Morales was elected new president with over 53% of the votes. In the Department of La Paz, which includes the city of El Alto, he received over 60% of the votes.

---

[1] Total population of the city El Alto in 2001: 640,958 persons; identified as indigenous: 393,224 persons (cf. INE [Instituto Nacional Estadístico], 2002. <http://www.ine.gov.bo>).

2. A Look at the City

In a newspaper interview in 1991, an anonymous interviewee characterized El Alto as follows: A "giant peripheral area of the metropolis La Paz, this city, with its misery, its legions of unemployed, its lack of urban infrastructure, its enormous population growth, and its dependence on outside forces, is the mirror image of all problems of our country" ("La Ciudad," my translation). At that point, El Alto was officially three years old and numbered roughly 500,000 inhabitants. In 2009, it numbered an estimated one million. In 1988, El Alto was recognized as an independent municipality and thus as a city of its own. Until then, this giant, wide-stretching agglomeration of settlements had been the poor suburb of La Paz, the seat of government situated in the mountain basin (cf. Ströbele-Gregor, "El Alto").

In line with its settlement history, a social differentiation emerged in El Alto that reflects the social geography of the city. The city is "un conglomerado híbrido de distintas experiencias comunales, artesanales, comerciales y obreras que se mueven en el espacio urbano y se entrecruzan cotidianamente de forma fragmentada" ["a hybrid conglomerate of distinct communal, artisan, commercial, and workers' experiences that move within the urban space and intersect in fragmented form on a daily basis"] (Zibechi 1).

The countless boroughs—that is, the spontaneous settlements and the few publicly planned residential areas—can be divided into three large zones with different social structures. In the southern zone, along the mountain basin, one can find a few factories as well as petty bourgeois areas of established migrants as well as villages that have been incorporated into the city. Small skilled-trades workshops and commerce, centering especially on the giant market on the Avenida 16 de Julio, dominate the northern zone. Many of the very poor *campesino* migrants live under extremely miserable conditions on the periphery of the northern zone. The central zone with the commercial and traffic hub Ceja forms the core of El Alto. Here, the city council, the new—similarly hard-won—university, hospitals, etc. are located. All transportation routes have their starting point here; from here the large rural roads depart, which connect La Paz with the other cities of the *altiplano* as well as with the borders to Peru and Chile. Those who live here have achieved a certain economic success. On the periphery of the continually extending central zone, one can find incorporated farm-steads and spontaneous settlements of poor *campesino* migrants. These settlements, too, lack a basic infrastructure. There are garbage and sewage all over the place, and drinking water can be obtained, if at all, from centrally located wells.

El Alto is a young city—not only on the grounds of its foundation history. The majority of the population is less than 30 years old. Who are the inhabitants of this young city?

3. Research Questions and Thesis

The following questions will guide my article:
How do the inhabitants—migrants—construct their identity as *Alteños*? What are the constitutive elements of that identity construction? What significance does this identity have for people's everyday lives and for the political sphere?

My argument is the following: El Alto is a heterogeneous society of migrants who construct their identity as *Alteños* on the basis of their cultures of origin, their precarious living conditions in El Alto, and their tension-ridden relationship to La Paz. Social organizations form an essential element in the *Alteños'* collective organization of life. These are the instruments by means of which people act in the political arena and represent their interests. The *Alteños* are decisive in carrying the political demands for a fundamental political change in Bolivia, for a Bolivia with an indigenous face.

4. Constitutive Elements of the Identity Construction as *Alteños*

4.1. El Alto: City of Migrants

The majority of *Alteños* are low-income indigenous migrants with a rural background. To understand El Alto, a brief look back to their migration history is necessary.

Before the national revolution of 1952, this region of the *altiplano* was mainly *hacienda* property. There were a few factories, the airport, and some scattered markets. Workers had settled here and along the rural roads. The first wave of migration to El Alto occurred during the 1960s. Mainly small-town dwellers and better-off peasants from the *altiplano* were looking for better job opportunities and living conditions as well as access to the educational system for their children in La Paz. Their goals included economic and social rise as well as social integration into the 'revolutionary national state,' constructed with the National Revolution of 1952.

Migration intensified on a massive scale during the 1970s and 1980s. Demographic growth, scarcity of land, ongoing periods of drought, and flood disasters drove poor *campesinos* into the cities—including El Alto. They, too, were looking for new sources of income. Until the end of the 1970s, the general economic situation generated a workforce demand. However, as they had little formal education and spoke insufficient Spanish, most *campesinos* were integrated into the labor market on a very low level. They found work especially within the skilled trades and as domestic servants for the middle and upper class in La Paz or as carriers on the markets. The goal of these migrants was to become independent merchants or to own a very small business. In the following years, the immensely large informal sector emerged from this migration movement. This sector characterizes the economy of El Alto.

The closing of the state-run mines in 1985 triggered a further migration wave. Thousands of families of laid-off miners (*relocalizados*) moved to El Alto (cf. Sandoval/Sostres; Ströbele-Gregor, "El Alto").

As the city council of La Paz provided only little means for expanding the basic infrastructure, living conditions in El Alto were extremely precarious. Therefore, the *Alteños* fought for years to gain independence as a municipality, hoping to thus better solve their problems.

This citizens' movement articulated a new identity of the migrants, now residents (*residentes*), as *Alteños*. This was embedded in the urban Aymara subculture (cf. Albó/Greaves/Sandoval, vols. 1 and 2) that had already emerged in La Paz. The characteristics of this subculture included independent forms of social organization with specific forms of expression, a distinct way of conducting business that included close ties to the communities of origin and the hinterland, an ambivalent attitude toward the state, and—last but not least—a creative drive that manifests itself in El Alto especially in the structure and shaping of the city.

4.2. Culture of Origin: Maintaining Relations to One's Community of Origin

For the *residentes* of peasant background, the community of origin (*comunidad*) and its local culture remain linchpins in their urban lives. Many of the *barrios* or spontaneous settlements have been named after the inhabitants' community of origin. For most of the *residentes*, participating in the Fiesta del Santo o la Santa—the holiday of the patron saint—of their *comunidad de orígen* is essential. This includes, among others, participating materially in the preparation of the holiday, in a dance group, in the traditional rituals and ceremonies. Hereby, the reciprocally organized relations between the people and their *comunidad* are renewed and confirmed. In the Andean context reciprocity is a fundamental principle of action in social, economic, political, and religious life. For the *residentes*, taking up traditional offices in the *comunidad* for a limited period of time is widespread and contributes to one's prestige. Marrying a partner from the *comunidad* or its local vicinity is similarly widespread. Economic relations are a key linking element here: *Residentes* work as merchants who deliver goods from the city to the *comunidad* and agricultural products in the opposite direction, in part for self-supply and in part for the urban markets in El Alto and La Paz. These merchants also serve as social brokers between the *comunidad* and political and service institutions in the city.

4.3. The Culture of Social Organization and *Ciudadanía*

The cultures of origin of the indigenous peasants and miners have marked the forms of urban organization: Here, the principles of organization of the Andean village community converge with those of the miners' movement. The different citizens' associations, in which almost all citizens are organized, are of central importance in El Alto. The task of these organizations is to articulate and represent the interests of the citizens toward municipal authorities, political parties, external sponsors, and the government with the goal of improving the city's infrastructure. These associations further coordinate the social organization of those infrastructure works the residents carry out themselves or in cooperation with external institutions, such as NGOs. These works include, for example, asphalting roads, enlarging schools, or constructing wells to provide drinking water. These citizens' associations range from neighborhood organizations (*Juntas Vecinales*) via borough organizations to the umbrella organization FEJUVE (*Federación de Juntas Vecinales*), the confederation of these associations (cf. Sandoval/Sostres). To these one can add organizations of street residents, in which neighbors both carry out infrastructure improvement works and provide security in their streets.

The other two decisive forms of self-organization include the labor unions and the numerous professional bodies, the *gremios* (for example of furniture makers, of fruit or fish vendors). They, too, have a pyramidal organization structure. Like the FEJUVE, these organizations perform tasks of representing citizens' interests toward municipal and state authorities and also provide and coordinate professional work regulations, regulate and mediate conflicts, and organize infrastructure work. A host of further organizations include mothers', youth, sports, and cultural associations among many others as well as religious communities—very often evangelical groups. There is probably no *Alteño* who does not belong to several organizations. Social organizations are thus central for performing citizenship (*ciudadanía*) in El Alto. Self-organization is the basis upon which *Alteños* shape their life world.

In El Alto, as in Bolivia generally, collective political action is carried out as a culture of a politics of the street (cf. Calderón/Smukler), manifesting itself in strikes, demonstrations, and road blockages that demonstrate assertiveness, but also fiesta parades that create and articulate community. These kinds of acts combine the exertion of pressure on institutions in charge on the one hand with negotiations with state representatives on the other. Based on the crucial historical experience of Bolivians that political representatives, even in times of democracy, mostly used state institutions to serve their own interests and that they rarely lent an attentive ear and granted justice to the subaltern social classes, self-organization is both a part of people's survival strategies and a prerequisite for participation in the political arena. Moreover, it articulates people's local and group-specific identity. In the case of El Alto this means simultaneously to comprehend oneself as *Alteño* and as a member of a professional and a neighborhood group, each with their own distinctive interests.

Scholars often describe El Alto as a rebellious city (cf. Lazar; Zebichi) and the forms of self-organization as 'indigenous democracy.' On this matter, a few critical remarks are in order: The high degree of self-organization and organizational discipline is a specific trait of the Aymara and Quechua and has its cultural roots in the Andean village community as well as in the miners' labor unions. The forms of participation within the socio-political organization are not democratic structures in the sense of a Western representative democracy, even though they include forms of direct democracy among others. One such example would be the participation in the *asamblea*, the plenary meeting that is a central element of all indigenous organizations and also shapes FEJUVE and the professional bodies. The *asamblea* is the place of debate and decision-making. However, the basic principle that participation in the *asamblea* is not voluntary but socially expected and that refusal of participation will be followed by sanctions (cf. Seoane/Nacci 103-04; Lazar 186-88) surely does not correspond to Western concepts of democracy. Yet, these are not what the political culture of the Aymara and Quechua is about. Rather than individuality, the guiding principles of living together are collectivity and group harmony as well as—derived from these—consensus decisions, reciprocity, service for the community, and dignity/respect. These principles also mark political culture in an urban context, even though they are weighted differently. Here, individual interests and competitiveness come to the fore more strongly. However, the principle of socially sanctioning deviant behavior, dissent, or non-fulfillment of an organization's decisions remains intact—with the goal of reestablishing harmony, a sense of community, and to reinforce collective strength and striking power. On the political level, this implies securing clout. There is no minority vote. A breach occurs whenever people prioritize individual interests or fail to achieve consensus, and often those who lose an argument move to another organization or found a new one.

Here, participation is embedded in vertical structures. People have to carry out the resolutions of the elected *dirigentes*, the representatives of the organizational level directly above their own. What renders this possible is organizational discipline, including the power to impose sanctions—in the associations of El Alto these mostly take the form of fines. Centralized planning and a compulsory organizational discipline make up a crucial element for the success of campaigns, such as the rural road blockages of October 2003—in that particular case meant to increase the pressure on the government, to effect the resignation of the president, and to force his successor to integrate the demands of the social movements into his government action.

The notion of representation as it forms the basis of representative democracy has little cultural hold in the 'modern' indigenous associations beyond the local level, even though it is formally and structurally integrated on the local, regional, national, and international levels (cf. Ströbele-Gregor, "Kanon"). The representatives of the FEJUVE or the professional bodies are elected by and accountable to the respective *asamblea*. Yet, the organizations have not internalized the translocal structures they adopted from the labor union movement in order to be able to represent the associations' interest toward the state and also toward international institutions. The social control of the *dirigente*, while largely working on the local level, proves to be unstable on the highest organizational levels. This opens up a space for pursuing individual interests, which fuels mistrust among the basis toward the *dirigentes* and political representatives in particular. This mistrust, however, goes hand in hand with the expectation, based on the principle of reciprocity, that representatives provide the communities they represent with social and material benefits. "Es corrupto pero hace

obras" ["he is corrupt but he gets work done"]—this assessment of a prefect characterizes an accepted form of reciprocity between politicians and community.

This political culture decisively shapes the *Alteños'* interactions, both in the
immediate area of the neighborhood or at work and with external actors, such as the
political parties, NGOs, and churches, and in particular with the state and the 'sister
city' of La Paz. I will discuss these translocal relations in the following.

5.   On Translocal Relations

Translocal relations are the lifeblood of El Alto. This articulates itself not only in the
already mentioned economic relations to the communities of origin of the *residentes*.
All in all, the economy is highly dependent on foreign trade and affected by global
developments. Here are a few brief examples: Currently, the textile and furniture
production in very small business nose-dives because of new import restrictions of the
United States. The companies are now looking for new markets. Another example:
Cocaine kitchens have been established in El Alto, and smuggling and black market
trade play an enormous role here. The functioning of these branches is similarly
dependent on numerous external factors, such as police control and external market
prices. Last but not least, the very widespread small- and smallest-scale informal trade
depends on how much money people have in their purses for consumption in times of
unemployment. Success and decline of business strategies are immediately reflected in
the appearance of the city, for example in the building activities and the increase or
decrease of street commerce.

6.   Tension-Ridden Relation to La Paz

It was La Paz that produced the migrant city El Alto with the face of a giant miserable
modern Andean settlement. For decades, the migrants' gaze was directed toward La
Paz. In the life plans of many, El Alto was only a stepping-stone in their economic and
social advancements. Their goal was an employment and a small house of their own in
one of the migrant quarters of La Paz. Therefore, they accepted the sometimes
miserable living conditions in El Alto for the time being. While this life plan materi-
alized for many of the early migrants, it increasingly failed to do so for those who
came during the 1980s. El Alto finally became the center of their lives. As a consequence, a distinct form of Andean urbanity emerged. At the same time, strong economic, political, social, and cultural relations remain between El Alto and La Paz,
especially as many *Alteños* work or study in the other city. From five o'clock in the
morning until the late evening one can witness an unbroken, never-ending stream of
minibuses going back and forth between El Alto and La Paz.

People have always directed their expectations and demands for a humane
shaping of El Alto to La Paz, the capital of the department and government seat.

Accordingly, both individuals and—in particular—social organizations are seeking contact with political representatives, state institutions, and external sponsors. They back up their demands with a politics of the street. Blackmailing the city in the mountain basin is easy: when *Alteños* block the few access roads, La Paz is lost. By that means, the *Alteños* have managed time and again to wrench the fulfillment of their demands from individual ministries or the government as a whole. The revolt of 2003 and the 2005 'Water War' of El Alto, in which the *Alteños* demanded the cancellation of the contract with the international water company, AISA (Aguas del Illimani S.A.), in which the French company Suez Lyonnaise des Eaux holds 54%, are examples of the power of this strategy. However, these radical measures are only one side of the coin. The other one is the interaction with external actors, especially the representatives of political parties, on the basis of reciprocity as the *Alteños* understand it. This interaction is about building up relations for mutual benefit. Understandably, this works in particular during the run-up to elections. The 'gift' of the *Alteños* is the votes a professional body or a neighborhood organization promises in return for the 'gift' of politicians of investing in their quarter. Demonstrations and citizens' activities accompany such negotiation processes to demonstrate the scale of votes at stake. Where necessity and poverty reign, people in El Alto are highly inventive.

7.   Summary

The symbolic construction of indigenous identity as *Alteños* and the shaping of an Aymara urbanity are rooted in the indigenous culture of the Andean village community, the political culture of migrant miners, and the complex and tension-ridden relation to La Paz. Economically, politically, socially, and culturally, the *Alteños* continue to be closely tied to that city. Even though they live in El Alto, many of them study and work in La Paz. *Alteños* on a daily basis experience the difference between their precarious city on the one hand and La Paz with its attractive center and the neat quarters of the affluent middle and upper classes on the other. Conscious of their extreme disadvantage, the *residentes* have constructed their own dignity as *Alteños* and demonstrate it with self-confidence whenever they deem it necessary. The second and third generations of migrants as well as the young people from rural areas, who have come to El Alto during the past years to study or work in the region, carry the new discourses of indigenous identity and the revitalization or reconstruction of the Aymara culture. Connected to this project is the political demand for a 're-founding' of Bolivia and for politically giving the country an indigenous face. The approval of the new constitution at the National Referendum in 2008 is an important step in that direction.

(Translated from the German by Astrid Haas)

Works Cited

Albó, Javier, Thomas Greaves, and Godofredo Sandoval. *Chukiyawu: La cara aymara de La Paz*. Vols. 1-4. Cuadernos CIPCA. La Paz: CIPCA, 1981; 1982; 1983; 1987.

Calderón, Fernando, and Alicia Szmukler. *La política en las calles*. La Paz: CERES/Plural, 2000.

Instituto Nacional Estadístico (INE). *Censo por población y vivienda*. 2001. <http://www.ine.gov.bo>.

Lazar, Sian. *El Alto, Rebel City: Self and Citizenship in Andean Bolivia*. Durham: Duke UP, 2007.

"La Ciudad El Alto." *Prensa Libre*, Guatemala, 1 Sept. 1991.

Sandoval, Godofredo, and Fernanda Sostres. *La ciudad prometida*. La Paz: Systems/ILDIS, 1989.

Seoane, José A., and María José Nacci. "Movimientos sociales y democracia en América Latina, frente al 'neoliberalismo de guerra.'" *Movimientos sociales y ciudadanía*. Ed. Manuel De la Fuente and Marc Hufty. La Paz: Plural/IUED/NCCR Norte Sud, 2007. 85-126.

Ströbele-Gregor, Juliana. "El Alto: Stadt der Zukunft." *Vom Elend der Metropolen: Lateinamerika—Analysen und Berichte* 14. Ed. Dietmar Dirmoser, Michael Ehrke, Tillmann Evers, Klaus Meschkat, Clarita Müller-Plantenberg, Michael Rediske, and Juliana Ströbele-Gregor. Hamburg: Junius Verlag, 1990. 84-107.

———. "Kanon mit Gegenstimmen: Soziale Bewegungen und Politik in Bolivien." *Jenseits von Subcomandante Marcos und Hugo Chávez: Soziale Bewegungen zwischen Autonomie und Staat: Festschrift für Dieter Boris*. Ed. Stefan Schmalz and Anne Tittor. Hamburg: VSA, 2008. 129-41.

Zibechi, Raul. "El Alto: Un mundo nuevo desde la diferencia." *Pensamiento Crítico*, 2005. <http://www.pensamientocritico.org/rauzibe200905.htm>.

Historic City Centers in Globalization Processes: Cultural Heritage, Urban Renewal, and Postcolonial Memories in the Americas

OLAF KALTMEIER

1. Introduction

It may seem paradoxical that in a phase of accelerated post-Fordist transnationalization processes and cultural hybridization due to more intense cultural interchange and mixture, heritage, or in Spanish *patrimonio*, is also becoming increasingly important. At first glance the conversation about material and non-material cultural elements of the past seems to be a desperate nostalgic effort to confront the transnational dynamics of postmodern *bricolage* and/or cultural homogenization. Nevertheless, heritage not only appeals to shared, pre-reflexive, and often affective dispositions of national and local identities; heritage is also a strategic element in the reconstruction of urban spaces and identities.

As cultural studies scholar George Yúdice has argued, we are today faced with an expediency of culture in the sense that culture itself has lost significance and cultural elements are only perceived and used in connection with economic or political aims. He argues that "culture is increasingly wielded as a resource for both socio-political and economic amelioration" (9). This interpretation of the instrumentalist use of culture echoes the critical readings of Max Horkheimer and Theodor W. Adorno on the culture industry (cf. 128-78). Nevertheless, Yúdice proposes a more ambivalent reading. He rejects a merely instrumental understanding of culture as a resource, as it may be used by rational choice theories, arguing that the "specific transformation of culture into resource epitomizes the emergence of a new episteme, in the Foucauldian sense" (28). Thus, nearly all social relations are understood in cultural terms, and the actors in the social fields are guided by a social imperative to perform their identities in order to maintain or improve their positions in different fields. Here I argue that the textual dimension of performativity that has often been characterized as an act which 'produces that which it names' may also be related to the imaginative production of the city and to its processes of materialization in space. These processes can be shown to be at work in the urban renewal of historic city centers in the Americas. In the following essay I want to explore the recent urban dynamics of a return to the center and of the re-colonialization of urban landscapes in the context of heritage. In doing so, I want to discuss the relation between heritage and urban cultural economies, focusing on the politics of memory and the representation of subaltern sectors in the city.

2.   Return to the Center

The renewed importance of culture is also observed in urban studies with the emergence of city marketing, branding, and urban cultural economy. While the Fordist era in industrialization envisaged a standard consumer and reduced him or her to a function of human needs, post-Fordist production flexibly addresses consumer identities that differ widely in their identitarian dispositions (cf. Bauman; García Canclini, *Consumidores*). This process actually leads corporate interests to foster the emergence of new marketable identities, and consequently makes commerce and com-modification crucial factors in identity politics (cf. Thies/Kaltmeier). Economic elites search for new trends in the creativity of everyday life and in popular culture in order to create consumer identities for specific target groups. This strategy implies that intellectual property rights and their expropriation, as well as the protection of com-mons and heritage sites, are important contested sites in the field of identity politics today. It can be argued that there exists an ongoing "de-differentiation between econ-omy and culture in late capitalist society" (Short/Kim 89) or, as George Yúdice puts it, an increasingly strategic use of culture for economic and political ends. The increasing importance of culture in the city can be identified in four ways (cf. Short/Kim 89; Zukin). First, with the rising entertainment industry, the arts and museum complex, the tourist sector, and the creative economy, we see the growing importance of cultural industries to the urban economy. Second, we have to point out the importance of urban spectacles (cf. Gotham, "Theorizing"; Debord), which finds its expression in festivals, fairs, sports, music and other cultural events, expositions, etc. Third, we can observe a rapid rise of aesthetic, cultural, and symbolic landscapes in the city. This includes processes of theming, imagineering, as well as urban renewal and regeneration. A fourth aspect is related to culture as governmental strategy, which refers to a wide array of practices from 'latte-macchiatoization' via surveillance, and eventually to gentrification and forced expulsion of 'dangerous populations.' In the practices of city marketing and the production of a unique image of the city, these tendencies are promoted by local and municipal governments that see a significant redevelopment strategy in the utilization of the cultural.

Recently, this cultural commodification of the city has met with another ongoing trend. While recent decades, particularly in America, have been characterized by enormous growth in urban populations, urban sprawl and decay, and a ghettoization of center districts and downtown areas, we are now witnessing a 'return to the center' (cf. Herzog; Rojas). 'Return to the center' means that hegemonic groups re-occupy urban space in the center districts—which often finds its expression in processes of gentrifi-cation, urban renewal, slum clearance, and new urban consumer lifestyles and iden-tities. Obviously, the idea of this recent return to the center is perceived from the perspective of the hegemonic middle and upper classes, as the center in fact was never abandoned. It can be argued that in the 20th century we saw a run to the center by subaltern, often indigenous peasants migrating from rural areas. Now, the middle-class and creative milieus return, and the subaltern sectors are expelled.

In a study of the Inter-American Development Bank, Eduardo Rojas and his collaborators Eduardo Rodríguez and Emiel Wegelin discuss theoretical approaches, instruments, and case studies of processes and projects that have the aim of urban renewal in central areas of the city. From their international perspective they discuss three categories of recuperation of central urban areas, all of which are related to the characteristics of the area. First, they identify programs of urban recuperation in central areas that have been abandoned, mainly by processes of de-industrialization. This is the case with Puerto Madero in Buenos Aires, the Elbe zone in Hamburg, and the docklands in London. The second category is constituted by programs of urban recuperation designed to modify the dynamics of the city in order to have an equilibrated growth. These interventions may be seen as directed processes of gentrification, as they try to renovate deteriorated neighborhoods by the stimulative impulse of a renewal program near the city centers. The third category comprises programs that recuperate central city areas. These interventions are complex and extensive and comprise the coordination of different programs in order to rehabilitate deteriorated central districts. Here, the report examines the cases of the east sector, Penn Quarter, of Washington, D.C., the eastern zone of Santiago de Chile, and the historic city center of Quito. As the authors note, this third category is of special importance for urban processes in Latin America, because nearly all Latin American countries face the problems of urban decay in city centers (cf. Rojas 130).

The renewed importance of city centers should be considered not only as a national issue, i.e., as the re-occupation of symbolic spaces by dominant groups in order to re-found national identities. In fact, this return to the center is also related to ongoing transnational processes which modify the governing capacities of nation states, placing more importance on global articulation in a worldwide network of informational and financial flows via global cities. However, the globalization of city centers is not limited to economically global cities that become nodal points in the informational world economy (cf. Sassen). In nearly all cities worldwide, we can point to translocal urban transformations in the wake of the ongoing processes of globalization.

In the case of historic city centers, we can argue that the two aspects of the concept, 'historic' and 'center,' are radically redefined by the ongoing processes of transnationalization. Actually—in the information age (cf. Castells)—historic city centers face a process of glocalization that expresses itself in three ways (cf. Carrión, *Centros* 91-92). First, in economic terms, the centrality with regard to infrastructure (services, technology), circulation (communication technologies, transport), human capital, administration, and—recently—to economic flows like international cooperation, remittances, and tourists remains an important resource for helping cities enter into transnational competition. Second, in cultural terms, the transnational promotion of specific local culture and the proliferation of authentic landscapes are of increasing importance for the positioning of a particular city within the transnational urban grid.

Third, in political terms, local governance, particularly the municipal government, is of growing importance due to the processes of decentralization, privatization, and denationalization in the context of the neoliberal policies since the 1980s, which finds its expression in new models of urban governance such as public-private partnerships. These processes lead to what urban studies scholar Fernando Carrión calls the return of the "ciudad construida" (*Centros* 93), which is conceived dialectically as a trans-local urban process beyond the global and the local, so that the "introspección, o el regreso a la ciudad construida, tiene como contraparte una cosmopolitización e internacionalización de la ciudad" (*Centros* 93).

3.   Heritage Cities and Coloniality

The social anthropologist Rolf Lindner has argued that we can distinguish cities on the basis of different habitus. He points out that cities have their own habitus, which becomes the generative principle of lifestyles. Following Pierre Bourdieu's approach, Lindner suggests classifying cities according to the quality and volume of their cultural, social, and economic capital, as well as according to their strategies of distinction vis-à-vis other competing cities (49). This anthropomorphic conception of the city is based on the idea of a homology between the hegemonic economic elites of a city and the emerging style of that city. Using the examples of Paris and Los Angeles, Lindner shows how two different lifestyle cities rely on cultural capital in order to create specific categories of distinction. Paris with its cultural industries, like the *haute couture*, has a sense of style and 'high culture.' Los Angeles, by contrast, is a city of glamorous appearance and post-modern cultural industry of the simulacra.

Here I argue that cities with a historic city center can rely on heritage as a primary way to distinguish themselves from other urban centers. With Bourdieu, it can be argued that the historic city centers are dispositions of the habitus of cities, which reflect their specific 'biographies.' The modes of activation of these dispositions, however, have changed profoundly: In the first half of the 20th century, the historic city centers were conceived as outmoded traditional areas of the city which constrained the process of modern urban development. But since the 1990s, in the realm of post-modernism, and the end of the grand narrative of modernity and development, a renewed interest in historic city centers has emerged. In the wake of cultural nostalgia and the hype of retro-fashion, historic centers are becoming marketable. Thus, we can identify a strong relation between the post-Fordist urban cultural economy and heritage in historic city centers.

One key component of urban cultural economies is the attraction of transnational tourist attention. Intercontinental transport options and low transport costs are drawing a transnational leisure class to culturally attractive cities all around the world, from Dubai and Bilbao via Singapore and Bejing to Paris and Florence. In this context, heritage assumes a strategic function with regard to urban development.

With respect to cultural capital, it is important to note that heritage, as an authentic feature of a certain city, can be marketed as a 'unique selling point' and can serve as an element of distinction. The quality of this cultural capital rises if it is internationally recognized, for example by means of an entry on the United Nation's list of cultural world heritage sites. Currently, the World Heritage List includes 679 properties of cultural heritage, 82 of which are in Latin America and the Caribbean.[1] Almost half of the Latin American cultural heritage sites are urban spaces such as historic city centers or outstanding urban ensembles and monuments. Yet, no city center or urban ensemble in the U.S.A., with the exception of La Fortaleza in Puerto Rico, has entered the list, while Canada is represented with Lunenburg and the city center of Quebec.

Although the combination of urban renewal and the tourism industry has been promoted in Latin America since the 1960s (cf. Azevedo 303), it was after the crisis of industrialization projects and the 'lost decade of the 1980s,' as well as with the emergence of a cosmopolitan leisure class, that the tourism industry became particularly attractive, especially in Latin American countries. In the United States, where the internal market for tourism has always been larger, cities like New Orleans have had a thriving tourism industry since the end of the 19th century, which in the 1960s led to a process of homogenization and rationalization of tourism (cf. Gotham, *Authentic*).

Despite the economic incentives provided by tourism, heritage and the marketing of heritage constitute a highly contested field of power. Questions arise in relation to the material appropriation of space, such as land-use conflicts, with the related problems such as gentrification, urban housing, and the informal sector. A further problem is related to the politics of memory and to the colonial condition of the Americas. The Americas as a geo-cultural entity are the result of a conquest and the subsequent colonization process that began in the 'long 16th century.' As Aníbal Quijano and Immanuel Wallerstein argue,

> [t]he modern world-system was born in the long sixteenth century. The Americas as a geosocial construct were born in the long sixteenth century. The creation of this geo-social entity, the Americas, was the constitutive act of the modern world-system. The Americas were not incorporated into an already existing capitalist world-economy. There could not have been a capitalist world-economy without the Americas. (549)

Thus, the Americas can be seen as the site of emergence of a capitalist world system that from the very beginning has been based on a racial divide between colonizers and colonized. Anibal Quijano argues that alongside economic and political conquest, a "coloniality of power" based on identity politics was established. In the classification of the 'racial' Other, the European self is constructed, while the construction of the 'racially inferior' Other served the needs of labor exploitation (cf. Quijano).

Other postcolonial scholars like Walter Mignolo, Silvia Rivera Cusicanqui, and José Carlos Mariategui have argued in the same way that the colonial situation cannot be reduced to a mere historical period; on the contrary, it can be argued that the

---

[1]   Cf. <http://whc.unesco.org/en/list/stat#s1>.

American societies are characterized by deep colonial structures that interfere with modern, republican layers. In terms of the racial divide and the exclusion of indigenous and African-American population(s), coloniality is still persistent. Therefore, the performative restoration of colonial urban landscapes is highly ideological and contested in terms of social imaginaries and the figuration of spaces of daily life. This performativity of coloniality is revealed in some of the urban projects in the context of 500 years of Conquista—many of them patronized by the Spanish Development corporation (cf. Agencia; Mutal 125), such as the renewal of the colonial center of Santo Domingo and the erection of a lighthouse honoring Columbus ('Faro a Colón'), which projects a giant cross of light in the Caribbean sky.

4.   The Field of Heritage in the Americas

The preoccupation with heritage lies at the heart of the consolidation of the nation in the Americas. In early 20th-century Latin America, the idea of the city as a monument helped sustain the process of inventing the national community (cf. Azevedo 297-303). Entire cities were declared to be national heritage, such as Panama in 1918 and Pátzcuaro and Mexico City in 1934. Particularly in the case of Mexico, this search for historic roots was strongly related to the *indigenismo* and its cultural politics promoted by the state with the attendant policies of nation-building through assimilation.

Nevertheless, the question of heritage entered a process of transnationalization after the devastation of Europe in World War II and with the emergence of international organizations such as the International Council on Monuments and Sites (ICOMOS, 1965) and the International Congress of Modern Architecture (CIAM, 1931) (cf. Bouchenaki). It can be argued that in the second half of the 20th century, a transnational field of heritage emerged, which is constituted by specific knowledges, actors, and practices, which are regulated by the *nomos* of 'conservation' or 'non-conservation.'

The second half of the 20th century brought about different approaches to heritage. An early approach put a premium on preserving single major monuments, with little consideration of the setting of these monuments. Later, more emphasis was placed on the preservation of historic ensembles within their specific local environments. A third and more recent approach involves the marketing of heritage themes, despite the fact that in the course of today's growing influence of urban governance, social politics and participation are included as well. This perception is to be seen in the context of a shift in the role of culture in different fields. In international regimes concerned with cultural preservation and heritage, a broad conceptualization of culture is applied, one that is expressed for example in the Mondiacult Declaration of 1982 as well as in the inclusion of immaterial cultural heritage in the UNESCO list in 2007. Despite the fact that popular and even subaltern features are thus included in hegemonic urban projects, we can observe a tension between heritage and subaltern actors in historic city centers, as the latter are for the most part reduced to the status of a problematic object, to being target groups for interventions, but not architects of urban landscapes.

The Mexican anthropologist Néstor García Canclini has brought to light the power relations entailed by the concept of heritage, which are often hidden under universalistic semantics:

> El patrimonio cultural sirve, así, como recurso para reproducir las diferencias entre los grupos sociales y la hegemonía de quienes logran un acceso preferente a la producción y distribución de los bienes. Los sectores dominantes no sólo definen cuáles bienes son superiores y merecen ser conservados; también disponen de medios económicos e intelectuales, tiempo de trabajo y de ocio, para imprimir a esos bienes mayor calidad y refinamiento. ("Los usos sociales" 18)

We can sum up that decisions about which sites are to be preserved depend on the possession of economic and technical resources as well as knowledge required for maintaining cultural heritage. Cultural heritage is therefore related to a fight over symbolic power, where the distribution of capitals—in quality and quantity—is highly unequal.

5. Urban Renewal, Gentrification and Control of Population

Over the last two centuries the urban subaltern populations of historic city centers of the Americas have been conceived of as a threat in terms of urban hygiene, delinquency, and social order (cf. Kingman, *Ciudad*). In a Foucauldian sense, control of the urban 'dangerous classes' has been central to conflicts about the material and symbolic appropriation of urban space. Certain strands of this discourse—e.g., discursive elements like criminality, order, public health, circulation, etc.—appear in the politics of urban renewal and the revitalization of historic city centers (cf. Kingman, "Patrimonio"). The spatial strategies applied in revitalization processes range from spatial control to violent displacement.

A major bone of contention has been how to deal with the mobile traders that populate public places in the centers, often since prehistoric times as in the cases of Quito and Cuzco. In Quito more that 8,000 merchants were relocated—after grueling negotiations—to new popular malls, transforming the vivid marketplace of San Francisco into an empty space (cf. Hanley/Ruthenburg 221-24). In Lima, the ambulant merchants of the informal sectors, 20,000 in total, were partly displaced by police forces in 1996 (cf. Dias 255). Although in the Norms of Quito of 1967 the expulsion of the poor population was outlawed, as a rule, the revitalization has served practically as a kind of 'slum clearance act.'

After the eradication of 'dangerous classes,' an entire array of strategies has been applied to maintain spatial control; we only have to think of surveillance cameras, illumination systems, or private security forces. In the aftermath of these first systematic interventions in urban renewal, we can often observe rising land prices and growing speculation on land. As a result, there has been a strong tendency towards converting monumental buildings: Churches and convents are used as libraries (Mexico) or hotels (San Juan de Puerto Rico); a bishop's palace becomes a restaurant (Quito);

residential houses are transformed into shops and boutiques; and a brewery is reused as a mall (New Orleans). Despite these transformations, we can often detect nostalgic traces of the former use: For example, the plaza San Francisco since pre-colonial times was the central marketplace, or *tiangez*, of Quito. In the process of urban re-vitalization, the informal street vendors were expelled and the place was cleared. Now there is only a fenced lifestyle café at the corner of the traditional marketplace where latte macchiato is sold and which is named Tiangez. This leads us to the problematic tension between Disneyfication and authenticity.

6.   Between Disneyfication and Authenticity

The modern utopia of urban planning and the eradication of the social and ethnic Other has never fully succeeded. And in those places where it was intended, it did not have the expected effects, neither in urban economy nor in the attraction of foreign tourists. This was clearly demonstrated by the revitalization project 'Plan ESSO' in Santo Domingo in the 1960s, as well as by the revitalization project in the Pelourinho in Salvador do Bahia, which tried to displace the urban population by remodeling the city center for touristic use (Azevedo 204-05).

Although these radical efforts to transform a historically grown space into an engineered theme park have never been completely realized in any of the historical city centers in the Americas, there are nonetheless dynamics of Disneyfication. This term refers primarily to security management, performative *mise-en-scène*, and monumental architectural features within an urban landscape. In the Calle La Ronda in Quito, revitalized in 2006, we see elements such as private security, lights at the iconic bridge, and a guidance system to direct the attention to the different features of the street—like small shops, art galleries, cafés, and bars. Several features are inspired by theme parks and themed malls, especially in the affective engineering to generate an atmosphere of security, *flâneuring*, and timelessness (cf. Gottdiener; Goss).

While postmodern theory has drawn attention to the fading of the real and the overwhelming dominance of simulacra (cf. Baudrillard), the search for the authentic— often linked to the exotic—is a predominant feature of postmodern consumer culture. Anticipating a cosmopolitan taste, we find an ambivalent tension between authenticity and universal features of consumption. The new urban spaces are characterized by both homogenization and a local sense of place, containing a mixture of latte-macchiatoization, as a feature of cosmopolitan consumer culture, and ethnic marketing.

Accordingly, in regenerated historical city centers we also find several elements of popular cultures, as hegemonic discourses about heritage have to fall back on everyday discourses and practices of identity in order to create authenticity. These politics of authenticity can rely on music—as in the cases of blues in Chicago, jazz in New Orleans, tango in Buenos Aires, and *pasillo* in Quito—, on urban spectacles like Mardi Gras in New Orleans and carnival in Rio de Janeiro, as well as on local food and other artifacts. As Raussert and Seeliger have shown in the case of Chicago, the imagined authenticity—in this case black blues—may differ from daily-life experience, where blues is performed by white underclass youth while the black youth prefers hip-hop.

In the aforementioned Calle La Ronda in Quito we see these elements of authenticity in spectacles of indigenous dance groups and performances of the 'real *quiteño pasillo*,' as well as in the small shops of the house-owners and tenants that sell traditional sweets, Ecuadorian food, and craft-work. Nevertheless, in the national press (*El Comercio*, *Hoy*) these people are not positioned as popular actors, but as an emerging economic group. The notions of individual engagement and entrepreneurship have been disseminated since the 1990s in the discussion about the *cholo* economy in Lima (cf. Ávila) as well as by neoliberal intellectuals like Hernando de Soto and programs of international cooperation that aim to foster and regulate the informal sector. This discourse can be understood in the vein of Michel Foucault in terms of a neoliberal governmentality, with the entrepreneurship of the self conceived as a strategy of self-control. With the politics of authenticity in the context of urban renewal and heritage, these entrepreneurs are ethnicized in order to make economic production more effective—by the use of social capital—and consumption more appealing to specific segments of consumers (cf. Crain). Thus, daily life is staged and has to be performed, while other features are not represented. Subalternity is visible only when framed by hegemonic discourses of cultural development.

7. Subaltern Voicelessness and Invisibility

Heritage is bound up with a politics of memory that is always based on the selection of memories from a certain contextualized perspective. "Vergangenes historisch artikulieren heißt nicht, es erkennen 'wie es denn eigentlich gewesen ist,'" Walter Benjamin argued against Leopold von Ranke (253). Instead, it is a reconstruction from the perspective of the present which reveals more about one's own values, norms, and identities than about those of a past society. In this sense, I want to point out the performative dimension of producing cultural identities in the context of heritage. Reconstructed urban landscapes narrate histories that are manufactured in a technical sense, often with direct or indirect relations to the concept of 'imagineering,' a new word that combines 'image' and 'engineering,' and 'theming,' the narration of a story, both promoted by Walt Disney and his company. In the case of the historic city centers in the Americas, and especially in Latin America, we can identify a colonial narrative and a material and imaginary re-colonization of the city. What is emphasized in this process are the references to colonial churches, which lead to the construction of the imaginary of a colonial urban landscape. Pre-Columbian elements are mainly framed in a neo-indigenist way as layers of a 'pre-historic' past that reinforce colonial authenticity as the 'true' image of the city. Obviously, we do not deal with colonialism as a specific historical period of European expansion, but with coloniality and its enduring principles of vision and division of the social world. In this sense, it is notable that Quito's *mise-en-scène* portrays it as the greatest colonial urban area in the Americas, although only a minor part of the material substance is of colonial origin.

The marketing of coloniality is translated into different constellations. On the one hand, it aims at a transnational level and at middle- and upper-class tourists with high cultural capital, especially from Europe and the United States, who praise the colonial monuments and the *mestizo* baroque on the basis of common historical roots. This European perspective also corresponds to the class position of experts in the field of heritage, such as those from the Inter-American Development Bank or the UNESCO.

On the other hand, coloniality appeals to the myths of a nation's founding, where the *criollo* groups, the heirs of the Spanish conquerors, are represented—especially in capitals—as *pars pro toto* for the national imaginary, forgetting the indigenous and African-American populations. This narration of the white nation's founding myth is highly problematic. Following Homi Bhabha, it can be argued that there is a gap between the signifier of the nation and the signified practices, discourses, and imaginaries of everyday life. Subaltern practices and discourses are thus not represented.

This practice of non-representation is not only constitutive for the narration of the nation and its tension between imagination and everyday life, but also for the nation's historic re-inventions. In recent debates on memory and the politics of the past, it has been pointed out that collective forgetting is required to constitute collective memories. This is certainly the case in the context of the recuperation of historic city centers in heritage projects. In general, the related narrative of the reconstructed past does not reveal the complexity of the conflictive construction of urban space and history. If they cannot be commodified, popular and subaltern positions are being forgotten. Without having to go into detail here, we only need to think of the indigenous or African-American presence in the cities, the experience of both ghettoization and urban decay, the contribution of workers—often in forced labor—in the construction of the built environment, or the shaping of daily urban life by popular dwellers. Not only because of the symbolic power of the hegemonic groups in the field of heritage, but also because of the complicated status of subaltern memories, the inclusion of these dimensions is precarious. Due to restricted access to circulating and conservational media and because of the limited depth of oral history (cf. García Canclini, "Patrimonio"), popular and subaltern practices, tactics, and imaginaries are usually 'forgotten.'

While heritage may serve as a source of resistance, as is the case with indigenous heritage, colonially semanticized contexts offer fewer opportunities for oppositional strategic positionings. Middle-class members such as those in New Orleans—where 97% of the population of the historic French Quarter are white (cf. Gotham, *Authentic* 144)— may confront Disneyfication, but indigenous immigrants in colonial city centers such as Quito or Lima have fewer options to rely on heritage in urban spaces. Socio-economically and culturally excluded, they are stereotyped as the 'rural, anti-modern and thus anti-urban Indians' and considered contaminants or "Fremdkörper" (Rüdiger Kunow in this volume) in the city. It is an open task for critical, postcolonial sociology to bring the subaltern back into urban imaginaries as well as into the material spaces of the city.

Works Cited

Agencia Española de Cooperación Internacional. *Programa de Patrimonio Cultural de la Cooperación Española*. 2002.

Ávila Molero, Javier. "Ciudad de los reyes (y plebeyos): Mapas de segregación y flujos translocales en Lima." *Ciudades translocales: Espacios, flujos, representación*. Ed. Rossana Reguillo and Marcial Godoy-Anativia. Guadalajara: ITESO, 2005. 109-39.

Azevedo, Paulo Ormindo de. "La lenta construcción de modelos de intervención en centros históricos americanos." *Centros históricos de América Latina y el Caribe*. Ed. Fernando Carrión. Quito: FLACSO, 2001. 297-316.

Baudrillard, Jean. *Simulacra and Simulation*. Ann Arbor: U of Michigan P, 1995.

Bauman, Zygmunt. *Consuming Life*. Cambridge: Polity P, 2007.

Benjamin, Walter. "Über den Begriff der Geschichte." *Illuminationen: Ausgewählte Schriften*. Frankfurt/M.: Suhrkamp, 1977. 251-62.

Bhabha, Homi. "Introduction: Narrating the Nation." *Nation and Narration*. Ed. Bhabha. London: Routledge, 1990. 1-7.

Bouchenaki, Mounier. "Organismos internacionales e instrumentos jurídicos para la preservación de los centros históricos." *Centros históricos de América Latina y el Caribe*. Ed. Fernando Carrión. Quito: FLACSO, 2001. 11-14.

Carrión, Fernando. *Centros históricos de América Latina y el Caribe*. Quito: FLACSO, 2001.

———. "El centro histórico como objeto de deseo." *Regeneración y revitalización urbana en las Américas: Hacia un estado estable*. Ed. Fernando Carrión and Lisa Hanley. Quito: FLACSO, 2005. 35-58.

———. "Los centros históricos en la era digital en América Latina." *Ciudades translocales: Espacios, flujos, representación*. Ed. Rossana Reguillo and Marcial Godoy-Anativia. Guadalajara: ITESO, 2005. 85-108.

———, and Lisa Hanley, eds. *Regeneración y revitalización urbana en la Américas: Hacia un estado estable*. Quito: FLACSO, 2005.

Castells, Manuel. *The Information Age: Economy, Society, and Culture*. Oxford: Blackwell, 1997.

Crain, Mary. "Negotiating Identities in Quito's Cultural Borderlands." *Cross-Cultural Consumption: Global Markets, Local Realities*. Ed. David Howes. London and New York: Routledge, 2001. 125-37.

Debord, Guy. *The Society of the Spectacle*. New York: Zone Books, 1995.

Dias Velarde, Patricia. "El espacio urbano en la recuperación del Centro Histórico de Lima." *Centros históricos de América Latina y el Caribe*. Ed. Fernando Carrión. Quito: FLACSO, 2001. 347-63.

García Canclini, Néstor. *Consumidores y ciudadanos*. Mexico City: Grijalbo, 1995.

———. "Los usos sociales del patrimonio cultural." *Patrimonio etnológico: Nuevas perspectivas de estudio*. Ed. Encarnación Aguilar Criado. Granada: Junta de Andalucía. Consejería de Cultura. Instituto Andaluz del Patrimonio Histórico, 1999. 16-33.

Goss, Jon. "The Magic of the Mall: An Analysis of Form, Function, and Meaning in the Contemporary Retail Built Environment." *Annals of the Association of American Geographers* 81.1 (1991): 18-47.

Gotham, Kevin Fox. *Authentic New Orleans: Tourism, Culture, and Race in the Big Easy.* New York and London: New York UP, 2007.

———. "Theorizing Urban Spectacles: Festivals, Tourism and the Transformation of Urban Space." *City* 9.2 (2005): 225-46.

Gottdiener, Mark. *Postmodern Semiotics: Material Culture and the Forms of Postmodern Life.* Oxford: Blackwell, 1995.

Hanley, Lisa, and Meg Ruthenburg. "Los impactos sociales de la renovación urbana: El caso de Quito, Ecuador." *Regeneración y revitalización urbana en la Américas: Hacia un estado estable.* Eds. Fernando Carrión and Lisa Hanley. Quito: FLACSO, 2005. 209-239.

Herzog, Lawrence A. *Return to the Center: Culture, Public Space, and City Building in a Global Era.* Austin: U of Texas P, 2006.

Horkheimer, Max, and Theodor W. Adorno. *Dialektik der Aufklärung.* Frankfurt/M.: Suhrkamp, 1988.

Kingman, Eduardo. "Patrimonio, políticas de la memoria e institucionalización de la cultura." *Iconos* 20 (2004): 26-34.

———. *La ciudad y los otros: Quito 1860-1940: Higienismo, ornato y policía.* Quito: FLACSO, 2006.

Lindner, Rolf. "Der Habitus der Stadt: Ein kulturgeographischer Versuch." *Petermanns Geographische Mitteilungen* 147.2 (2003): 46-53.

Mignolo, Walter. *Local Histories/Global Designs.* Princeton: Princeton UP, 2000.

Mutal, Sylvio. "Ciudades y centros históricos de América Latina y el Caribe: 50 años de trayectoria (1950-1999)." *Centros históricos de América Latina y el Caribe.* Ed. Fernando Carrión. Quito: FLACSO, 2001. 113-38.

Quijano, Aníbal. "Colonialidad del poder, eurocentrismo y América Latina." *Colonialidad del saber, eurocentrismo y ciencias sociales.* Ed. Edgardo Lander. Buenos Aires: CLACSO-UNESCO, 2000. 202-46.

———, and Immanuel Wallerstein. "Americanity as a Concept, or the Americas in the Imaginary of the Modern World-System." *International Journal of Social Science* 134 (1992): 549-59.

Raussert, Wilfried, and Christina Seeliger. "What did I do to be so Global and Blue?—Blues as a Commodity: Tourism, Politics of Authenticity, and Blues Clubs in Chicago Today." *Selling EthniCity: Urban Cultural Politics in the Americas.* Ed. Olaf Kaltmeier. Farnham: Ashgate, 2011. 39-52 (forthcoming).

Reguillo, Rossana, and Marcial Godoy-Anativia. *Ciudades translocales: Espacios, flujos, representación.* Guadalajara: ITESO, 2005.

Rojas, Eduardo. *Volver al centro: La recuperación de áreas urbanas centrales.* Washington, D.C.: Inter-American Development Bank, 2004.

Sassen, Saskia. *The Global City: New York, London, Tokyo.* Princeton: Princeton UP, 1991.

Short, John Rennie, and Yeong-Hyun Kim. *Globalization and the City*. Harlow: Prentice Hall, 1999.

Soto, Hernando de. *The Other Path: The Invisible Revolution in the Third World*. New York: Harper & Row, 1989.

Thies, Sebastian and Olaf Kaltmeier. "From the Flap of a Butterfly's Wing in Brazil to a Tornado in Texas?: Approaching the Field of Identity Politics and Its Fractal Topography." *E Pluribus Unum? National and Transnational Identities in the Americas*. Ed. Sebastian Thies and Josef Raab. Münster and Tempe: LIT and Bilingual P, 2009. 25-48.

Yúdice, George. *The Expediency of Culture*. Durham: Duke UP, 2003.

Zukin, Sharon. *The Cultures of Cities*. London: Blackwell, 1995.

The Construction of Ethnic Identities in Street Art

EVA MARSCH

1. Introduction

Until fairly recently, graffiti and other forms of urban art were usually considered a disfigurement and blight of urban environments. However, for a number of years now, a shift in the perception of graffiti and resembling forms of 'vandalism' has been recognizable; books on graffiti and street art around the world (London, New York, Berlin, Paris, Miami, and many more) have emerged; exhibitions concerned with street art attract large audiences, and works of celebrated painters or writers at well-known auction houses fetch enormous prices. Along with this growing popularity came an equally growing interest in the subject among scholars of popular culture, who began to explore in detail the forms and, more importantly, the functions of street art and other forms of urban cultural expression in their specific environments.

Among these functions, the role of street art in expressing and shaping group identities—especially those of marginalized groups—seems to be particularly prominent. Indeed, one can identify a large branch of 'ethnic street art' featuring specifically 'ethnic' imagery and symbolism to foster individual and collective ethnic identities. Street art thus seems to be one of the central means of expression of ethnic minorities (which may particularly be due to its inherently subversive character). Therefore, in broaching the subject of street art's cultural impact, it may be fruitful to explore why exactly ethnic identity seems to be such an important theme in street art all over the world. Studying classic as well as more recent developments in this area, this paper aims to provide answers to this question by exploring the role of street art or post-graffiti as a specifically urban means of communication in processes of ethnic identity formation.

I will begin my argument with some theoretical considerations on the role and function of street art in negotiating ethnic identities in urban space, which are informed by several approaches to street art as well as by the notion of 'strategic essentialism' and its functionalization of exaggerated alleged 'ethnic' characteristics to achieve a collective awareness of belonging to an ethnic group. I will then outline a model to classify some of the functions of street art in the dynamics of urban surroundings by adapting Hubert Zapf's model of the functions of literature to the realm of urban culture. Finally, I would like to illustrate this approach to ethnic identities in street art with a number of examples, beginning with the *murales* tradition.

2. 'We Were Here and This is Who We Are': On Street Art, Urban Space, and (Ethnic) Identity

It is in the nature of human beings to try to influence and form their surroundings according to individual or collective wishes, ideas, and needs. One domain in which these needs are expressed is art on and in the streets. In contemporary urban studies, street art is centrally regarded as a new urban form of expressing identity and the self (cf. Stevenson 5).

One prominent form of street art is graffiti. Although the term 'graffiti' etymologically stems from the Greek word *graphein*, meaning 'to write,' and in a strict sense only denotes written letters on walls, 'graffiti' is nowadays used in a broader sense and includes all writing as well as figurative images found in streets (cf. Philips 40). The term 'street art' (also post-graffiti or urban art) refers to any kind of artistic installations found in public places such as sculptures, arrangements of stickers, murals, graffiti in the original sense (as described above), and many more. Generally, the term is used to describe the most recent developments of mostly illegal arts in urban environments. Because of the wide range of its subject matters and different forms of expression, it is not possible to define the exact boundaries of street art and of its strategies of representation.

Graffiti (like any other form of street art) is specifically tied to its place of production—the streets of a city—as it incorporates the concrete surroundings (walls and streets) into its body. The location of works and pieces not only earns their creators tremendous respect (e.g., when a piece is planted on a specifically 'dangerous' place like a highly frequented public place or spot of touristic interest), but also adds individual style and meaning to them. The city's surface is therefore integrated into the pieces not only as a passive background or canvas but in a way actively involved in the creation of meaning: "The coding and decoding of these meanings is an interactive process with the users of the city being actively engaged in a dialogue with its spaces" (Stevenson 60). Against this backdrop, graffiti (as well as street art in general) can be regarded as a subversive form of individual engagement with the concrete material surroundings.

What adds to the potential of graffiti as an art form is the fact that its expressive power as a medium for communication lies somewhere between language and (visual) art and takes advantage of the semiotic possibilities of both (cf. Philips 38-40). Since images and pictures influence human self-perception and how we perceive our environment (cf. Müller 13), enormous potential influence and manipulative force are attributed to visual arts. Thus, street art and visual images have been established as means to foster an exchange of ideas, to influence perceptions of the world and to negotiate (ethnic) identities. In this vein, Rotman certainly has a point when he argues that "[street art and its] multi-faceted expression reflects the many personalities of the city: its counter-cultural left-leaning politics, dramatic ethnic diversity, gay and lesbian activism, [and] entrepreneurial hipster energy" (5). Ethnic diversity and affiliation shape and define everyday life and the daily living together of people and find expression in spatial appropriations. The condition and the appearance of the built environment in any given area become this area's public face and thus its most immediate aspect (cf. Kim 13).

Thus, it would be far too simplistic to conceive of graffiti merely as an indication of crime and unsatisfactory living conditions in an area (which is still a prevailing notion; cf. Kim 13). Instead, street art in general should rather be considered a means of social and individual self-expression and communication among members of various subcultures (cf. Siegl 63). Especially recent developments in the street art scene express a great potential of critical reflection on our social and environmental changes and developments.

Against the backdrop of this communicative function of street art, it is urban space in particular which functions as an arena of actions and interactions of individuals and collectives, first of all, as the very physical location of street art, but also—and even more importantly—as a surface of contact and friction, in the sense of a city user's 'interface.' In other words: Street art might be one way of appropriating the city's materiality and spatiality for people's own needs and purposes, that is to say in this case for the expression of a cultural or ethnic identity, be it individual or collective.

Among the many means these cultural appropriations employ to emphasize and strengthen ethnic unity, 'strategic essentialism' (cf. Verkuyten 126) plays a particularly important role. This concept implies that, although significant differences may exist between members of an ethnic group, it can be advantageous for certain purposes to temporarily 'essentialize' some physical features in order to establish a group identity. Essentializing in this context means that physical features are simplified and overgeneralized to form some stereotypical group affiliation (cf. Mann 378). In street art, strategic essentialism is used to create certain bonds of affiliation among groups through the exaggeration of certain 'ethnic' physical features (such as skin color, the shape of faces, a particular style of clothing etc.), which are, at times, flaunted to the point of caricature. This mechanism of establishing a group identity, which can also be maintained by portraying iconic figures (e.g., Bob Marley, Ché Guevara) belonging to the target group or by visualizing collective symbols (e.g., the Aztec serpent and eagle, the *Pachuco, la Virgen*), can both be used to threaten others and exclude them from the established group (as for example in gang graffiti) or be utilized to suggest a shared past or history in the sense of a Pan-American unity, as is common in the *murales* tradition (with Diego Rivera's *Pan-American Unity* as a famous example).

After having briefly sketched some of the major themes and potentials of street art as regards the negotiation of ethnic identities, I would now like to propose a model allowing me to describe the functions of street art in closer detail. It starts from the assumption that urban culture can generally be argued to play a central role within the dynamics of urban systems. According to Gurr and Butler, urban culture indeed works as an 'integrating force' in urban systems due to its *seismographic* (diagnostic) and *catalytic* (processing) function. In their approach, they draw on Hubert Zapf's concept of literature as cultural ecology, applying it to the urban realm (cf. Gurr/Butler 147-51). Zapf's concept highlights the similarities of the functions of literature with those of ecological systems. According to Zapf, literature functions as "an ecological force within culture" due to the "specific ways in which it has evolved as a unique form of textuality that ... employs procedures analogous to ecological principles" (93). This concept, as Gurr and Butler argue, may also be used to analyze and describe forms and functions of cultural expression in urban environments (cf. 147-51).

In keeping with their argument, I would like to apply it to street art, which, accordingly, can take on the following functions: Firstly—in Zapf's terminology—, street art can function as "cultural-critical meta-discourse," meaning that typical deficits and contradictions of almost all areas of (human) life, whether political, social, economic, or ecological, can be represented and discussed with close reference to their location. Secondly, it lends itself to creating an "imaginative counter-discourse" by visualizing all that is marginalized, neglected or repressed in urban agglomerations like cultural or ethnic heritage of Mexicans, African Americans, Latin American indigenous peoples, and many others. This also includes the utopian function of art. According to this model, art can be a form of exploring possible alternative worlds and scenarios. Thirdly, it is a means to reintegrate all that is repressed and denied in popular culture into the collective consciousness by functioning as "re-integrative inter-discourse" (cf. Zapf 85-93).

3.   Ethnic Identities and Street Art: Model Analyses

In the following, I will apply my theoretical notions on the function of street art in negotiating urban ethnic identities in a discussion of a number of examples, beginning with a brief introduction to the Mexican *murales* tradition. The Mexican mural movement started in the 1920s in the aftermath of the Mexican revolution and was initially patronized by the government. The murals were supposed to express the government's ideology and to represent their vision of history. The artists believed that art as the highest form of human expression could be a key force in social revolution (cf. Gómez-Málaga). Artists like Diego Rivera, José Clemente Orozco, and David Alfaro Siqueiros should be mentioned as a prolific force in the mural renaissance (cf. Tréguer). These artists painted magnificent frescos stylistically reminiscent of the artistic expressions of mythological Aztec drawings, thereby evoking their cultural ancestry and roots. It is also these artists' legacy that such murals are not only to be found in Mexico anymore but also spread to the U.S. This merging of street art and wall painting is especially tied and connected to the collective or shared memory of 'Chicanos' indicating political consciousness (cf. Kim 15). One example of this tradition is a piece called *We Are Not A Minority*, which was created in East Los Angeles in 1978 (cf. fig. 1). It refers to the struggle of Latinos for their civil rights in the United States. The lettering shows different styles of graffiti writings, indicating variety and individuality among Americans. The iconic Ché Guevara as a symbol of struggle against economic inequalities and social injustice points and looks directly at the observer to suggest a direct appeal. His posture and gesture remind the onlooker of the famous Uncle Sam poster to recruit soldiers for the U.S. army (*I Want You For U.S. Army*). Moreover, the shape of the article 'A' in the mural could be interpreted as a stylized Mesoamerican pyramid, an Indigenist symbol that alludes to their status of being descendants from the Aztec or Mayan civilizations and linking their heritage to the alleged greatness of ancient empires like Rome and Greece (cf. Latorre 75-78).

Fig. 1: El Congreso de Artistas Cosmicos de las Americas de San Diego, *We Are Not A Minority*, Mural Estrada Courts Housing Project, East L.A., 1978. Photograph © Josef Raab.

This mural especially draws on the still existent ethnic distinction between 'whites,' 'blacks,' or 'browns,' but then again aims at including them in the community. With its 'slogan' and the pointing finger, it turns out to be a somewhat aggressive attempt at drawing attention to the exclusion of ethnic groups from public life and politics because of their (alleged) minority status. Thus, in Zapf's terminology, it indeed functions as 'cultural-critical meta-discourse' by presenting their still prevalent status as a minority in the U.S., reinforcing demands for political representation and equal integration of Chicanos or Latinos. In addition, it also functions as part of an 'imaginative counter-discourse' in that it suggests a possible alternative to a marginalized minority status.

The muralist Peter Quezada, a Chicano artist living in L.A., creates various murals in his neighborhood which even more clearly emphasize the potential of street art to create an 'imaginative counter-discourse.' Quezada specifically makes everyday life and experiences of his immediate neighborhood the subject of his work. Using various motifs and styles, he embeds his actual experiences in his collage-like murals. In Quezada's decorative street art, community identity and political ideology merge in multiple layers of symbolism and images composed to produce little (hi)stories (cf. Philips 40). In his remarkable murals Quezada combines images and words to convey his message. He negotiates various topics and themes in his drawings, paintings, and characters, for example gang violence and crime, religious motifs, and also ethnic affiliation, and specifically incorporates his Chicano heritage in his murals.

Quezada's mural *Pray to End Gang Violence* (cf. fig. 2) is a very good example of his art and technique. On the right, a man in chains kneels in front of the surveillance tower of a prison. His posture and the flames surrounding him suggest despair and devastation. The folded hands with the rosary—which here closely echo Dürer's ubiquitous 1508 drawing of the praying hands—are a motif that is commonly used among Chicanos in tattoos made in prison and show the prevalence of their Catholic roots.

Fig. 2: Peter Quezada, *Pray to End Gang Violence*,
Esmeralda Street/Huntington Drive, L.A. (Kim 69).

The expression on the face of the woman mirrors the man's facial expression and suggests the sorrow and grief of the families affected by gang activities. The dove as the classic symbol of peace corresponds to the flames, creating an association with the dichotomy of heaven and hell. The lettering is 'Old English,' a style which is used by gang members for tattoo inscriptions as well as for gang graffiti, and which is especially employed to write the gang's name—creating the impression of an easily recognizable logo or trademark (cf. Philips 106, 118). The mural clearly hints at a better world without gang violence, thus establishing an 'imaginative counter-discourse' to the everyday experience of gang activity. Some of Quezada's murals include texts like "Peace Brothers, It's The Only Way If We Are To Survive" or "End The Insanity.

Have The Courage To Say No To Gangs" (cf. Kim 7-9). The phrase "There Will Be Peace In The Valley" painted across a wall in Los Angeles also evokes a hopeful utopia of the future.

Quezada's murals are valid examples of both the *seismographic* and the *catalytic* functions of street art (cf. Gurr/Butler 146). By emphasizing a 'Chicano' group identity, they establish the notion of togetherness to strongly evoke the feeling of belonging and community, thus fostering a personalized connection to the youths in question. Quezada's works raise awareness of the social problems common among Chicano youths (such as gang violence) and thus identify the vicious circle these youths are stuck in. At the same time, and in addition to this diagnostic function of his art, his pieces also evoke a hopeful utopia by projecting a life without gang violence. In doing so, they conjure up alternatives to a seemingly hopeless situation and may thus contribute to a change of ideas (which might be considered the *catalytic* potential of his art).

To establish a collective ethnic identity in his murals, Quezada relies on symbols which are linked to Chicano identity in the collective memory of Mexican Americans, namely Aztec imagery, the *Pachuco*, or the figure of *la Virgen de Guadalupe* as the most important religious symbol, and the *Dia de los Muertos* as the most important religious festival in Mexico, thereby reintegrating the repressed—the Mexican heritage—into the system of cultural discourse ('re-integrative inter-discourse'). The symbols he uses to raise awareness of ethnic membership are also frequently used by other artists and writers as well in L.A. and in other U.S. cities.

Another form of street art as a specifically urban form of expressing individual or collective identities is gang graffiti. These graffiti are specifically meant to draw a demarcation line between 'us' and 'them,' 'insiders' and 'outsiders,' in other words: They are supposed to establish relationships of inclusion or exclusion. More often than not, they are intended to scare people and can even be used to 'kill' a person symbolically by crossing out his or her name (cf. Philips 129). By thus threatening those who do not belong to the 'in-group,' gang graffiti perfectly underline notions of exclusive membership to gangs such as Santa Monica 17th or Sotel 13 in West L.A. (cf. Philips 119).

Gang graffiti also lend themselves to manipulating a person's position within the gang or their gang's position within the local gang community: "Gang members use graffiti to weave themselves into their neighborhoods and to delimit the boundaries of the larger gang's social system and their place within it" (Philips 125). Consequently, gang graffiti are used to establish identity, firstly, by communicating membership in social groups, in this case the Chicano gangs, and, secondly, by tying this identity to the immediate surroundings, thus linking gang identity with the gang's specific urban location. Furthermore, in what Hernández calls the "discourse of reclamation" (116), they are used as a symbolic gesture to reclaim the streets of their territory, either from another gang or from the government.

Yet, rather than distinguishing ethnic groups from each other, street art can also be a means of fostering a more inclusive sense of belonging to a larger identity group. In the sense of a 're-integrative inter-discourse,' it may establish a utopian view of a pan-American unity, as in Diego Rivera's famous mural in San Francisco (cf. fig. 7, opposite page). Along comparable lines, the graffiti painted by Florida crew[1] Graff Armada (Bane, Sege, Crome, Five, Dask, and Prisco) creates an image of social and cultural coherence among people in North America by depicting the continent as an integrated whole; thus, it functions both as 'imaginative counter-discourse' and as 're-integrative inter-discourse' (cf. fig. 8, opposite page).The background of the piece is dominated by a stylized sea chart as used during the 15th century and later. On the right, a European ship is approaching the coastal line of (northern) America (cf. fig. 4), clearly indicated by the outline of Florida stretching towards the ship (cf. fig. 3).

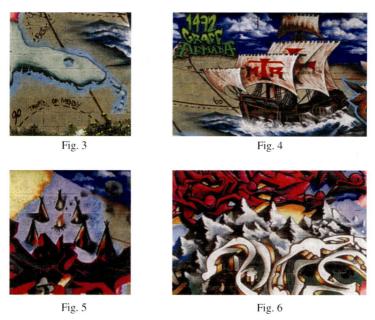

Fig. 3   Fig. 4

Fig. 5   Fig. 6

Figs. 3, 4, 5, 6: Miami murals, details (Murray/Murray 42-43).

---

[1] One alternative to gang activities is to join a 'crew.' Crews take up some of the functions of gangs like ethnic group identification and camaraderie but avoid the self-destructive forces of the gang (cf. Hernández 108).

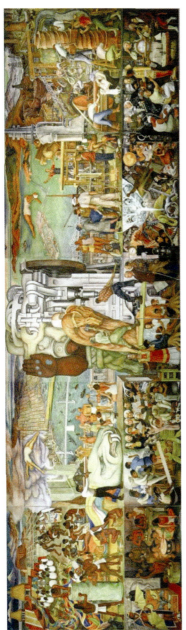

Fig. 7: Diego Rivera, *Pan-American Unity*, City College of San Francisco. (<http://www.redtreetimes.com/2010/06/18/pan-american-unity>).

Fig. 8: Miami mural (Murray/Murray 42-43).

At the upper margin of the sea chart, the year 1492 extends into the sky and reminds the onlooker of the arrival of Christopher Columbus in America (cf. fig. 4). Above Florida one can see prairie teepees used especially by Native American tribes of the Great Plains arranged in a circle around a fire (cf. fig. 5). The continent is covered with the names of the artists who thus weave themselves into the picture and into the community it evokes (cf. fig. 8). The middle of the continent is dominated by the ridge of the Rocky Mountains (cf. fig. 6). The drawing of the continent is completed by a totem pole and an outline of the western coastline (cf. fig. 8). These totem poles were typically erected by Native American and First Nation Canadian tribes of the north-west coast of North America.

In the center of the picture Native Americans of several tribes (indicated by their variant hairstyles) are depicted while negotiating with Europeans (cf. fig. 8). These representatives of different tribes in conjunction with the depicted housing customs of Native Americans of the Great Plains and typical totem poles from the west coast evoke an integrationist understanding of Native Americans. It can be regarded as a revised version of Diego Rivera's famous mural *Pan-American Unity* and arguably evokes and creates a shared North American indigenous history and community similar to the concept of the Aztlán nation (cf. Latorre 68-71).

In conclusion, I would like to argue that street art can adopt various functions in the tactics of everyday life and especially in the communication of ethnic identity or identities. Artistic forms of expression can serve as 'cultural-critical meta-discourse' on ongoing political and social changes (*Pray to End Gang Violence, We Are Not A Minority*) and therefore function as a diagnostic tool. They can create an 'imaginary counter-discourse' in the sense of proposing utopian ideas and wishes in an attempt to act as a trigger or a catalytic force. Thus, street art contributes to creating what Hubert Zapf calls a 're-integrative inter-discourse' by "feeding back and reintegrating of the repressed into the whole system of cultural discourses" (Zapf, qtd. in Gurr 249). Street art as a means of cultural expression and communication can indeed serve various purposes in our everyday urban surroundings: It originates from both the social and the material urban conditions and should be regarded as a subversive form of individual engagement with the concrete material surroundings of the metropolis.

Works Cited

Gómez-Málaga, María Cardalliaguet. "The Mexican and Chicano Mural Movements." <http://www.yale.edu/ynhti/curriculum/units/2006/2/06.02.01.x.html>.

Gurr, Jens Martin. "Urbanity, Urban Culture and the European Metropolis." *Britannien und Europa: Studien zur Literatur-, Geistes- und Kulturgeschichte: Festschrift für Jürgen Klein*. Ed. Michael Szczekall. Frankfurt/M.: Lang, 2010. 241-55.

———, and Martin Butler. "Against the 'Erasure of Memory' in Los Angeles City Planning: Strategies of Re-Ethnicizing L.A. in Digital Fiction." *Selling EthniCity: Urban Cultural*

Politics in the Americas. Ed. Olaf Kaltmeier. London: Ashgate, 2011. 145-63 (forthcoming).

Hernández, Rod. "Battling in L.A.: Chicano Graffiti Poetics and Technologies of Vision." *The Americas Review: A Review of Hispanic Literature and Art of the USA*. 23.3-4 (1995): 107-32.

Kim, Sojin. *Chicano Graffiti and Murals: The Neighborhood Art of Peter Quezada*. Jackson: UP of Mississippi, 1995.

Latorre, Guisela. *Walls of Empowerment: Chicana/o Indigenist Murals of California*. Austin: U of Texas P, 2008.

Lewisohn, Cedar. *Street Art: The Graffiti Revolution*. London: Tate Publishing, 2008.

Mann, Michael, ed. *The International Encyclopedia of Sociology*. New York: Macmillan, 1984.

Müller, Marion G. *Grundlagen der visuellen Kommunikation*. Konstanz: UTB, 2003.

Murray, James, and Karla Murray. *Miami Graffiti*. New York: Prestel, 2009.

Philips, Susan A. *Wallbangin': Graffiti and Gangs in L.A.* Chicago: U of Chicago P, 1999.

Rotman, Steve. *San Francisco Street Art*. New York: Prestel, 2009.

Siegl, Norbert. "Kulturphänomen Graffiti: Das Wiener Modell der Graffiti-Forschung." *Der Graffiti-Reader*. Ed. Susanne Schaefer-Wiery and Norbert Siegl. Wien: Institut für Graffiti Forschung (ifg), graffiti edition, 2006.

Stevenson, Deborah. *Cities and Urban Cultures*. Philadelphia: Open UP, 2003.

Tréguer, Annick. "Chicanos Paint their Way Back." <http://www.unesco.org/courier/1993_03/uk/apprend/txt1.htm>.

Verkuyten, Maykel. *The Social Psychology of Ethnic Identity*. New York: Psychology P, 2005.

Zapf, Hubert. "Literature as Cultural Ecology: Notes Towards a Functional Theory of Imaginative Texts with Examples from American Literature." *Literary History/Cultural History: Force-Fields and Tensions*. Ed. Herbert Grabes. Tübingen: Gunter Narr, 2001.

Latino Mural Cityscapes: A Reflection on Public Art, History, and Community in Chicago after World War II

MARC SIMON RODRIGUEZ

Chicago is a city known for its longstanding public mural tradition as well as its community murals movement based in the African-American, Mexican-American, and Puerto-Rican neighborhoods of the city. While the murals often depict the struggles of distinct communities, the artists reflect diversity not easily reduced to racial or ethnic categories. As its many authors and artists have shown, Chicago is a city that does not easily fit delimitation or categorization. This essay is an effort to consider the art of Latinos in Chicago from the perspective of a historian in an effort to situate them in terms of their meaning (that is the things the art appears to represent or the narratives the art appears to reveal) and their place in the city (historically) and their continuing location in an environment defined by gentrification and the destruction and rebirth of communities in Chicago, a city long washed by waves of immigrants. I have made a particular effort in this essay to refrain from discussions of cultural theory and use such materials sparingly.[1]

Fig. 1: *Wall of Respect*, photograph courtesy of Mark Rogovin.

---

[1] This is an interpretive essay and a historical reflection. It is meant as a starting point for further thinking on the issues of art, Latino identity, urban history, and historical representation in public murals and not an exhaustive consideration of the state of the field or of recent theoretical currents in public art analysis. The author wishes to thank Sari Samp for her assistance in locating and photographing several of these murals.

In 1968, artist Mario Castillo created *Metaphysics (Peace)*, a mural considered by most to be the first Chicano outdoor mural of the Chicano era of art and politics in the United States. Painted on the Urban Progress Center on South Halstead Street and 19th, this mural was painted just a year after William Walker and a group of African-American youths, artists, and others painted *Wall of Respect* to honor community heroes and make the city a nicer place to live. This cross-community effort to create accessible art where the artist and members of the community worked together to create outdoor murals on the sides of buildings exposed as a result of urban renewal, decay, and the wrecking ball touched both the African-American and Mexican-American communities almost simultaneously. Organizations like the Urban Progress Center, a War on Poverty agency, operated in African-American, Mexican-American, and Appalachian migrant neighborhoods. There was certainly cooperation between activists and organizations in the late 1960s as minorities were living in cities that were facing economic, structural, and community decline. As the broader community fought for civil rights and a commitment to urban life, artists played a role in documenting the struggles of urban living as they simultaneously sought to beautify cities scarred by the social policies of Post-World-War-II America. Mario Castillo's work, now destroyed, was the opening volley in what became a decade's long commitment to community-based Chicano and Latino public art (cf. Sorrell; Huebner).

Fig. 2: Artist's Group Photo, 1968, *Metaphysics (Peace)*, photograph courtesy of Mario Castillo. Photograph from the Mario Castillo papers, Julian Samora Library, Institute for Latino Studies, University of Notre Dame.

1.   Shifting Demographics and the Latino City

Chicago's mural movements reflected the changing demographics of the city. Latinos lived in three distinct areas of the city in the late 1960s and 1970s. Mexican-ancestry Latinos tended to live in two distinct areas of the city. On the city's south side in the shadow of the United States Steel South Works, Mexican immigrants poured into Chicago in the early 20th century to meet the demands of the steel industry. In an area south of 78th street on the north, Interstate 90 on the west, and bounded on the east by the lake and the U.S. Steel plant, Mexican immigrants and their children established churches and became a part of the local fabric of this industrial, multi-ethnic, and multi-racial city. On the city's southwest side, Mexican Americans and immigrants settled in Pilsen near the industrial area established around the McCormick Reaper Works in a neighborhood originally settled by Austrians, Bohemians, and Germans, and made famous by its relationship to the labor struggles of the late 19th century, most famously the Haymarket Square Riot of 1886 and other battles between those seeking to establish labor unions and the police, military, and company soldiers. Much of the world celebrates the martyrs of these battles each May Day/International Workers day. Because of gentrification, which began in Lincoln Park, Puerto Ricans settled further west in the 1960s on the Near Northwest side. Living at the heart of the 'Polish Triangle' at the cross streets of Division, Milwaukee, and Ashland, Puerto Ricans settled in an area which was the early 20th century's cultural and civic heart of immigrant Polish life in Chicago and the location of many of Nelson Algren's famous novels including *The Man with the Golden Arm*. While still heavily Polish and Ukrainian in ethnic makeup in the 1960s and 1970s, this area commonly known as West Town had become the center of Puerto Rican community life. The *barrio* extended west along Division Street to Humboldt Park, named in honor of German naturalist Friedrich Alexander von Humboldt, in a neighborhood that was once largely Norwegian and German in the late 19th century. Latinos reinvigorated neighborhoods established by immigrants in wave after wave of migration to Chicago (cf. Lucas; Latino Institute; Betancur).

Into these neighborhoods, facing years of settlement and resettlement by immigrants and migrants, Latinos came during the early 1970s. In a city facing the onslaught of deindustrialization and hard-hit by the regional transfer of manufacturing work from the Midwest's so-called Rust Belt cities of Chicago, Detroit, Milwaukee, and Cleveland to the Sunbelt cities of the South, and to 'Third-World' manufacturing zones, Latinos and other minorities increasingly fought for a space in the declining metropolis of 19th- and early 20th-century industrial capitalism.

Fig. 3: Resurrection Project Murals, Virgin of Guadalupe,
18th and Paulina, Pilsen, Chicago, IL. Photograph © Marc Simon Rodriguez.

The outdoor art movement was one component in this dramatic series of events. Castillo's *Metaphysics (Peace)* was merely the first spark in a Latino mural movement. In Lincoln Park, where Puerto Ricans faced the onslaught of urban renewal under the 'Chicago 21 Plan,' which ushered in the first wave of gentrification in Chicago, artists painted a mural detailing the history of Puerto Rico and its main independence leaders on the walls of People's Church at Armitage and Dayton Avenues in Lincoln Park. Soon, the building became the national headquarters of the Young Lords Organization, a militant Puerto Rican civil rights organization modeled on the Black Panther Party even as urban renewal displaced the bulk of the Puerto Rican community from that neighborhood into nearby West Town and Humboldt Park (cf. Natalie Voorhees Center; Jeffries).

In Pilsen, the largest concentration of Mexican-ancestry people in the United States outside of Los Angeles, the Chicano Movement grew in the late 1960s and gave birth to related arts movements, which continued well into the next decade. On 18th street, the main commercial street of Pilsen, in a former Bohemian settlement house the Brown Berets established a community organization that became Casa Aztlán. At Casa Aztlán, Ray Patlan, a Vietnam veteran, began a project to paint a series of murals in the interior rooms. Much like its Puerto Rican counterpart at People's Church, the mural depicted historical events of importance to Latinos. The Patlan mural depicted the history of Mexico, of Mexican workers in both farm and industrial work, as well as a portrait of United Farm Workers Organizing Committee (UFWOC) president, Cesar Chavez. Patlan's work at Casa Aztlán eventually incorporated both the internal and external facades of the building and wrapped it in a retelling of Mexican and Mexican-American history through art. From the exterior, the building paid homage to heroes and—much like *Metaphysics (Peace)*—incorporated images based on Aztec, Mayan, and other Amerindian archetypes. Murals became a site for community celebration, storytelling, and historical representation and critique.

The Chicano muralists of the 1960s and 1970s in particular saw themselves as the modern descendents of Mexican muralists David Alfaro Siqueiros, Diego Rivera, and Jose Clemente Orozco and thus borrowed from the works of these masters as they created new art to fit the urban landscape in Chicago. The 1970s became a period of expansion and experimentation in Chicago's mural movement as the Latino and African-American communities as well as others, including the Polish-American community, commissioned murals or painted murals on their own on the urban canvas of exposed brick walls often left open to view by the demolition of 19th-century buildings across the city. In the decades before the widespread reinvestment in cities and the rampant gentrification of low-income communities, Latino and other ethnic communities tried to beautify and claim the urban landscape through public art, while at the same time cities often tore down 'blighted' buildings exposing ever more brick to the painter's brush. In some ways, the mural movement of the 1960s and 1970s grew in tandem with urban renewal *and* in opposition to it, filling in the spaces left by the destruction of the built environment.

2.   Case Study: Community Organization, Art Defense, Art Activism

The Humboldt Park community was the site of sustained activism in the middle and late 1960s, and this movement continued into the 1970s. The efforts of several waves of artists to alter the visual landscape of the city came into direct conflict with public and private efforts to redevelop sections of the city deemed blighted or considered worthy of private redevelopment. On June 12, 1966, following a routine arrest, two hundred Chicago police officers fought what the *Chicago Defender* termed a "pitched battle" at the corner of Division Street and Damen Avenue against Puerto-Rican community residents in an affair that left several dead and caused significant damage ("Police Leaders"). The *Defender* then went on to provide its readers a bit of history on the racial and ethnic diversity of the Puerto-Rican community, its specific dialect of Spanish, and the fact that the city had not considered the Near Northwest side of Chicago an area where there were racial and ethnic tensions. Reverend Martin Luther King, Jr. called for a meeting in Chicago to "totally free all minority groups" as it became clear that much of the violence had to do with police firing into the crowd, using night sticks to hit people, and the release of attack dogs ("King Calls").

Fig. 4: John Weber, *Breaking the Chains,* 1971. Note the logo of the Latin American Defense
Organization (LADO) at the top of the mural. Photograph © Marc Simon Rodriguez.

Over a decade later, following sustained community activism and a related mural
movement, Humboldt Park residents fought to defend murals, which themselves represented the struggles of the community. One such mural, titled *Breaking the Chains*,
became the subject of sustained activism in 1978 as residents engaged in street protests
and twenty-four hour vigils to protect a building from demolition by the city. The city
of Chicago, in seeking to clear abandoned buildings, hired a contractor to tear down a
building at 1456 North Rockwell Street. However, the mobilization in defense of
community art and the preservation of building structures succeeded and preserved one
of the most militant murals in the neighborhood. *Breaking the Chains*, which still exists,
is about the struggles of minority people to cast off oppression in favor of liberty and
community and shows black, white, and brown hands working to free themselves from
bondage. The community group that led the mural preservation effort also sought to
renovate and rehabilitate the property to provide housing for fourteen families and
criticized the rapid destruction of city structures rather than renovation. This became a
trend in resistance across the city as communities who increasingly felt boxed in by the
wrecking ball, public and private neglect as well as other forms of oppression organized

to improve and preserve their neighborhoods ("Citizens"). This activism prompted the *Chicago Tribune* to investigate further the mural movement in the city, and led to an article that celebrated the murals of Chicago for creating a "museum of the streets" for residents. The *Tribune* also noted that several of the murals which embodied the greater meaning of the public mural movement had been demolished. The article also linked the mural movements of Latinos, African Americans, and white artists to the greats of the Mexican muralist movement, including Siqueiros, who had worked in Chicago and trained some of the muralists active in the late 1970s ("The Walls"). These protection movements, followed by decades of preservation, were common features of the urban public mural movement of the 1970s.

The Chicago public art movement was well organized. They hosted artists from other countries and cities, published manuals on how to prepare exterior walls for painting, and held workshops to train community members in the selection of paints well suited to the often harsh winters common in Chicago. In many ways, the institutionalization of this movement, often with the support of non-profit organizations, led to a professionalization of the practice of public art and public art instruction, even as the actual execution of the art projects themselves required community support, and as time progressed became a part of the political and social fabric of many of Chicago's communities (cf. Rogovin).

Fig. 5: *Sea of Flags*, Various Artists, Near Northwest Neighborhood Network, 2004. Photograph © Marc Simon Rodriguez.

Latino urban murals in Chicago and elsewhere represent civil rights struggle as a visual narrative and become the subject of community social movements as the buildings on which they are often painted continue to be the target of urban renewal and gentrification. Both urban renewal in the decades of the 1960s and 1970s and gentrification in the late 20th and early 21st centuries work on the physical landscape in similar ways. Old buildings are torn down, and the community often undergoes a passive form of ethnic and racial cleansing as low-income minority and ethnic communities are pushed out of neighborhoods due to a lack of income to maintain homes, pay inflated rents, and—as new buildings are erected—an inability to purchase housing in these newly upscale communities. What has happened in Chicago has happened nationwide as empty lots are sold, new housing and businesses are constructed, and murals are lost to the march of progress. Some murals have outlived the communities they once represented surrounded by the new businesses and residents of the gentrified city. For example, the corner of Division and Damen in Chicago is home to few Puerto Rican or Polish immigrants and has become the epicenter of a gentrified neighborhood on Chicago's West Side. Yet, some of the murals painted by artists in the 1970s remain, such as *Unidos Para Triunfar* at Division and Hoyne. One might also consider the fact that the depopulation of the once working-class and middle-class sections of the city which led to property abandonment and the demolition of buildings, which in turn exposed brick walls to the view of residents, was itself an opportunity, brief as it may have been, created by white flight to the suburbs. If this is the case, the white flight into cities that expanded in the late 20th century has led to both an erasure of these distinctive urban spaces common in the late 1960s and early 1970s as well as to the creation of new opportunities for Latino residents, who still live in more diverse population groups in many of the neighborhoods they populated after World War II. This position has meant that Latinos are now politically represented in a city that has a great number of Latino aldermanic office holders, state representatives, and a congressional representative. Moreover, some members of the new urban gentrification populations actually desire the preservation of diversity in their recently adopted neighborhoods and work to preserve historic murals.[2]

---

[2] This is not a statement of acceptance on my part of the geography (low culture)/art (high culture) divide noted by Sanchez-Tranquilino.

Fig. 6: John Weber, *Unidos Para Triunfar*, Division and Hoyne,
Wicker Park, Chicago, IL. Photograph © Marc Simon Rodriguez.

3.   Conclusion

The consideration of public art and Latino muralists has continued to focus on the
important community-based mural movements of California, yet Chicago, as a birthplace of Latino art, cross-ethnic, cross-racial muralist movements continues to be
understudied and neglected by comparison. In this brief reflective essay, I have tried to
make the case for a lived and visually important resistance and public art movement in
Chicago, which should become a part of a national narrative of public Latino art. Art
historians and social historians alike should seek to incorporate these two rich muralist
movement histories as they attempt to present a national history of Chicano and Latino
art in the United States. Moreover, in places like Chicago and New York City, both
home to diverse pan-Latino communities, the incorporation of Puerto-Rican and other
artists must be part of any effort to document this rich history. Within this milieu of
artists and civil rights activists, many non-Latinos played significant roles as artists,
coordinators, and participants, and the diversity of a movement that produced art that
was distinctly Latino also needs to be recognized. In the case of Chicago, non-Latinos
often made mural art that embodied the history of the city's Latino and African-
American communities and relied on coalitions of community members and artists as
planners, volunteers, and participants. The history of Chicano and Latino muralism
and its relationship to broader changes in American society and the history of ethnic
civil rights history is a rich field not only for documentation and comparison, but also

one that increasingly has international and transnational linkages that scholars must explore in relation to one another.

As history, the murals are often a combination of myth and historical documentation and must be seen as an effort to present and explore memory and history in distinct ethnic or racial communities. As time has progressed from the more radical 1960s, the art has become more abstract, yet a thread of resistance still permeates much of the work, and the activism and history represented in the murals is often joined with preservation activities that seek to engage both an effort to preserve the art, the structure, and the open space created by the demolition movement of the 1960s-1980s in the face of the gentrification and building boom of the late 1990s and early 21st century. It remains to be seen whether the economic collapse of the early 21st century has put an end to the nearly four-decade-long process of urban renewal and gentrification or if it has merely paused it, a process which may lead to renewed efforts to destroy buildings, and the art that has been on the exterior walls of buildings in Humboldt Park and Pilsen in Chicago.

Fig. 7: Salvador Jimenez, lead artist, 18th and Blue Island, Pilsen, Chicago, IL.
Photograph © Marc Simon Rodriguez.

Works Cited

Betancur, John J. "The Settlement Experience of Latinos in Chicago: Segregation, Speculation, and the Ecology Model." *Social Forces* 74.4 (1996): 1299-324.

"Citizens keep Round the Clock Vigil on Threatened Mural Site." *Chicago Tribune* 13 April 1978.

Huebner, Jeff. "The Outlaw Artist of 18th Street Marcos Raya: His Life, His Work, His Demon." *Chicago Reader* 1 Feb. 1996.

Jeffries, Judson. "From Gang-Bangers to Urban Revolutionaries: The Young Lords of Chicago." *Journal of the Illinois State Historical Society* 96.3 (2003): 288-304.

"King Calls for Puerto Rican Meet." *Chicago Defender* 15 June 1966.

Lucas, Isidro. "A Walk through the Latino City." *Chicago Tribune* 1 Nov. 1981.

Latino Institute. *Latinos in Metropolitan Chicago: A Study of Housing and Employment.* Chicago: Latino Institute, 1983.

Rogovin, Mark. *Mural Manual: How to Paint Murals for the Classroom, Community Center, and Street Corner.* Boston: Beacon P, 1975.

Sanchez-Tranquilino, Marcos. "Murales del Movimiento: Chicano Murals and the Discourses of Art and Americanization." *Signs from the Heart: California Chicano Murals.* Ed. Eva Sperling Cockcroft and Holly Barnet-Sanchez. Albuquerque: U of New Mexico P, 1990: 84-101.

Sorrell, Victor A. "Barrio Murals in Chicago: Painting the Hispanic American Experience on 'Our Community' Walls." *Revista Chicano-Riqueña* 4.4 (1976): 50-72.

Natalie Voorhees Center for Neighborhood and Community Improvement. *Gentrification in West Town: Contested Ground.* Chicago: U of Illinois, 2001.

"Police Leaders Huddle to Cool Riot Zone." *Chicago Defender* 14 June 1966.

"The Walls of the City Blossom into a Museum of the Streets." *Chicago Tribune* 5 May 1978.

The Plaza de las Tres Culturas in Mexico City as a Point of Crystallization for Urban Cultural and Ethnic Identity

CERSTIN BAUER-FUNKE

1. Introduction

For more than 500 years, the Plaza de las Tres Culturas in Mexico City has been a symbolic site where important cultural and ethnic clashes, hybridizations, and fusions have taken place. First of all, this site was an important religious and economic center of the Aztec Empire. Following the Aztec name of the place and the city, it is also called Tlatelolco. In 1521, it became one of the battlefields during the great confrontation between Cortés and the Aztecs. Furthermore, it is an important place where the Mexican nation was born from the melting of two different cultures—the Aztec and the Spanish cultures—, which is still visible in the Plaza's architectural design. Throughout the history of Mexico, the place—as an everlasting urban landmark—therefore became a *lieu de mémoire* as it symbolizes the hybridization which has always characterized and still characterizes Mexican culture: the violent juxtaposition and melting of pre-Columbian, colonial, and modern Mexico.

After a short survey of the different periods which mark the process of this cultural and ethnic hybridization and *mestizaje*, I will focus on another historic event which took place on this Plaza: the student revolt in 1968 and the massacre in Tlatelolco on the second of October of the same year. Like over four centuries earlier, the place was again stained with the blood of the Mexican people. My contribution will then focus on the way in which cultural and ethnic identity, symbolized by the architectonic construction of the Plaza, are discussed in a theater play, a song, a poem, and in the testimonial literature about the massacre. The literary works to be analyzed are Juan Miguel de Mora's play *Plaza de las tres culturas: Tlatelolco* (1968), Judith Reyes's *corrido* "Tragedia de la Plaza de las Tres Culturas" (1968), Rosario Castellanos's poem "Memorial de Tlatelolco" (1971), and Elena Poniatowska's compilation of eye-witness's recollections of the massacre in her book *La noche de Tlatelolco* (1971).

2. Historical, Cultural, and Ethnic Significance of the Plaza de las Tres Culturas

The Plaza de la Tres Culturas is the actual name of a large square in the northern part of Mexico City, which is situated in a *colonia* called Tlatelolco. Ever since modern Mexico City emerged from the fusion of the ancient Aztec cities—especially of

Tlatelolco and Tenochtitlán—this place has been an important landmark in the urban landscape because it had a significant function as a point of crystallization for historical, cultural, and ethnic events and changes. So, as an introduction to my analysis of the four literary testimonies of the massacre mentioned above, I will present a short historical survey in order to explain its trans-epochal significance.

After a long walk from their mythic region Aztlán, a tribe called Mexicas arrived at the valley where Mexico City is now situated. They settled in Chapultepec in 1276, and some time later moved to the lake named Texcoco, where they founded a city called Tenochtitlán in 1325 (cf. Bernecker/Pietschmann/Tobler 13-20). In the immediate neighborhood they founded another city named Tlatelolco. Tlatelolco formerly was an independent city of the Aztec Empire, but since both cities were only separated by a canal, as they grew, they became united into one big Aztec city in 1473 (cf. Thomas 678; Ruhl/Ibarra García 50-55). While Tenochtitlán was the religious, political, and military center, Tlatelolco became the economic center. The market of Tlatelolco was very famous because it was the biggest market in Meso-America before and still at the time of the arrival of the Spaniards, as Bernal Díaz del Castillo, a soldier in Hernán Cortés's army, described it (cf. esp. chapters XCI-XCII; Bernecker/Pietschmann/Tobler 19).

In addition to this, Tlatelolco had an important religious function because the place was also used for sacrificing young people to Huitzilopochtli, the God of the Sun and of War (cf. Ruhl/Ibarra García 51-52). According to the Aztec belief, every day Huitzilopochtli needed the hearts and the blood of young people to keep the rhythm of day and night going. Furthermore, Tlatelolco was the only bulwark the Mexicas had to protect themselves and to defend their freedom against other tribes. So the place also had an important symbolic function as a place of freedom. Architectonically, the place of Tlatelolco—in Náhuatl, Tlatelolco means 'Mound of Earth'—was characterized by many ramps and stairways, which joined at the pyramid of Tlatelolco. The many small surrounding buildings may have been small temples or platforms for ritual fights.

In 1521, a decisive intercultural and ethnic clash took place on this site which later became the Plaza de las Tres Culturas: The final battle between Cortés and the Aztecs, led by Cuauthémoc, which caused the destruction of the Aztec Empire. The place was consequently soaked with the blood of both Spaniards and Indígenas; following different sources about that event, between 40,000 and 240,000 Aztec men, women, and children are supposed to have died in this battle (cf. Thomas 649-706, esp. 703-04). Thus, its symbolic baptism as a site of tragic bloodshed was completed.

After the destruction of the Aztec Empire, the Spaniards used the stones of the Aztec market and the temples to construct a church on that same place: They built Santiago Tlatelolco, a church whose interior is decorated with a painting showing Santiago Mataindios ["Indian-slayer"] in a brutal gesture treading on Indians. As an annex to the church, in the 16th century Fray Pedro de Gante built El Colegio de la Santa Cruz for Aztec children. The famous defender of the Indians, Fray Bernardino de Sahagún, worked there as a teacher of Aztec pupils.

The Metropolitan Cathedral in Tenochtitlán was also constructed with the stones of the Templo Mayor from 1573 on; so was the huge Palacio Nacional. Cortés himself used the debris of Montezuma's Palace to build his house. In 1978, during works to lay new cables next to the Metropolitan Cathedral, workers discovered the sunken Templo Mayor. But even before that date, already in the years 1964 and 1965, workers had discovered the Aztec market of Tlatelolco. Thus, the actual Plaza de las Tres Culturas was chronologically the first place of the destroyed Aztec Empire to reappear in contemporary Mexico (cf. Thieme-Sachse 496, 500-06). The reason for these large-scale works was the construction of a huge residential area for more than 50,000 people, consisting of 102 enormous blocks of flats which surround the Plaza. Furthermore, a big tower was added to this immense complex called 'Nonoalco-Tlatelolco,' the Tower of Tlatelolco (1964-1966), which housed the State Department until 2005 (cf. Dussel/ Wemhöner 675-76, 678-81). Thus, since the 1960s the place has been known as the Plaza de las Tres Culturas because of its architectonic composition of the ruins of the pre-Hispanic town of Tlatelolco, the church of the colonial period, as well as the complex of 102 modern buildings and the tower constructed by the famous architect Mario Pani to represent modern Mexico.

The second enormous tragedy after 1521 took place on the second of October in 1968. During the summer of that year, Mexican students started their protests and showed their non-conformity with the Mexican political system. They demanded an open dialogue with the regime, a process of democratization, human rights, freedom of speech, and justice. The government reacted with arrests, abduction, torture, and murder, as they wanted to nip in the bud any democratic and leftist movement. The protests intensified in September, as workers and students planned to use for their purposes the international attention focused on Mexico because of the Olympic Games, which were to begin in Mexico City on October 12. October 12 is a highly symbolic date, because it is celebrated in the Hispanic world as the *Día de la Hispanidad* or *Día de la Raza* to commemorate the discovery of the New World.[1] An important meeting was announced for the evening of the second of October on the Plaza de las Tres Culturas. Thousands of people arrived on the Plaza—among them students, workers, artists, mothers with their children, street traders, and journalists from foreign countries like the Italian star journalist Oriana Fallaci—to listen to the speeches of political dissidents and labor representatives. At 5:30 pm helicopters appeared; green Bengal lights announced the attack: The Mexican government under president Gustavo Día Ordaz had ordered about five thousand soldiers, policemen, and a kind of paramilitary group wearing white gloves to attack the peaceful demonstration. For more than 30 minutes, the people sitting and standing on the Plaza were under massive machine-gun fire. The shooting diminished later, but continued for another hour. Eyewitnesses and victims wounded in the attack speak of an 'inferno.' Officially, the number of the dead was never counted. While the state-controlled press only wrote

---

[1] For the following chronology of the events of that day in October, cf. Poniatowska; Caistor 134-38; Ruhl/Ibarra García 195-96; Bernecker/Pietschmann/Tobler 316-17.

about some 30 victims, the foreign press and eye witnesses spoke about more than 500 victims. As a reaction to the massacre, Octavio Paz stepped down from his position as Mexican ambassador in India.

The third immense tragedy that took place on this Plaza was the strong earthquake in the morning of September 19 in 1985 (cf. Dussel/Wemhöner 687-88): Due to widespread corruption, the huge modern buildings were not built in line with earthquake safety standards, so that they collapsed immediately after the first tremor, burying thousands of people. For a long time, homeless people lived in tents among the ruins of Tlatelolco. One can hence imagine that the Plaza de las Tres Culturas has become, by a terrible historical coincidence, the site on which the three most severe tragedies in Mexican history have taken place.

As a summary of this first part, I would like to underline the most important aspects of Mexican ethnic and cultural identity inscribed into the Plaza's history and architectural design: In pre-Columbian times, the place was, first, defined by economic functions, and second, it was a symbolic place of freedom, of ritual fights and, third, of intense bloodshed due to the sacrifices to the God Huitzilopochtli. In 1521, it once more became the site of war, destruction, and bloodshed when the two cultures clashed, and immediately after that, it came to symbolize the building of a nation: The re-use and re-functionalization of the ancient Aztec stones to build the church Santiago Tlatelolco are an example of cultural hybridization as the beginning of the *mestizaje* in Mexico. The last step of this cultural and ethnic hybridization took place when the modern, faceless buildings, which appeared to lack a specific identity, were constructed on the Plaza. The Tlatelolco buildings stand for a modern Mexico that is part of globalization and for the sell-out of ethnic and cultural identity. The events of 1968 and especially the massacre of October 1968 mark a crucial turning point in the political history of Mexico, because the strong party dictatorship received a decisive blow. This again marks the beginning of the slow process of loss of power of the PRI (Partido Revolucionario Institucional)[2] and an increasing awareness among Mexican intellectuals of the cultural sell-out. Thus, it is important to state that every re-shaping and re-construction of this plaza in a very decisive way marks a turn to a new epoch and a changed cultural and ethnic identity in Mexican history. Furthermore, the Plaza is an important urban memorial 'silhouette,' an omnipresent witness of the everlasting presence of the past: Because of its hybrid character and its highly symbolic value, it allows for a simultaneous glimpse of the past and the present, and it is therefore a site of hybridization *par excellence*.

In addition to this, the massacre of October 1968 had a very important impact on the idea of a historical foundation of the cultural identity of the Mexican people: All of a sudden and in a very drastic way, the place regained its significance as a trans-epochal point of crystallization of memory and thus became a very important *lieu de mémoire* (*sensu* Nora). Moreover, it was immediately associated with bloodshed and

---

[2]   This party held power in Mexico from 1929 until 2000.

death, both of which appear to be the trans-historical link between the three cultures which succeeded one another on this very same site: the pre-Columbian, the colonial, and the modern Mexican cultures and their respective ethnic repercussions.

These important aspects will now guide me through my analysis of four Mexican literary and musical works of art written about the tragedy of the second of October of 1968. The works of art I will consider are very interesting in the way in which they use the multifarious historical, cultural, and religious meanings of the site. It is also very striking to observe the tremendous degree to which all texts coincide in their use of specific cultural and ethnic symbols.

3.   Literary Works on The Plaza de las Tres Culturas

3.1.   Juan Miguel de Mora: *Plaza de las tres culturas: Tlatelolco* (1968)

The play *Plaza de las tres culturas: Tlatelolco* was written in 1968 by the Mexican author, Sanskrit professor, and human rights activist Juan Miguel de Mora (*1921), who until recent years published a long series of literary and essayistic works in which he denounces the corrupt and unjust political system in Mexico.[3] The author attacks those responsible for the massacre and in an extremely harsh way criticizes the Mexican political system of the 1960s as well as the reaction of the ruling class to the student demonstrations.

Every sentence, every allusion, every image of his play *Plaza de las tres culturas: Tlatelolco* is soaked with his protest against the oppressive regime, the sell-out of Mexican culture, and the concomitant loss of identity. In his play, de Mora also uses all the different symbolic meanings of the Plaza already mentioned above and ties them together in a dramaturgically and thematically interesting way. Much more than the other works discussed later, he uses the urban space of the plaza as the point of crystallization of Mexican cultural and ethnic identity. Thus, many scenes of the play cannot be understood if one is not familiar with Mexican history, and especially with the history of the Plaza de Tlatelolco. The play reconstructs the trans-epochal signifi-cance of the place on which cultures fought against each other and struggled for their survival. The Aztec use of Tlatelolco as a ritual battlefield teleologically determines the whole action of the play.

Furthermore, de Mora uses the personification of Death as a central and omni-present dramatic figure. This is also the reason why all the characters are characterized as *agonistas* ["fighters"], but the word *agonizante* ["agonizing"] also immediately comes to mind as it introduces the thematic field of oppression, torture, death, and political murder.[4]

---

[3]   For biographical information about de Mora, cf. Ocampo, vol. V, 460-66.

[4]   All English translations are my own.

The description of the stage decoration, too, is deeply marked by death because the dramatist prescribes the use of illustrations by the Mexican artist José Guadalupe Posada (1854-1913), who might be called the 'specialist' for Mexican death (cf. Topete de Valle; Barajas Durán). Guadalupe Posada and his engravings symbolically stand for the Mexican Revolution. He was the artist of the people, of the oppressed, and the poor. His most famous figure is "La Catrina"; his *calaveras*, i.e., the skulls and skeletons he engraved, have an enormous impact on Mexican identity, and they also have a tremendous influence on the Mexican *Día de los Muertos* on November 2. These elements of the stage decoration form an integral part of Mexican cultural and ethnic identity.[5]

Moreover, de Mora prescribes a 'hybrid' and *mestizo* site: He mixes figures, symbols, and settings of the three cultures on the same plaza to create a trans-historical collage. This trans-historical collage is underlined in a sharp way by the omnipresence of death in all three cultures, here already illustrated by the stage decoration:

> Escenografía: Los dioses de la muerte del México prehispánico ... se revuelven y entremezclan con calaveras del dibujante y grabador Guadalupe Posada, ... y con una selección de cristos ensangrentados ... Muerte en su forma indígena, muerte en su forma mestiza, muerte en su forma criolla, española, pero en su esencia muerte. (121)

> ["Stage decoration: The pre-Hispanic Mexican Gods of Death ... are moving and mixing with the *calaveras* of the illustrator Guadalupe Posada ... and with a selection of bloody Christs ... Death in its indigenous form, Death in its mestizo form, Death in its criollo and Spanish form, but in its essence Death."]

De Mora here uses the popularity as well as the importance of José Guadalupe Posada's illustrations of Death in line with the Mexicans' strong relation to death, and combines it with one of the main themes: the bloodshed on the Plaza de las Tres Culturas.

Because of its dramaturgical and formal aspects, the play belongs to the highly political theater of agitation and propaganda: stereotypical figures, allegories, and personifications appear and in short scenes illustrate Mexico's long way from the Aztec culture to the year 1968, or, to be more precise, to October 2, 1968. Traditional Mexican songs and music, some Beatles and Rolling Stones songs, Chopin's "Etude révolutionnaire," Beethoven's "Funeral March" of the *Eroica* constitute the acoustic fore- and background, whereas graffiti, photos of Che Guevara, banners, and newspaper pictures establish the visual context in order to transmit the highly political message as well as the *mestizo* identity of modern Mexico. The action is structured in three acts, which consist of a collage of several short and independent scenes succeeding each other in a rapid rhythm. Marked by an aesthetic of violence, the play is extremely brutal and shocking. The following summary of the acts will show how de Mora stages the different symbolic functions of the Plaza de las Tres Culturas as a point of crystallization for Mexican ethnic and cultural identity.

---

[5]   Interestingly, Guadalupe Posada is also used by Judith Reyes in her song, which will later be discussed because of its reference to the Mexican revolution and the *corrido*.

In the first act, a boy and a voice from the off discuss the issue of what precisely is "lo latinoamericano" and how to grasp Latin-American uniqueness. In keeping with the trans-historical organization of the play, they go back to the pre-Columbian epoch in order to find the roots of Mexican cultural and ethnic identity: "Para entender al mexicano de hoy hay que conocer un poco la historia anterior de México" (137) ["If you want to understand the Mexican of today, you have to know a little about the ancient history of Mexico"]. In short scenes taking place on the Plaza, we see an Aztec emperor who oppresses his people; we see a ritual sacrifice scene in which the priest is calling on "Huitzilopochtli, Dios de la Muerte, señor de los aztecas" (138) in order to consecrate this place to the God of Death. The scene ends with the stabbing of a young boy and a young girl so that the plaza is baptized with the blood of the young generation. The next allegorical scene is dedicated to the *Conquista*, the subordination of the Indians, and the plundering of all the treasures the Spaniards found in the New World. The following scene shows the wars of independence in the 19th century. Finally 'Uncle Sam' appears and introduces a new form of colonization to Mexico.[6] The loss of pride and of political and cultural independence are visualized by a woman who presents herself as a prostitute and tries to seduce 'Uncle Sam.' The Mexican revolution also shows up, musically accompanied by the very famous *corrido* "La Adelita." The act ends with a kind of political speech that parodies the Mexican president, who, besides, is responsible for the Tlatelolco massacre: the typical PRI-rhetoric of the Mexican revolution and, above all, the opening of Mexico to the international, U.S.-dominated trade system. Thus, for de Mora, this third culture is profoundly neo-colonial rather than post-colonial, due to Mexico's (economic) dependence on the United States of America.

The second act is dedicated to the oppression of the student generation in Mexico in the 1960s. Some students respect the orders from 'above,' others demand a process of democratization, freedom of speech, and the human and civil rights discussed by students all over the world at the time. We see how the revolutionary spirit awakes among the students and how the official representatives of the PRI react to these claims. In the next scene, a dissident student is tortured and killed directly in front of the Mexican president and an old, gold-covered whore who personifies the Mexican revolution. The final scene of the act is a very significant one, too: Female personifications of the three cultures—named "la Cultura Indígena," "la Cultura Colonial," and "la Cultura Híbrida"—are discussing which of the three is the most valuable. They agree on having a song contest in order to find out who is the best one. However, after the contest, they begin to quarrel because each of them thinks she is the best. At that moment, a very old woman enters the stage. The three cultures ask her to give her opinion, but as an answer, the old woman shows who she really is: she is Death and shoots down all three Cultures. This personification of Death is obviously inspired by the engravings of José Guadalupe Posada. Students, a boy, an old woman, a worker, a

---

[6] De Mora here hints at the essay *Ariel* written by José Enrique Rodó in 1900 as a protest against the U.S.-American influence in Latin America.

pregnant woman, and a girl start arriving at the plaza, and, just like on the engravings of Guadalupe Posada, Death walks around among the people and repeats a conspiracy date like a refrain: "¡La cita es en la Plaza de las Tres Culturas!" (180-82) ["The meeting is on the Plaza de las Tres Culturas!"]

The third act opens with a scene that takes place only moments before the massacre begins. A foreign reporter takes pictures which are immediately destroyed by a soldier; the pregnant woman goes around; a boy arrives; a foreign journalist shows up; some students walk around. They discuss why they are here on the Plaza de las Tres Culturas, why they protest against the political system of the PRI, and why they fight for a democratic and independent Mexico. Then the first soldiers and the policemen in civil clothes with their white gloves appear; machine-gun fire starts; screaming and shooting are heard, and, one after the other and isolated by a spotlight, the characters who were 'invited' by Death to come to the plaza die in the gunfire. After the murder of the student, the scene is abruptly illuminated so that all corpses lying in their blood are revealed. The last scene continues on this battlefield covered with all the dead bodies. A beautiful girl named "Sociedad de Consumo" on the plaza meets a certain "Sr. Gris Eterno Conformista"; they then step over the corpses on their way to the opening celebration of the Olympic Games—this last scene recalls the painting in the church Santiago Tlatelolco: Santiago Mataindios stepping over the corpses of the Indians—while photos of the student revolt in Berlin and Paris as well as photos of tortured people in Vietnam can be seen on the projection surface. Then a bomb explodes over the heads of the spectators and hundreds of photos of a killed boy come down. This scene is especially brutal and touching at the same time; the picture of the boy also appears in other works about the massacre, as, for instance, in Judith Reyes's song and Elena Poniatowska's testimonial book. The following analysis will underline how de Mora and the other artists use all the above-mentioned aspects for their critical purposes; the last chapter then discusses the importance of de Mora's play in the process of (dis)remembering the trans-epochal significance of the Plaza de las Tres Culturas.

3.2. Judith Reyes: "Tragedia de la Plaza de las Tres Culturas" (1968/1969)

Another very strong voice in Mexico who protested against violence, oppression, exploitation, and an unjust political and social system was the composer and singer Judith Reyes (1924-1988). She was born in Chihuahua, which was the center of the Mexican Revolution. She used a musical form, the traditional *corrido*, to formulate her social and political protest. Because of her struggle against the political system in the context of the student revolt in 1968, Reyes was arrested and tortured in 1969; as she received threats on her life, she left Mexico after her release and stayed in Europe and the United States of America for some years before returning to Mexico, where she continued her protests against the 'dirty war' ["guerra sucia"] against democratic and leftist activists.[7]

The *corrido*, like the *canción ranchera* of the Mariachi orchestras, is a popular Mexican literary and musical genre which is particularly associated with the Mexican Revolution of 1910. It was a very important medium to spread political information and to inform the masses. It expressed the struggle for freedom of the Mexican peasants and their fight for an agrarian reform. So the *corrido* is thematically deeply connected with revolution, war, freedom, and with protest against the mighty landlords and the ruling upper class. From a literary point of view, the *corrido* is a variation of the Spanish romance. It is a lyrical and epic, ballad-like poem structured in 20 or 30 quartets of eight syllables per line and accompanied by a guitar or a *requinto*, a small orchestra. The content is divided into six parts: address to the public, definition of the place, the date, and the name of the hero, description of the events, message or moral, farewell to the hero, and goodbye of the singer.[8]

During the Mexican Revolution, the *corrido* was the most important chronicle of the revolutionary events, and it became the direct expression of the historical consciousness of the peasants. The *corridos* also criticized the landing of U.S.-American troops; they celebrated the heroic actions of Pancho Villa, the rebel and avenger of the poor, and Emiliano Zapata, the leader of the *agrarista* movement whose battle cry was "Land and Freedom." As so-called *corridos agraristas*, these songs protested against the unjust distribution of the land and the exploitation of the peasants. These *corridos agraristas* were, consequently, an open declaration of war. They circulated orally and in little booklets, illustrated in many cases by the wood engravings of José Guadalupe Posada. The most popular *corridos* of the Mexican Revolution were "La Cucaracha," "La Valentina," and "La Adelita," and Guadalupe Posada illustrated these figures with his engravings (cf. Topete de Valle; Barajas Durán).

This information on the literary and musical genre of the *corrido*, the Mexican revolution, and Guadalupe Posada's engravings is necessary to understand how Judith Reyes combines this cultural heritage in her *corrido* on the massacre called "Tragedia de la Plaza de las Tres Culturas."[9] Reyes wrote and composed this *corrido* some days after the massacre of October 2, 1968. In very sharp contrast to the content of the song, the music is waltz-like, soft, and cheerful. Judith Reyes describes the peaceful meeting and the sudden assault by the police and the military in 15 quartets. She also hints at the men with white gloves who fired into the crowd of people. She speaks about a twelve-year-old boy who died next to her; she tells about Oriana Fallaci and how she

---

[7]   For biographical information about Judith Reyes, cf. Marsh.

[8]   For the history, form, and importance of the *corrido*, cf. Mendoza; Custodio; Herrera-Sobek.

[9]   In her openly political *corridos*, she speaks about the heroes of the Revolution, about Che Guevara, about violence, oppression, exploitation, an unjust political and social system, and about the sell-out of Mexico's independence in its relation to the U.S. Reyes composed ten *corridos* for her *Cronología del Movimiento Estudiantil* published in 1969.

was wounded. Her main theme, however, is the rebellion of the students against the corrupt political system.

The most important effect of this song is its conservation of images that focus on the inhuman act against the Mexican people. The images she recalls in her *corrido* are the twelve-year-old boy, young men with their heads against the wall, heaps of dead and wounded bodies, and young men who show the Victory sign. These images effectively evoke the massacre's brutality; they are no fictional invention. In Poniatowska's book published two years later, one can find all these brutal and shocking images. Like de Mora, Reyes uses these violent pictures to touch the listeners of her song emotionally and to recollect the memories of that sad day. Along with these images, she also uses the imagery of the bloodshed that we will later see in the testimonies compiled by Poniatowska. Thus, Judith Reyes sings: "Como te escurre la sangre / Plaza de las tres culturas" ["Plaza de las Tres Culturas, look how you are soaked in blood"]. By using these images, Reyes connects her description of the massacre to the different religious and historical significations the place had during the pre-Hispanic and the colonial epochs. Like de Mora, she puts emphasis on the trans-epochal and therefore constant elements of Mexican cultural and ethnic identity. That is why the words "acordarme" and "recordará" ["I/he/she will remember"] are used again and again like leitmotifs to underline the necessity not only of protesting against this horrible crime and of denouncing the guilty, but, most of all, of not forgetting what happened on the Plaza de las Tres Culturas, because what happened there in 1968 has ever since determined and forever will determine the cultural and ethnic identity of the Mexican people.

3.3. Elena Poniatowska: *La noche de Tlateloclo* (1971)

In her testimonial book *La noche de Tlatelolco*, published in 1971, Elena Poniatowska (*1932), the Grande Dame of Mexican literature,[10] gives a voice to the victims of the massacre: She presents a lot of newspaper clippings as well as graffiti and, what is most important, she directly quotes innumerable reports and memories of many eyewitnesses, victims, and relatives of victims, which she compiled between 1968 and 1970. Most of the reports focus on the individual suffering during and immediately after the massacre, and it is worth remarking that nearly all of the witnesses and victims stress the inconceivable quantity of blood they saw everywhere: on themselves, on the people surrounding them, on heaps of shoes lying around, on the plaza, and also on the ancient Aztec stones and ruins that where covered in blood. Poniatowska does not analyze the events; she just pieces together statements from students, teachers, workers, neighbors, women and children, soldiers, and official representatives of the regime.

Poniatowska's book marks an important moment in the history of Mexican literature not only because of its content—the book became a strong counterpart to the silence of the official media—, but also because of its new form: the testimonial genre, which

---

[10] For biographical information about Elena Poniatowska, cf. Ocampo, vol. VI, 547-71.

is situated on the crossroads between journalism and literary fiction (cf. Jorgensen; Abeyta; Gelpí; Unnold).

In the context of my analysis of different works dealing with the massacre, Poniatowska's book is very important as it underlines the authenticity of the images created in the literary and musical works; this can also be said about the photos published in the book. Furthermore, it confirms the trans-epochal significance of the place from the Aztec Empire to modern Mexico.

3.4. Rosario Castellanos: "Memorial de Tlatelolco" (1971)

In her poem "Memorial de Tlatelolco" written for and published in Poniatowska's *La noche de Tlatelolco* (1971), the very prominent Mexican author and poet Rosario Castellanos (1925-1974) evokes the same main themes also voiced by Elena Poniatowska, Judith Reyes, and Juan de Mora in their works. Like Elena Poniatowska and Octavio Paz, Rosario Castellanos was also a very important political figure. She was the Mexican ambassador in Israel, where she died in an accident in 1974.[11]

Rosario Castellanos belongs to the most famous Mexican writers; in her novels she adopts the perspective of the exploited *indígenas* and criticizes the unjust social system. In her poem "Memorial de Tlatelolco," she asks a lot of questions as a way of grasping the inconceivable and to prevent disremembering. She puts the emphasis on how the political representatives tried to hide the crime: There were no news about the massacre in the newspaper, television, and radio; archives were empty; dead and wounded people disappeared; and the blood which soaked the ancient stones was quickly washed away. All traces were rapidly erased. But she raises her voice to ensure that all the blood and all the images 'survive' both in the memory of those who eye-witnessed what had happened and in Mexican collective memory.

Like Judith Reyes and Juan de Mora, Castellanos contributes to transforming the Plaza into a *lieu de mémoire*, a site of memory, by recalling the original function of the Plaza de Tlatelolco when she interprets the massacre as a sacrifice to the ancient Aztec goddess Coatlicue, who is Huitzilopochtli's mother: "No busques lo que no hay: huellas, cadáveres / Que todo se le ha dado como ofrenda a una diosa" (163) ["Don't search for things that do not exist: traces, dead corpses / because all this has been given as a sacrifice to the Goddess"]. And she, too, underlines the bloodshed which has profoundly marked the plaza throughout the times. Finally, Castellanos also uses the words "recuerdo, recordamos" ["I remember, we remember"] as leitmotifs in order to formulate her protest and to express her opposition to the Mexican political system and the ruthless government.

In 1993, a plaque was installed on the Plaza de las Tres Culturas to commemorate the massacre. Rosario Castellanos's poem "Memorial de Tlatelolco" is engraved on this plaque. Thus, her wish to contribute to the collective memory of this sad day

---

[11] For biographical information about Rosario Castellanos, cf. Ocampo, vol. I, 333-43.

and to the Plaza's character as a *lieu de mémoire* finally became reality many years after her death.

4. The Trans-Epochal Importance of the Plaza de las Tres Culturas as a Point of Crystallization for Urban Cultural and Ethnic Identity

When we look at the aspect of cultural and ethnic identity, in all three literary texts— the play, the *corrido*, and the poem—the *Plaza de Tlatelolco* seems to be the place where cultural and ethnic identity are both confirmed and questioned at the same time: On the one hand, we see the suffering of the oppressed people, and on the other hand we have the *conquistadores* and the ruling *junta* who sacrifice the Mexican people for their own purposes: The belief in the Aztec God, it seems, has been replaced by the belief in a modern 'God,' i.e., a merciless system of worldwide economic exploitation, based on the dynamics of globalization and neo-colonization, which finally leads to the above-mentioned sell-out of cultural identity. This loss is staged in the urban space of Tlatelolco so as to visualize its political, economic, cultural, religious, and ethnic significance. As I have shown, Juan Miguel de Mora uses all the different significations and functions of the Plaza de las Tres Culturas: He establishes the bloody ritual function the place had at the time of the Aztecs as a trans-historical constant of Mexican cultural and ethnic identity; he parallels the bloody rite of Huitzilopochtli with the sacrifice of the young student generation struggling for freedom and human rights; he uses the hybrid death cult of the Mexicans, which incorporates Aztec and Christian elements, to also establish links between the major events in the process of the building of a nation between 1521 and 1968. Thus, like in Aztec times, the plaza functions as a battlefield and, at the same time, is the place for decisive turning points in the process of the formation of a national cultural and ethnic identity. In addition to this, Juan Miguel de Mora relocates the strategic function of the ancient Plaza as the market center of Mesoamérica to a very modern context in order to emphasize his criticism of the U.S.-dominated capitalist system in Latin America and to hint at the neo-colonial rather than post-colonial situation of modern, 'independent' Mexico, thus alluding to a new form of colonization that is taking place, represented by the newly invented God "Pepsicoatl" as a symbol of the global McDonaldization.

Consequently, the *Plaza* functions as a point of crystallization on which all these numerous and different but interlinked aspects converge. This seems to confirm de Mora's opinion that Mexican ethnic and cultural identity is indeed a hybrid, *mestizo* one. The Aztec ruins and the colonial church on the Plaza have the function of safeguarding the monumental, indestructible origins of the Mexican culture and nation. The stones are mute eyewitnesses of all the bloodshed; in 1968, when they were riddled with bullets, even they once more became as wounded as the Mexican people still is today. The Plaza de las Tres Culturas has been transformed into an aesthetic *memento mori*. All these symbolic functions and meanings of the place condensed into de Mora's theater play are one reason for its uniqueness. Another reason for this is the fact that the dramatist gives the main role to the Plaza itself. He explained in his play why the Plaza for 500 years has been and still is—even today—an open wound in the heart of Mexico. The works of Judith Reyes and Rosario Castellanos as well as the recollections published by Elena Poniatowska confirm and underline this interpretation of the Plaza, which therefore became a *lieu de mémoire par excellence.*

As a testimony of the massacre, de Mora's play is an important document of the political theater of the 1960s, which tried to explain the country's way through history up to this traumatic moment. At the same time, it is chronologically the first Mexican drama that treated this subject. A drama written only one year after the tragedy, Pilar Campesino's *Octubre terminó hace mucho tiempo* ["October ended a long time ago"] could not be staged in 1969 because of alleged political and moral doubts. According to the aesthetic patterns of the genres they used, Judith Reyes, Rosario Castellanos, and Elena Poniatowska also present testimonies of the massacre. Thus, this massacre appears to be the decisive event that binds together the trans-epochal significance of the Plaza de las Tres Culturas on which this constant struggle for cultural and ethnic identity emerges. The voices raised by de Mora, Reyes, Castellanos, and Poniatowska are unique and shocking in their plaintive and accusatory power. In the following years, very few Mexican authors dared to write against the officially dictated silence. The plays written later on, like Adam Guevara's *Me enseñaste a querer* (1988; "You taught me how to love"), José Vásquez Torre's *Idos de octubre* (1993; "The dead of October") or Miguel Angel Tenorio's *68: Las heridas y los recuerdos* (1998; "68: The wounds and the memories") look back at the massacre and rather show the psychological effects of this collective trauma (cf. Küppers).

The silence dictated from 'above' for decades prevented work on cultural memory. Only very slowly did the 'literature of Tlatelolco' become an important element of the process of remembering. The novels and plays reclaim the cultural memory by autobiographic remembrance and collective commemoration. In this process, the Plaza de las Tres Culturas is not only an urban landmark, but above all a trans-epochal symbol and visual *lieu de mémoire* of Mexican history, culture, and identity, evoking memories of the nation's most tragic moments.

Works Cited

Abeyta, Michael. "Un cuadro sincrónico del cuerpo en *La noche de Tlatelolco* y en *Visión de los vencidos.*" *Relaciones: Estudios de Historia y Sociedad* 82.21 (2000): 177-98.

Barajas Durán, Rafael. *Posada: Mito y mitote: La caricatura política de José Guadalupe Posada y Manuel Alfonso Manila.* México, D.F.: Fondo de Cultura Económica, 2009.

Bernecker, Walther L., Horst Pietschmann, and Hans Werner Tobler. *Eine kleine Geschichte Mexikos.* Frankfurt/M.: Suhrkamp, 2007.

Caistor, Nick. *Mexico City: A Cultural and Literary Companion.* New York and Northampton: Interlink Books, 2000.

Castellanos, Rosario. "Memorial de Tlatelolco." Elena Poniatowska. *La noche de Tlatelolco.*
México, D.F.: Ediciones Era 1991, 11th printing of the 2nd, revised edition, 1998. 163-
64.

Custodio, Alvaro. *El corrido popular mexicano: Su historia, sus temas, sus intérpretes.*
Madrid: Ediciones Júcar, 1976.

Díaz del Castillo, Bernal. *Historia verdadera de la conquista de la Nueva España.* (Manu-
scrito "Guatemala"). Ed. José Antonio Barbón Rodríguez. México, D.F.: El Colegio de
México, Universidad Nacional Autónoma de México, 2005.

Dussel, Susanne, and Antje Wemhöner. "Architektur in Mexiko im 20. Jahrhundert: Zwischen
Internationalismus und Nationalismus." *Mexiko heute: Politik, Wirtschaft, Kultur.* Ed.
Walther L. Bernecker, Marianne Braig, Karl Hölz, and Klaus Zimmermann. Frankfurt/M.:
Vervuert, ³2004. 663-96.

Gelpí, Juan G. "Testimonio periodístico y cultura urbana en *La noche de Tlatelolco* de Elena
Poniatowska." *Celehis: Revista del Centro de Letras Hispanoamericanas* 9.12 (2000):
285-308.

Herrera-Sobek, María. *The Mexican Corrido: A Feminist Analysis.* Bloomington: Indiana UP,
1990.

Jorgensen, Beth E. "Framing Questions: The Role of the Editor in Elena Poniatowska's *La
noche de Tlatelolco.*" *Latin American Perspectives* 18.3 (1991): 80-90.

Küppers, Gaby. *Tlatelolco 30 Jahre danach: Erinnerungstheater an das Massaker an der Stu-
dentInnenbewegung in Mexico.* <http://www.ila-web.de/theaterszene/274mex_tlatelolco.
htm>.

Marsh, Hazel. "'Writing Our History in Songs': Judith Reyes, Popular Music and the Student
Movement of 1968." *Bulletin of Latin American Research* 29.1 (2010): 144-59.

Mendoza, Vicente T. *El corrido de la Revolución Mexicana.* México, D.F.: Fondo de Cultura
Económica, ²1974.

de Mora, Juan Miguel. *Plaza de las tres culturas: Tlatelolco: El teatro en la Ciudad de
México.* Vol.: *La Ciudad de México.* México, D.F.: Escenología, 1997. 115-205.

Ocampo, Aurora M., ed. *Diccionario de escritores mexicanos, siglo XX.* México, D.F.:
Universidad Nacional Autónoma de México, 2002.

Poniatowska, Elena. *La noche de Tlatelolco.* México, D.F.: Ediciones Era 1991, 11th printing
of the 2nd, revised edition, 1998.

Reyes, Judith. "Tragedia de la Plaza de las Tres Culturas." *Cantaré: Songs aus Lateinamerika.* Ed. Carlos Rincón and Gerda Schattenberg-Rincón. Ost-Berlin: Verlag Neues
Leben, 1978. 422-26.

Ruhl, Klaus-Jörg, and Laura Ibarra García. *Kleine Geschichte Mexikos von der Frühzeit bis
zur Gegenwart.* München: Beck, 2000.

Thieme-Sachse, Ursula. "Archäologie und Denkmalpflege." *Mexiko heute: Politik, Wirtschaft,
Kultur.* Ed. Walther L. Bernecker, Marianne Braig, Karl Hölz, and Klaus Zimmermann.
Frankfurt/M.: Vervuert, ³2004. 493-516.

Thomas, Hugh. *Die Eroberung Mexikos: Cortés und Montezuma.* Frankfurt/M.: S. Fischer
Verlag, ²1998.

Topete de Valle, Alejandro, ed. *José Guadalupe Posada: Prócer de la gráfica popular mexicana*. Aguascalientes: Universidad Autónoma, 2007.

Unnold, Yvonne. "El testimonio y *La Noche de Tlatelolco*." *Revista de Literatura Mexicana Contemporánea* 6.13 (2000): 26-31.

II. ETHNICITIES ON THE MOVE

MIGRATIONS, MOBILITIES, AND THE METROPOLIS

A New Founding of Lima in the City Center of Santiago de Chile?: Structure and Problems of Peruvian Immigration to the Chilean Capital

AXEL BORSDORF AND ALOISIA GÓMEZ SEGOVIA

1. Introduction

"Nosotros no podemos permitir que los peruanos estén fundando Lima en el centro de Santiago" ["We cannot allow the Peruvians to found Lima in the center of Santiago"], Iván Moreira, a conservative member of the Chilean Parliament, declared on 19 February, 2009.

Immigration from Peru to Chile has risen remarkably in the last decades. One might, on the one hand, wonder about the motives of the migrants, the demographic and social structure, the activities in which they are involved in Santiago, or their relationship to the host city and host population; on the other hand, one might be curious about the opinions and attitudes of the Chileans with regard to the Peruvians.

Although the phenomenon is highly visible and frequently discussed in the main Chilean newspapers, there are at present only few scholarly studies of the topic. Most of them are written by Chilean authors (Martínez Pizarro, *El encanto*, "Magnitude"; Martínez Pizarro/Vono; Stefoni, *Immigracion peruana en Chile*, "La migración"; Luque Brazan). There is only one study by Peruvians (De los Rios/Rueda), and another study published in Ecuador (Altamirano, "El Perú"). Altamirano published a study as early as 1992, republished in 2000, dealing with the Peruvian exodus at that time. In most of these studies, the quantitative dimension, the motives, social structures, and conflicts are analyzed, but there is only one approach that deals with the spatial dimension (Schiappacasse). Torres and Hidalgo concentrate their analysis on lower-class case study areas (Santiago, Recoleta Independencia), but they do not consider the concentration of female Peruvian immigrants in the wealthy municipalities of the metropolitan area. Other authors look at the effects of globalization as a driver of migration (Muñoz). Haferkamp, Holzapfel, and Rummenhöller analyzed the motives of Peruvian migrants, as Altamirano had already done in his general analysis in 1992 and later De los Rios and Rueda. Martínez Pizarro and Vono give an overview of interregional migration in Latin America. Our contribution will also have a spatial orientation, but will include an overview of the metropolitan area as well as case studies of the most affected municipalities (Santiago and Las Condes).[1]

The share of people born in other countries in the current Chilean population (15.1 million) is 1.2% (185,000, cf. INE 2002). On the other hand, 487,000 Chileans are living in other countries. The largest group of foreigners in Chile are Argentineans (26%); Peruvians constitute the second largest group (21%, registered immigrants only, cf. INE 2002). There is no xenophobia against Argentineans, but there is a strong resistance against Peruvians, not only among some *Santiaguinos* but also in the press and on television. In 2002, 38,000 Peruvians were legally registered as living in Chile (cf. INE 2002); it could be estimated that twice as many Peruvian immigrants are living undocumented in Chile (cf. Gómez Segovia). These figures are contradicted by the Peruvian statistics. Altamirano ("El Perú") stated that between 1990 and 2003 alone, 180,544 Peruvians immigrated to Chile. Even if this figure is correct and we add those Peruvians who had immigrated to Chile earlier, the share of Peruvians living in Chile is small, and is not, for example, comparable to the number and percentage of Turks, Greeks, or Bosnians living in Germany or Austria.

However, the concentration of Peruvians in the Chilean capital Santiago is remarkable. About 80% of the registered immigrants coming from the northern neighbor country of Chile live in Santiago (cf. Stefoni, "La migracion"). What is more, they are locally concentrated in only three municipalities of Greater Santiago. Their numbers increased significantly during the 1990s (cf. fig. 1).

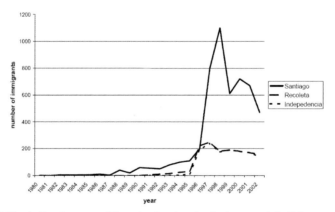

Fig. 1: Development of Peruvian immigration in three municipalities of Santiago de Chile, 1980-2002 (Torres/Hidalgo, fig. 2, modified).

---

[1] This study is based on the diploma thesis of Aloisia Gómez Segovia (2008), supervised by Axel Borsdorf, and complemented by fieldwork by Axel Borsdorf, carried out in cooperation with Rodrigo Hidalgo, Santiago de Chile.

The focal questions of this article are: What is the impact of Peruvian immigration on spatial, social, and economic structures in Santiago de Chile? Which problems arise with regard to integration and gender? How do Chileans and the Chilean mass media react to the Peruvian immigration?

2.   Theoretical Framework

Overviews of the theories of migration and transnational mobility are manifold (cf., e.g., Fassmann; Han; Parnreiter). We will concentrate on only a few of these. In his work on the dual labor market, Piore argued that capitalism tended to develop a secondary labor segment of cheap foreign workers, who act as a reserve army of capitalism. From a spatial point of view, Scholz interprets fragmentation as an element of capitalistic development, leading to a socially and spatially segregated and fragmented space (cf. fig. 2).

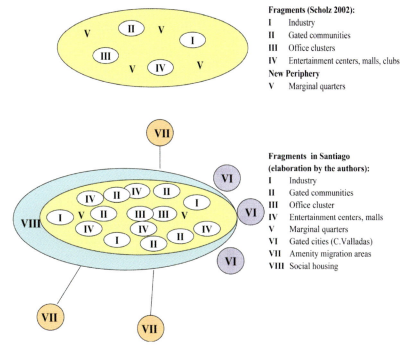

Fig. 2: The model of fragmented development (Scholz) modified and applied to Santiago de Chile by the authors.

In 1971, Zelinsky had already noticed a change of mobility patterns and implemented this in his model of mobility transformation, which was complemented by Borsdorf, who included the development trends of the last few decades. More moderate is the estimation by Glick Schiller, Basch, and Szanton-Blanc. They see foreign immigration as building a bridge between source and target nation, forming a 'both-and' or 'as well as' identity. Following this argument, Fassmann and Mydel even see the ethnic networks among immigrants as favorable to integration. They are also very important for subsequent Peruvian immigrants.

The oldest theory on migration was elaborated by Ravenstein in 1889 and further developed by Lee in 1966 with his push-and-pull model. In the specific case at hand, the push factors in Peru are economic depression, political repression (specifically under the Fujimori administration and the activities of the Sendero Luminoso guerilla movement), poverty and the low standard of living, the traditional structures in Peru, and the poor living conditions in the Andean country. Pull factors in Chile are the progress in society and economy, political liberty, the comparative well-being of the Chilean population, the high standard and quality of life, the modern infrastructure, and the higher incomes.

Tables 1 and 2 give some indicators of socio-economic levels in Chile and Peru (in table 1 compared to Austria).

Country	Austria	Chile	Peru
Human Development Index (HDI)	High	High	Medium
HDI value	0.948	0.867	0.773
Life expectancy	79.4	78.3	70.0
Index of life expectancy	0.907	0.889	0.761
GDP/capita (U.S.$)	33,700	12,027	6,039
Index GDP/capita	0.971	0.799	0.684
Education index	0.966	0.914	0.872

Table 1: HDI indicators for Austria, Chile and Peru 2005
(*Fischer Weltalmanach*).

Country	Chile	Peru
Malnutrition (% of total population) 1990/92	8	42
Malnutrition (% of total population) 2002/04	4	12
Unemployment rate 2005	6.9	11.4
Poverty index 2005	3.7	11.6
Literacy rate	95.7	87.9

Table 2: Socio-economic indicators for Chile and Peru
(*Fischer Weltalmanach*).

3.   The Immigration of Peruvians to Santiago de Chile

The migration between Peru and Chile is characterized by historical, economic and political conditions. From colonial times until 1985, Peru was a main target region for migrants from Europe, for instance, for Spaniards, Italians, or Germans. Due to the colonial triangle trade, Africans were brought to Peru as slaves and in the 19th century Chinese workers immigrated to Peru as workers in the transport system. Until 1985 there was only little emigration from Peru to other countries to be observed. However, since then the situation has changed and an increasing number of Peruvians have left their country for economic and later for political reasons.

Altamirano ("El Perú") has documented this new emigration trend (cf. fig. 3). De los Rios and Rueda estimated that 50.7% of the Peruvian emigrants live in the United States, 7.3% in Argentina, 6.8% in Venezuela, 6.5% in Spain, 5% in Italy, and 4.7% in Chile.

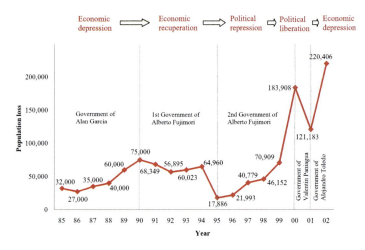

Fig. 3: Migration balance of Peru, 1985-2002
(Altamirano "El Perú," modified).

In the years 1990 to 2007 the U.S. lost its outstanding status as the target region for Peruvian emigrants, but remained the overall most important target: 30.6% of the migrants still went to the United States. Countries with the largest gain in migrants from Peru are Argentina with a share of 14% of the Peruvian emigration, Spain with 13%, Italy with 10.3%, and Chile, which attracted 9.3% of the migrants (figures courtesy of DIGEMIN, Dirección General de Migraciones y Naturalización, Lima). In this period Venezuela lost its status as an attractive target due to changes in the economic and political situation. Only 3.1% of Peruvian migrants went there, mostly for family reasons.

To a certain degree, Peruvian emigration to Chile demonstrates similarities to the rural exodus which characterized inner-Chilean mobility in the 1960s and 1970s (cf. Borsdorf). The migrants formerly lived in rural areas and the majority is female: 55.9% of the Peruvians who immigrated to Chile between 1990 and 2007 are women. This is the largest percentage of Peruvian female emigrants in relation to other Latin American target regions. In Greater Santiago the share of Peruvian women is even larger: 61.06% of the migrants are female.

4.   Demographic Structure, Spatial Distribution, and Economic Activities of the Peruvian Immigrants in Santiago de Chile

The age pyramids of the Peruvian immigrants demonstrate the predominance of the female population and of the age groups of 20 to 40 years. While in the central municipalities the gender relation is more or less balanced, in the municipality of Las Condes, where the rich Chileans live, there is a female predominance to be observed (cf. fig. 4). This is the result of the demand for domestic personnel there. Almost 80% of the Peruvians living in Las Condes are domestic employees.

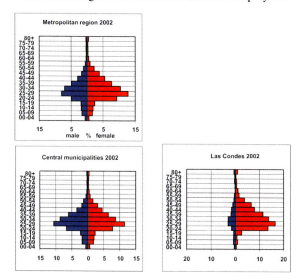

Fig. 4: Age and gender structure of Peruvian immigrants (Gómez Segovia, 49-51).

In the metropolitan region of Santiago, the gainful employment of Peruvians is much more balanced. 43% are domestic employees, 46% legal workers, 3% businessme and 8% self-employed persons. It has to be considered that these figures only include the legal immigrants; illegal migrants mainly work in the informal sector. As measured by their level of education, Peruvians are not appropriately occupied: 18% possess a university degree, 22% have finished a professional degree, and 44% have a high school education (cf. INE 2002). This points to the poor employment and income conditions in Peru.

The spatial distribution shows certain disparities among the municipalities of Greater Santiago. There are high concentrations of Peruvians in the central districts, in the living areas of the high and upper middle class municipalities, and in one poor district of Santiago (cf. fig. 5). With reference to gender structure, these disparities are even more significant (cf. fig. 6).

Axel Borsdorf and Aloisia Gómez Segovia

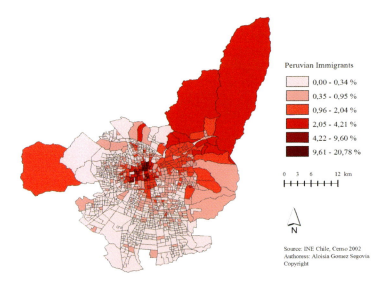

Fig. 5: Spatial distribution of Peruvian immigrants in Greater Santiago 2002 (Gómez Segovia 36).

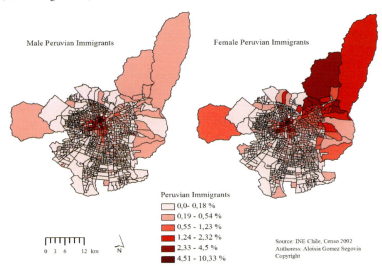

Fig. 6: Spatial gender distribution of Peruvian immigrants in Greater Santiago 2002 (Gómez Segovia 37).

Especially in the central municipality of Santiago, living conditions are quite precarious. Figure 7 shows the distribution of Peruvians in comparison with some socio-economic indicators. Peruvians often share their rooms with two or more persons and the standard of living in the districts they inhabit is quite low. 62% of the Peruvians live in only one room, 20.5% in an apartment, 12% in a *conventillo* ["inner urban marginal quarter"].

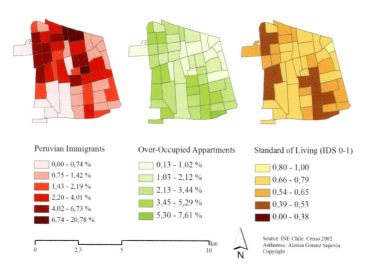

Fig. 7: Socio-economic indicators in the city center of Santiago (Gómez Segovia 44).

5. Integration

When the first Peruvians moved to Chile, they immediately founded their own social organizations. In the beginning of the 20th century, the Club Peruano was founded, followed by the Asociación de Damas Peruanas in 1964 and the Grupo Parakas, an association for businessmen, in 1990. These organizations mainly cater to Peruvians with a high social status. The first interest groups of lower-status immigrants were founded in the 1990s when the massive immigration from Peru started. The Amigos de la Vida only existed between 1993 and 1994, the Casa Andina de la Solidaridad from 1994 to 1998, and the Grupo de las Ocho Familias from 1994 to 1995. Since then the Programa Andino para la Dignidad Humana, founded in 1997, is the most powerful association of Peruvian immigrants in Santiago.

Beside these social groups, some religious and political organizations were founded, too (cf. Luque Brazan). Among the religious associations, the Comunidad Cristiana Santa Rosa de Lima, founded in 1994, the Hermanidad del Señor de los Milagros (1994), and the Pentecostal Comunidad Evangélica Peruana América para

Cristo (2000) can be mentioned. Clearly political objectives are brought forward by the Asociación de Peruanos Residentes en Chile (1997), the Comité de Refugiados Políticos Peruanos (1997), the Círculo de Estudio y Trangaja César Vallejo (2000), the Asociación de Exiliados Políticos Peruanos en Chile (2002), and the Comisión por la Libertad de Presos Políticos Peruanos Micaela Bastidas (2004). While these organizations also pursue their ideologies with the aim of changing the political situation in their mother country, the syndicates of Peruvians aim to improve the labor conditions of Peruvians in Chile. Three organizations are acting in this sense: The Asociación de Peruanos en Santiago (2001), the Sindicato Asamblea de Trabajadores Migrantes (2003), and the Asociación de Trujillanos Organizados en Santiago (2004).

Some more organizations have clearly defined cultural objectives in order to preserve the Peruvian culture and sports in Chile. Peruvian folklore, theater, and soccer are among the activities offered by these clubs.

All these organizations play an important role for Peruvian identity in Chile and for the dialogue with the dominant society.

6.   Reactions in the Chilean Mass Media

In an analysis of the coverage of the Peruvians living in Santiago in Chilean mass media realized in 2006, Arriagada and Granifo found more than 200 news items from June to December 2006. From June to September, 45% of the items were neutral, 44% negative, 11% ironical. In the last months of the year, this changed only little: 44% were neutral, 43% negative, 13% ironical. The negative topics reported on were crimes and illegality; negative to neutral were reports on integration, migration policy, the situation of women, and on arts and culture. None of the reports could be classified as positive.

This result is surprising since even in Europe, where immigrants generally differ in religion, language, and level of education, the media coverage is not that negative. The Peruvians in Chile do not differ in any of these items, and in terms of education they frequently correspond to the average or even higher-than-average Chilean. The Peruvians are only 'visible' because of their different appearance and some different customs and patterns of behavior.

7.   Theoretical Reflection

The analysis has shown that the traditional model of push and pull factors is still an appropriate way to explain the migration of Peruvians to Chile. They migrate because of the poor conditions in their homeland and come to Chile in the hope of a better life, better economic conditions, and political liberty. The model of mobility transformation has to be modified, as international migration has increased all over the world since

1971, when Zelinsky elaborated his theory. The Peruvian out-migration is only a regional branch of this global trend.

The spatial distribution of Peruvians in Santiago clearly shows elements of fragmentation and segregation, not only of the Peruvians in total, but also on a gender level. Although a number of Peruvian associations were founded in order to conserve their identity and to strive for better integration into the Chilean society, there is still a remarkable resistance on the part of Chileans against their immigrated neighbors, and this opposition is even strengthened by the mass media. So far, the optimistic assumptions of Fassmann and Mydel or Glick Schiller et al. cannot be confirmed.

Works Cited

Altamirano, Teófilo. *Liderazgo y organizaciones de peruanos en el exterior*. Culturas transnacionales e imaginarios sobre el desarrollo 1. Lima: Pontificia Universidad Católica del Perú, Fondo Editorial, 2000.

―――. "El Perú y el Ecuador: Nuevos países de emigración." *Revista Aportes Andinos* 7 (2003). <http://www.uasb.edu.ec/padh>.

Arriagada, Camilo, and Helvia Granifo. "Monitoreo de medios sobre noticias referidas a migrantes internacionales: El caso de Santiago de Chile." MIUub/AL—Observatorio experimental sobre las migraciones internacionales en las áreas urbanas de América Latina. <http://www.miurbal.net/documents/Santiago03_August07.pdf>.

―――. "Monitoreo de medios sobre noticias referidas a migrantes internacionales: El caso de Santiago de Chile." Periodo Octubre-Diciembre 2007. MIUub/AL—Observatorio experimental sobre las migraciones internacionales en las áreas urbanas de América Latina. <http://www.miurbal.net/documents/Santiago05_DIC07.pdf>.

Borsdorf, Axel "Landflucht als Teil der Mobilitätstransformation: Das Beispiel Lateinamerika." *Praxis Geographie* 7-8 (2004): 9-14.

De los Rios, Juan, and Carlos Rueda. "¿Por qué migran los Peruanos al exterior?: Un estudio sobre los determinantes económicos y no económicos de los flujos de migración internacional entre 1994 y 2003." *Economía y Sociedad* 58 (2005): 7-14.

Departamento de Extranjería y Migración del Ministerio del Interior 2005. "Evolución de la gestión gubernamental desde 1991: Desarrollo del fenómeno de las migraciones en Chile." Santiago de Chile. <http://www.extranjeria.gov.cl/filesapp/migraciones.pdf>.

Fassmann, Heinz. "Transnationale Mobilität: Empirische Befunde und theoretische Überlegungen." *Leviathan* 3 (2002): 345-59.

―――, and Raimund Mydel. "Zuwanderung und transnationale Pendlerwanderung am Beispiel der Polen in Wien." *Mitteilungen der Österreichischen Geographischen Gesellschaft* 144 (2002): 81-100.

Fischer Weltalmanach 2008. Frankfurt/M.: Fischer, 2008.

Glick Schiller, Nina, Linda Basch, and Cristina Blanc-Szanton. eds. *Toward a Transnational Perspective of Migration: Race, Class, Ethnicity and Nationalism Reconsidered*. New York: New York Academy of Sciences, 1992.

Gómez Segovia, Aloisia. *Peruanische Immigration in Santiago de Chile*. Dipl. thesis, Universität Wien, 2008.

Haferkamp, Rose, Annette Holzapfel, and Klaus Rummenhöller. *Auf der Suche nach besserem Leben: Migranten aus Peru*. Unkel/Rhein, Bad Honnef: Horlemann-Verlag, 1995.

Han, Petrus. *Theorien zur internationalen Migration*. Stuttgart: UTB, 2006.

Husa, Karl, Christof Parnreiter, and Irene Stacher, eds. *Internationale Migration: Die globale Herausforderung des 21. Jahrhunderts*. Frankfurt/M.: Brandes & Apsel, 2000.

INE (Instituto Nacional de Estadísticas). *Censos de población*. Santiago de Chile: INE, 2002.

INEI-DIGEMIN-OIM. *Perú, estadísticas de la migración internacional de Peruanos 1990-2007*. Lima: INEI-DIGEMIN-OIM, 2008.

Lee, Everett. "A Theory of Migration." *Demography* 3 (1966): 47-57.

Luque Brazan, José Carlos. "Asociaciones políticas de inmigrantes peruanos y la 'Lima Chica' en Santiago de Chile." *Migraciones Internacionales* 4.2 (2007): 121-50.

Martinez Pizarro, Jorge. *El encanto de los datos: Sociodemografia de la inmigracion en Chile según el censo de 2002*. Serie Población y Desarrollo 49. Santiago de Chile: CEPAL, 2003.

———. "Magnitude and Dynamics of Chilean Immigration, according to the Census of 2002." *Papeles de Población, Mexico* 44 (2005): 103-36.

———, and Daniela Vono. "Geografía migratoria intrarregional de América Latina y el Caribe al comienzo del siglo XXI." *Revista de Geografía Norte Grande* 34 (2005): 39-52.

Muñoz, Alma Rosa. "Efectos de la globalización en las migraciones internacionales." *Revista Papeles de Población, Mexico* 33 (2002): 10-45.

Parnreiter, Christof. "Theorien und Forschungsansätze zu Migration." *Internationale Migration: Die globale Herausforderung des 21. Jahrhunderts*. Ed. Karl Husa, Parnreiter, and Irene Stacher. Frankfurt/M.: Brandes & Apsel, 2000, 25-52.

Piore, Michael. "Upward Mobility, Job Monotony and Labor Market Structure." *Work and the Duality of Life*. Ed. James O'Toole. Cambridge, MA: MIT P, 1974. 73-87.

Ravenstein, Ernest George. "The Laws of Migration." *Journal of the Royal Statistical Society* 53 (1889): 241-301.

Schiappacasse, Paulina. "Segregación residencial y nichos étnicos de los inmigrantes internacionales en el Área Metropolitana de Santiago." *Revista de Geografía Norte Grande* 39 (2008): 21-38.

Scholz, Fred. "Die Theorie der 'fragmentierenden Entwicklung.'" *Geographische Rundschau* 54.10 (2002): 6-11.

Stefoni, Carolina. *Inmigración peruana en Chile: Una oportunidad a la integración*. Santiago de Chile: Editorial Universitaria, 2002.

———. "La migración en la agenda chileno-peruana: Un camino por construir." *El caso Enron: Principales aspectos contables de auditoría y de gobierno corporativo*. Ed. C. Bastidas Mendez. Santiago de Chile: RIL Editores, 2007. 551-64.

Torres, Alma, and Rodrigo Hidalgo. "Los peruanos en Santiago de Chile: Transformaciones urbanas y percepción de los inmigrantes." *Polis: Revista de la Universidad Bolivariana* 22 (2009). <http://www.revistapolis.cl/polis%20final/22/art17.htm>.

Zelinsky, Wilbur. "The Hypothesis of the Mobility Transition." *Geographical Review* 61 (1971): 219-49.

A Segmentary Society in the City: Urban Ethnification of Mapuche in Santiago de Chile

WALTER ALEJANDRO IMILAN

1. A Segmentary Society Migrates to the City

These days, many Latin American cities are beacons of diversity. Since large-scale mass migration from the countryside to the cities began in the middle of the 20th century, the actions of migrants have played a distinct role in reconfiguring the urban landscape.

To concentrate on the dynamics of migration is more than ever essential in order to understand the recent trajectory of Latin American cities. First of all, the experience of migration is part of the biography of a large majority of their current inhabitants. Second, the relationship with the places of origin has been instrumental in building social networks that allow access to resources for integration into the city. The link between migrants and the people in their place of origin is of fundamental importance in many cases: It is a way of maintaining and reterritorializing a network of relationships of support and cooperation. As expressed by Golte for the Peruvian case:

> The migratory movements that were widespread at the end of the first half of the 20th century did not mean that the people lost their bonds to their social groups of origin. The migration from peasant villages to other agricultural areas, mines and cities did not mean a break in the social networks, then, but its reterritorialization. Wherever migrants arrived, they recreated in formal and informal associations the cohesion of groups that shared a common origin and organized the interrelationship with their countrymen and relatives in villages. (60, my translation)

Indeed, this phenomenon of reproduction of the original bonds and their formalization through associations of migrants can also be observed elsewhere in the subcontinent, for instance in Mexico City, where an intense flow has been identified between rural and urban areas since the 1970s, permitting the reorganization of the original relations in the city. In fact, it has been ascertained that the possibilities of migrants' success in urban integration is directly related to the strength of traditional communitarianism in their villages of origin. The more communitarianism, the greater the possibility of re-producing better access to benefits in the city (cf. Velasco 205).

In general, the character of the migration process influences the ethnic relation-ships which in part propel the redefinition of a city's character. Formal and informal associations intended to fortify and strengthen the required resources for integration into the urban setting are the primary factors in the gradual increase in networked social structures of mutual aid and solidarity. These social networks manifest themselves in the urban space in the form of *barrios* and economic activities based on ethnic associations (cf. Golte/Adams). Despite exclusion and discrimination on the part of the established urban dwellers, migrants have managed to construct their own urban spaces.

The reterritorialization of social relationships based on the place of origin has become the general model—a *folk concept*[1]—used to observe the integration process of the urban indigenous: a point of view which aids researchers and political activists in assessing ethnic relationships in an urban setting to develop appropriate and effective policies affecting these social groups. Nevertheless, there are other types of processes, such as in the case of Mapuche migration to Santiago, which have proven to be quite different. Mapuche migration to Santiago has resulted neither in *barrios* nor in controlled economies as a function of their ethnic origin. The reterritorialization of filial relationships or forged alliances under the auspices of the community was not a significant factor at the beginning of the Mapuche migration. It is likely that this is the reason why, despite their large numbers, the urban Mapuche have been an invisible oppressed group over such a long period of time (cf. Montecinos 30). Consequently, the current methods that the Mapuche society has of constructing its own urban ethnicity differ from other widely documented cases in Latin America.

The history of the Mapuche people provides an important vantage point from which one may arrive at a better understanding of some distinct elements of their migration process and previous urbanization. The fact that they have a long tradition of lacking hierarchical power structures in their societies is essential. Mapuche society was a segmented society based on lineages, which only permit the formation of major alliances if they fulfill certain criteria. The underlying hypothesis of this essay posits that this experience of non-subordination, particular to a segmentary society such as the Mapuche, has had a strong impact on their subsequent migration patterns and their alliance-building strategies in urban life. Examining the existence of long-term structures is by no means intended to lay the groundwork for a search for ahistorical or essentialist aspects. There is no intention of negating the fact that an ethnic society is in permanent construction; rather, it is an effort to observe how social relationships are formed over the course of a long period of time, how they have culminated into their contemporary form, and which of them at present play a relevant role in articulating a society from within and its relationship to its context as a whole.

Ethnicity has a double aspect: On one hand, it refers to a process of social differentiation allowing for the creation of identities and senses of belonging. On the other hand, ethnicity exists as mediation between an entire spectrum of identities and

---

[1]   Wacquant refers to the folk concept as a general model used to explain and convey widely publicized images and concepts. These phenomena relating to identity are employed by policy makers and development experts to form the basis of public policy and mediations. The hegemony of this folk concept often influences political analysis and scientific research as well (cf. 8).

their political space (cf. Martucelli 41). Overall, the ethnicity of the urban Mapuche has already been examined up to the present, but the essay at hand seeks to explore the first, hitherto less documented aspect. To begin to understand it from this angle, it is first necessary to place the migration process in its historical context. This text puts forward the argument that Mapuche society's segmented character has been an obstacle to the formation of urban associations which could have directed the process of collective migration. During the second half of the 20th century, urban Mapuche associations were extremely rare. Only since the Indigenous Law of 1993 was enacted have organizations begun to proliferate in Santiago, creating a dynamic organizational topology in the city. These organizations, the role of which will also be discussed in this essay, are now considered to be the primary ethnic space. At the same time, in a less institutionalized space, second-generation migrants have begun to shape the urban horizon in the last decade as primary actors in this process. This new generation, primarily a young population, is actively demanding ethnic identity with access to a variety of resources. These youth are constructing a Mapuche ethnicity whose principal experience is urban. In effect, in order to be able to comprehend the Mapuche urban subject, this essay intends to observe three social spaces: migration, present organizations, and present youth ethnification practices.

The rise of the Mapuche *warriache* ["people of the city"], recognized by Mapuche society as a new social segment, speaks of a possible Mapuche existence not connected to a traditional community, but instead relating to a product of social differentiation in an urban environment.[2] Even though this discussion is shaped by Mapuche intellectual discourse from contradicting perspectives,[3] it is a significant contribution to the debate on how to better understand indigenous ethnicity in contemporary Latin American society.

2.   The War of Occupation and the Post-Reductional Society

In 1881, the Chilean Army initiated the last military occupation of the Mapuche territory. The so-called 'Pacification of the Araucanía,' the war of the Chilean state against the Mapuche, put an end to territorial control of Mapuche society.

Up to the military defeat, filial units based on lineage controlled the territory, each one relatively autonomous in relation to the others. The *Wallmapu*[4] ["Mapuche

---

[2] Traditionally, Mapuche society has typically acknowledged its own existence by means of social segments based on land acquisitions. The drawing of delimiters and the determination of territorial boundaries has been a historically varied process. However, groups such as the *Lafkenche, Huilliche,* and *Pewenche,* among others, have been identified as the basis of the Mapuche society as a whole.

[3] For general discussions on this topic, cf., e.g., Ancan/Calfio; Marimán.

[4] "Mapuche country" is a reference to all Mapuche territory before the occupation by both the Chilean and Argentine states.

country"] was a conglomeration of lineages forging temporary political alliances based on specific objectives. In particular, activities such as trade, internal disputes, military alliances, or peace treaties resulted in such alliances. Consequently, the entire Mapuche territory was governed by the articulation of a number of family units, often with divergent interests and varying cultural terms, although sharing the same tradition.

The political direction of the Mapuche society was formed by *lonkos* ["chiefdoms"]. The administration of Mapuche society was not a fixed social stratum. The *lonko* and their lineage formed a social unit. The *lonkos'* power stemmed from their ability to persuade and convince. A *lonko* could not exercise coercion over another *lonko*. In this vein, the primary criterion of Mapuche political power was rhetorical capacity and the ability to negotiate. The negotiating body was the so-called *xawün* (or *coyán*, later known as *parlamentos*). A series of assistants and messengers accompanied the *lonkos* to these meetings; several hundred people would sometimes be present at the *xawün*, which would be held over days or weeks (cf. Contreras Painemal 55).

In spite of the regularity and institutionalization of the *xawün*, these took on the character of a specific event as an instance of discussion, conflict resolution, and alliance-building. Each *lonko* was responsible for fulfilling the decisions adopted at these meetings to which it subscribed. Among other things, this meant that the *xawün* never became permanent bureaucratic structures; nor did they possess the logic of a state. In fact, in reference to the political organization of the *Wallmapu*, Pablo Marimán postulated:

> We can say that politically, socially, and culturally their way of being is more related to the principles of equality, reciprocity, redistribution, and horizontalism. This impeded practices which were more related to the verticality of power and its hierarchization as well as social stratification and the subsequent accumulation of wealth in a few hands. (65, my translation)

Mapuche society never had a formal state. As a result, the construction of actors of negotiation was transformed into a mechanism by which to organize internal diversity.

The negotiating bodies best documented by historians are the *parlamentos*: meetings between Mapuche and *winkas* ["foreigners"]. The first foreigners were representatives of the Spanish Crown, subsequently from the Chilean State. The *parlamentos* established territorial boundaries and trade regulations. For instance, in 1647, the Spanish Crown and the Mapuche nation signed the treaty of Killin, in which the Spanish Empire recognized the territorial autonomy of the Mapuche nation to the south of the Bio-Bio river (500 km south of Santiago). In the two hundred years which followed, Mapuche and Spaniards signed 28 treaties as confirmation of this border. This political negotiation process between nations distinguished the Mapuche situation in the Latin American context. For the same reason, the invasion of the Chilean Army during the second half of the 19th century can be viewed as an illegitimate war of occupation.[5]

---

[5] Currently, the *parlamentos* are receiving great attention from historians. They were an instance of negotiation between nations, so they had the character of an international

Over the course of the first decades of occupation, Mapuche society found itself in a new context of life on the reservation, witnesses to the obligatory modification of the economic structures, subjected to a sentiment of defeat and humiliation, and confronted with the necessity to fight with a Chilean *mestizo* society submerged in violence following the end of the war. In the years after the war, the Mapuche experienced a social catastrophe, which would not end with military defeat. Rather, it continued with the reservations and formed the basis of the profound social crisis the region of Araucanía fell into by the end of the 19th century.

Upon the war's end, a process of expropriation and mass expulsion of the population from their territories began, so that the lands could be bought and sold to the colonists. For its part, the Chilean government applied a reductional or reservation regime on the Mapuche population. In other words, limited extensions of land were given to individual families for their settlement. 90% of Mapuche territory was expropriated. Five million hectares were auctioned off between the Malleko River and Valdivia. The Mapuche were forced to reside in reservations not even totaling 500,000 hectares. The massive resettlement took place at the beginning of the 20th century, when the almost 100,000 Mapuche recorded in the 1907 census[6]—survivors of the first decades of the military occupation of their territory—were subjected to a process of territorial reductionism comprised of three thousand plots of land handed over by way of *Títulos de Merced* ["land deeds"] to heads of families. As a result, Mapuche society became atomized, with each head of family put on equal terms with the other, thus putting an end to the times of large alliances formed for the purpose of negotiation or to defend the communities against the Spanish or the Chileans. In this manner, Mapuche society entered into a process of restructuring in which new communities and new leaderships were formed. As a consequence, a new social form emerged—the so-called 'post-reductional society.'[7]

---

treaty. Thus, the Mapuche nation has an inalienable right—as a nation with international recognition before the Chilean state—to the recovery of their historical territory (cf. Contreras Painemal; Lincoqueo).

[6] The first modern census was conducted in 1907 and supervised by Tomas Guevara, Principal of Liceo de Temuco.

[7] According to Saavedra, the reductional process had the following consequences for the territory of Araucanía and for the Mapuche population: A) The military defeat and the subsequent military occupation and control by the Chilean and Argentinean armies; B) The political appropriation of the territory occupied by the Mapuche, and the auctioning of their land to landowners and Chilean foreign settlers; C) The formation of a network of fortresses and towns and private estates; D) In the exercise of political power of the state, such as sovereignty over the defeated Mapuche population, the Mapuche are forced to transform from members of ethnic autonomous corporations to citizens of the Chilean and Argentinean States, under a foreign law in the definition of which they had never participated; E) The installation of Mapuche families on bounded land granted as a 'mercy' (residence in reductions); F) The transfer of land to individuals (cf. *Los mapuche* 59-60).

The reductional process gave birth to a new social, economic, and cultural structure: the community. From that time on, the community became the organizational reference of Mapuche society. In effect, the very concept of a collective, of society, was transformed. The traditional leaderships not only changed in form but in substance as well. The *lonko* as the head of a lineage was transformed into the *lonko* as the head of a family (authority of a reservation) and bearer of a *Título de Merced* under which his nuclear family and parts of his extended family resided. Moreover, however, *lonkos*, *ülmenes* (rich and prestigious Mapuche), and *konas* (warriors) were socially equal in terms of their right to possess community land. Referring to this structural socio-political change, Caniuqueo concluded: "Collectivism gave way to the realization of an individualism which developed throughout the course of the 20th century, initiating a gradual breakdown of Mapuche territoriality into more basic units" (160, my translation).

The amount of land owned by Mapuche, an average of just 6.2 hectares per person, decreased in the years following the creation of the reservations. Thereafter the Mapuche experienced the appropriation of a part of their properties, and whole families lost their lands as the result of confusing negotiations, frauds, and violent occupations. Since the period of *Títulos de Merced,* Mapuche land found itself under the permanent pressure from *latifundistas*, colonizers, and Chilean farmers who, thanks to irregular legal hearings and scams, seized the Mapuche properties in the face of a by and large unconcerned judicial system. The systematic impoverishment of the Mapuche population on the reservations entered into crisis in the 1930s. Whereas the first post-reductional generation had remained in the communities, the second generation saw its opportunities to possess a piece of land increasingly reduced. This proved to be the main motive of expulsion from the communities and the beginning of the migratory process to the urban centers.

3.   Migration into Santiago

The migration of a significant proportion of the Mapuche population to urban centers was already visible in the communities by the 1960s. At that time, few studies reported about the state of migration. A study on agricultural development carried out by CIDA in 1966 on 26 Mapuche farms established that 16 of these farms could register at least one male Mapuche who had migrated to an urban center. From a total of 146 persons who lived on these farms, 30 had left the community in search of better prospects. In statistical terms, this represented 20% of the population. Other studies of this time estimated Mapuche migration to be at 15% to 20% of the population (cf. Saavedra, *La cuestión* 180). This much is certain: Mapuche migration to urban centers began to grow steadily as of the 1960s. A study carried out at the beginning of the 1980s with 200 families from the Cautín Province revealed that 49% of the women over 16 years of age had definitively left the community. In the case of men, that percentage was slightly lower at 44% (cf. Bengoa/Valenzuela 45).

According to the National Census of 1992, 60% of the Mapuche population have migrated into cities. Just as it was the center of attraction for other national migrations over decades, Santiago has been the principal migration goal of the Mapuche from the very beginning. Today nearly 30% of the Mapuche population in Chile live in the capital city.[8] These facts point to the massive character of this migration and are highly significant for the reproduction of the contemporary Mapuche society.

The migrants experienced the fate of being expelled from the community. Although they maintained contact to their families, there was no space for them back home. Louis Faron noted this situation in his field work during the 1950s:

> In legal theory, those who have migrated can have access to rights over land when the community has divided, but this rarely happens. What really happens is that the family opposes the rights over land of the migrated family members not for purely economic reasons but out of moral considerations, too; in the mind of the Mapuche, those who have migrated now find themselves outside of Mapuche society. (25, my translation)

By observing the arrival itineraries of Mapuche to Santiago, it is possible to distinguish two ways of getting settled in the city, either by way of a *chain migration* or autonomously. The chain migration is characterized by the initial assistance offered by family members in the search and acquisition of housing and employment, generally at the location where the assisting migrants also work (cf. MacDonald/MacDonald 227). The following narration of a migrant in the late 1970s provides insight into this phenomenon:

> When I arrived in Santiago for the first time, I met a cousin who was also Mapuche, a nephew of my father. He was the son to the brother of my father who worked as cook in a restaurant. He got me a job there. About nine months I worked there *indoors*, I never got out. … Later I got to the bakery thanks to my brother-in-law. My brother-in-law worked there. He placed a job for me and exactly at the time that they were searching for someone, that is when I got there. Of course, at that time I started as cleaning help; one day a baker was absent, and so they let me work as baker. And there I stayed until now.[9]

It could be claimed that a chain migration was established during the second half of the 20th century, which made it possible for Mapuche to find employment and housing in Santiago. The integration into the city mainly took place through a system of relations consisting of the extended family and articulated by the first migrants which settled in the city. Although this system was dominant, it did not exclude other formal mechanisms of job application. Rather, both systems complemented each other. Most of the first jobs which Mapuche got in the city offered a system of *puertas adentro* ["indoors system"], which allowed the Mapuche to start working in the city without already having to have a place to live. In fact, the migrants could live in the bakeries, restaurants, and houses where they worked. It is possible that other work sectors, such

---

[8] According to the National Census 2002.

[9] Interview with migrant Mapuche man. June 22, 2007, my translation.

as that of female housemaids, are structured in a similar form. Additionally, part of their payment included a daily ration of food, which permitted them to save money on food costs.

In the first phase of Mapuche migration to Santiago, the residence depended in large part on where the jobs were located. This led to the dispersion of the Mapuche throughout the city. They were not concentrated in any specific neighborhood. If they were able to rent their own space, it was in industrial districts where poor Chileans lived. In effect, migrant organizations set up to receive newly arrived Mapuche migrants did not exist in these neighborhoods.

Despite spatial dispersion in the city and the autonomous work, an attempt is made to maintain family bonds, and brothers, cousins, uncles visit each other regularly. In some cases, these relationships end up being a migrant's only circles of trust. However, these relations do not represent a territorial character in the city. Although the relationships are fundamentally between Mapuche, mostly within the family, Mapudungún is rarely spoken, and Spanish is the language used in these encounters.

A chain migration constitutes an initial situation which makes it possible for the migrants to initially settle in the city and to begin to integrate themselves into city life. But did this chain exist longer than this first moment, as the migrants began to reside in Santiago? It can be stated that this chain migration did not give way to a migratory network. In this case, a network is different from a chain in that it signals a process of higher formalization in the relationships based upon kinship or friendship, thus permitting an increase in the migratory movement and access to more and better resources of integration (cf. Han 17). Generally, at least insofar as can be gleaned from studies of transnational migration, the migratory networks can give way to ethnic economies and/or ethnically segregated neighborhoods in the center of the city as a way of achieving control of a specific socio-economic space.

The Mapuche living in Santiago never forget their communities. Once the migrants establish themselves in Santiago, they maintain relations with their community of origin. Although this fact has been stated in a great part of the literature dealing with the urban Mapuche, particularly in Santiago, we still lack a clear characterization of this relation (cf. Abarca Cariman; Aravena; Cumina; Gissi). Although the migrants frequently visit their communities, such visits do not play a relevant role in the internal dynamics of the community. The emigrated Mapuche do not construct exchange mechanisms of a relative institutionalization between community and city. The visits of the Mapuche *warriache* to their communities of origin are generally made in the summer months, when the weather is favorable, and when it is the time for harvest and for the *Nguillatún* (the main religious ritual of the Mapuche). But, above all, they take advantage of the summer vacations, which generally overlap with the vacations of other family members, thus facilitating the possibility of important family meetings. Another migrant's account describes this type of relationship:

> My mom told me, "When you are one year, you are six months there (in Santiago), you come and see me." I never went back. I got lost. I got used to earning a bit of money,

getting dressed, going out with friends. I was about 30, 35 years old, and I never went back to the countryside. Later I started going again. I visit during my vacation time, then I go there in February, in March. To go see my mom, my family, my mother-in-law, all living there.[10]

Likewise, the death of a family member, especially of the older members of the family who remained in the community, is an occasion that permits the reunion of brothers, uncles, and cousins who find themselves spread out over different places. These encounters take place in the context of a visit. The migrants generally do not work during their visits. At the same time, the circle of affective relations has broadened for the migrants, a great part of which are found outside of the community.

Product exchange is very restricted between the city and the community. While personal gifts are taken to the family members of the communities, upon returning to the city, the migrants bring with them a few goods from back home, especially food products. Otherwise, there is no exchange of products from the communities to the city, and the migrants rarely send money or goods from the city to the countryside. Product exchange between the two groups generally remains personal and infrequent.

One of the most studied impacts in the area of transnational migrations is the current dynamic of the remittances, i.e., the money sent by migrants to their places of origin. The dimension that this transnational economy has reached finds its base in the gigantic income differences between host countries and the countries of origin of the migrants. In fact, the surplus that the majority of the Mapuche can generate in the city is quite restricted and, in comparison to the transnational phenomenon, could not become an economic support for the local rural economies. This does not mean that urban Mapuche do not support their communities through financial assistance. Rather, their support is limited to special situations. Indeed, it is often the case that the migrant Mapuche try to pay for the costs of their visits so as not to be a burden on their families.

The longing for the community, for country life, is broadly documented and is not just limited to cases of translocal or transnational migration in which the migrant constantly guards the hope of returning to his society of origin. In the case of Chile, largely in reference to the first-generation migrants who came to the city from the countryside, authors such as Bengoa broadened the idea of longing for the "lost community" to include the whole urban society in Chile (5). The truth is that the longing for a return hardly ever turns into reality. The main obstacle is the lack of land in the communities, which forces migrant Mapuche to buy land or to invest in new productive systems on the available land. Yet both options require financial resources. Enough capitalization to permit a comfortable return to the community is almost impossible due to the unfair conditions under which the great majority of Mapuche in Santiago are employed. But even if the circumstances made it possible, after having

---

[10] Interview with migrant Mapuche man. March 21, 2007, my translation.

gotten used to city life, despite the difficulties, the precarious situation, and discrimination which are part of it, a return is very much improbable.

The development of a model of permanent residency by the Mapuche in Santiago limits contacts with the community to the social space of the 'event.' Although these events can become spaces of renovation for the communitarian relationships, especially those linked to religious rituals, their character (frequency, distance, type of activities) determines that—in social terms—Mapuche society occupies two clearly separated and strongly contrasting spaces: that of the community and that of urban Santiago. The Mapuche migrants can identify themselves with their communities of origin, but cannot participate in the relevant aspects which determine the future of these communities.

4. Association in the City

The first urban Mapuche organizations of the post-reductional society adopted alliances based on workers solidarity. Their primary objectives were defense against discriminatory practices and the demand for the same legal rights the Chilean citizen had. The names of the first organizations illustrate their defensive nature. For example: Sociedad Caupolicán de Defensora de la Araucanía ["Caupolican Society in Defense of the Araucanía"], Sociedad Mapuche de Proteccion Mutua ["Mapuche Society of Mutual Protection"], or Sociedad Defensora de Indígenas de Osorno ["Society in Defense of the Indigenous of Osorno"]. All are organizations that were founded at the beginning of the 20th century by Mapuche who resided in the emerging cities of the Araucanía region and who were generally linked to the field of education, i.e., teachers. Their leaders were a small urban elite with a relatively high level of education, a fact which permitted them to feel comfortable among both Mapuche and *winkas* ["Chilean society"] alike. They directed their efforts at legal recognition, thus providing a platform from which it was possible to access formal venues of negotiation with the Chilean state.[11] Up until the coup of 1973, Mapuche organizations worked in conjunction with national political movements. In the last three decades, the Mapuche movements have aimed to obtain more autonomy from Chilean political forces.

The Mapuche organizations of the 20th century were based in the cities, but did not direct their objectives to an urban population. Unlike many other migratory processes from rural to urban areas on the continent, Mapuche urban organizations did not develop with the objective of aiding the integration of migrants into the city by supplying housing or work.[12]

The proliferation of urban Mapuche organizations at the beginning of the 21st century, however, poses a new scenario. First, due the 1993 Indigenous Law, these

---

[11] The election of three Mapuche National deputies in the 1920s and 1930s is an example of such active political participation. Each one was backed by various political parties.

[12] For the Peruvian case, cf. Steinhauf; Paerregaard.

organizations have arisen under the legal figure of indigenous associations with a special statute, which recognizes them as legal institutions for the development of cultural and/or economic objectives. Second, these new organizations are portrayed as venues of 'cultural refuge' rather than as institutions with political aims. In other words, they are spaces where it is possible to reproduce the original culture—'tradition'—at the margins of Chilean society. In consequence, scholars suggest that such organizations have taken on the role of the post-reductional community in urban space, i.e., that they have become spaces where the reproduction of Mapuche culture is sustained. Post-reductional communities represent the place where Mapuche society has held on to its traditions with a survival instinct and where the culture of resistance which currently characterizes this society has been forged (cf. Saavedra, *Los mapuche* 64). According to some scholars (cf. Aravena, Gissi), the indigenous organization fulfills the same objective of rural community, thus turning into a sort of neo-community. In this context, the urban organization is the principal space of construction of Mapuche ethnic identity in the city; social spaces closed within themselves which, due to their characteristic of being identifiable as units and structured as organizations, become privileged spaces to observe the process of urban ethnification by scholars.

The urban organizations are the vessel through which the migrants can share their feeling of detachment—the organization as a cultural refuge; but it is also a way of restructuring ethnicity in a new space. This process is possible because the urban indigenous organization is transformed into a neo-community. The reference to the community is a reference to the ancestral, traditional, original community. What now emerges is the possibility of reproducing this cultural space in the city; it becomes a place in the city where that which is ethnic can be expressed in its utmost 'purity,' as a highly structured social space.

The current urban Mapuche organizations resulted out of the 1993 Indigenous Law.[13] The Mapuche organizations and collectives primarily existed within the structures set out by the law. According to the CONADI (National Corporation for Indigenous Development) registers, the 101 indigenous Mapuche organizations in Santiago counted a total of 5,407 members in 2004, which translates into an average of some 50 members per organization. This figure represents 3% of Santiago's Mapuche population. It must be pointed out, however, that many held dual memberships, i.e., they were members of more than one organization. At the same time, a distinction must be made between active members, who participate in a permanent form, and passive members, who only take part in specific activities of the organization. According to estimates, the percentage of active members represented approximately 50% of the members of an organization (cf. Millaleo 113). Seen from a statistical perspective, the

---

[13] The Indigenous Law recognizes two forms of association for indigenous peoples. One is the indigenous community in rural regions. The other is the indigenous associations, whose character is functional; that is, its objectives are aimed at carrying out productive or cultural projects. The Mapuche in the city may only found urban indigenous associations. In this text, urban organization refers to the legal figure of urban indigenous associations.

urban Mapuche organizations do not represent a massive movement. From a historical perspective, however, the increase in the number of organizations over the last few years is a relevant phenomenon. Only three formalized collectives existed in Santiago as of 1985; 19 organizations were identified by 1999; six years later, in 2005, that number had reached over 100 (cf. Huaiquilaf 12).

The explosive increase in the number of associations over the last ten years has brought forth a very diverse yet highly fragmented landscape, fragmentation here referring to the permanent division which each organization experiences. Although this division process can be understood as a diversification of choice, Millaleo puts forth that the concept of fragmentation denotes a landscape of organizations comprised of small collectives which position themselves more in terms of competition than in terms of collaboration. The internal division of the associations is produced not only through disputes brought about by the differences in orientation proper to every organization, but principally because of the inadequate administration of projects. The survival of the majority of the organizations, which is based on projects financed by the CONADI, ensures a quasi-dependence on state funding. However, this financing has proved to be an important incentive for participation, and probably is one of the causes for the recent increase in the number of organizations (cf. 148).

Typically, researchers focused on urban Mapuche organizations with the aim of describing a political discourse of placing demands. Certainly, a discourse has been developed in the past few years which not only pertains to solidarity with rural Mapuche, but also to the Mapuche *warriache* in respect to aiding initiatives around traditional healthcare or bilingual education. However, my focus lies more on elucidating methods of understanding organization in everyday life in order to test the validity claim of the hypothesis that an urban organization is a neo-community. Based on field notes, I describe two activities which allow us to appreciate the organization in Santiago as a space of quotidian meetings.

The first one refers to a weaving workshop. In the summer of 2005/06, indigenous association Kai-Kai[14] organized a *witral* project, a traditional loom-weaving technique. The basics of this technique were taught over a period of several weeks, and the course ended with the weaving of a *trarilonko* (headband worn by men). A teacher was hired from a Mapuche organization from another area of the city. The project was financed by CONADI.

Over a period of two months, around 15 women met once a week on Saturday afternoons in order to learn or perfect the *witral* technique. A loom was made available to each of the participants, who sat side by side. The majority of the participants possessed some knowledge of the *witral* technique; only a few had no knowledge of it at all. Some remembered having seen their mothers or grandmothers weaving, and for some, it was a completely new challenge to learn the craft. They brought their children with them, and some were accompanied by their spouses, who sat around a fire set up

---

[14] Name changed.

in the garden and talked. Towards the end of the afternoon, the participants got together in the interior of the *ruka* (traditional house) where they shared *mate* (tee drink), *sopaipillas* (fried bread), and sandwiches. The conversations revolved around family issues. Usually, friends or relatives came and visited during the afternoon. As some of them participated in other Mapuche organizations, it was an opportunity to talk about Santiago's organizational landscape. As I mentioned previously, the organizations in Santiago are in permanent transformation; their members circulate among the different organizations, and the organizations are constantly dissolving and splitting. Thus, news about the transformations of the organizational landscape is shared at each meeting. Two sources are identified as the roots of the problems which the organizations go through: the disputes for leadership and the implementation of projects. Whether in terms of leadership or participation, the foundation of the organization is always family-based. This means that quarrels over leadership are family disputes as well. A more recent development is the idea that the leadership of the organizations must not be in the hands of the *winkas*, i.e., the *winka* spouses of Mapuche should not be allowed to act as formal leaders. This is a controversial point in terms of leadership and recognition between the organizations. Another source of conflict—perhaps the most important of all—involves the 'projects.' The problems arising from the administration of resources are a permanent threat to the stability of the organizations. In fact, projects financed by the state must be carefully supervised, and the financial administration of such projects, in particular the distribution of benefits and their administration, is a constant source of disputes. Some sectors criticize that access to benefits from projects is the principal purpose behind the formation of some organizations, which, as a result, generates numerous misunderstandings.

The flexibility in participation allows members and leaders to be in permanent movement. Generally, it is a whole family who either joins or leaves an organization. Despite this, it is fair to point out that the conflicts in Mapuche organizations around the administration of resources for projects are probably not very different from those of other social organizations. The leaders know that the best method to manage these conflicts is by carrying out short-term initiatives with tangible results, such as in the case of the *witral* workshop.

The second activity I describe is a workshop about Mapuche *Weltanschauung*. The organization Kalfulikán developed a project during the second half of 2006; a seminar on the topic of *cosmovisión mapuche* ["Mapuche *Weltanschauung*"]. The course was financed by CONADI and took place in a small meeting room used by social organizations at the indigenous municipal office of the La Florida neighborhood. The course was held in municipal facilities because it was open to the public. It took place in four sessions, around two hours per session, in which the basic elements of Mapuche *Weltanschauung* were taught.

Machi[15] Lincovil taught the seminar. At the first session, *machi* Lincovil stood in front of a group of eight participants sitting around a table. At the beginning he clarified that the contents he was going to teach, the Mapuche *Weltanschauung*, were based on the knowledge he had acquired in his community of origin and that therefore there might be differences from those originating with other communities. The specific origin of the instructor is of utmost importance, owing to the fact that the participants hail from various Mapuche territories. Some come from the *Lafquenche* communities located along the Pacific coast. Others come from *Williche*, originating from Mapuche territories in the farthest south. Apart from the diversity in territories of origin, participants have had different experiences with regard to Mapuche culture. Some spent most of their lives in a rural community and have only recently migrated, others migrated when they were young, while yet others were born, raised, and always lived in Santiago.

The first session consisted of an explanation of the concept of *pellé*, translated as 'energy,' which is comprised of eleven further elements. After explaining each of the types of energy, *machi* presented the concept of *moguen*: "It is the materialization of energy. It is all of existence, what we see, know and believe. It transcends death," he explained in a calm tone. In this way, concept after concept succeeded each other on the chalkboard, and his explanations were illustrated through expressions in Mapudungún. The teacher permanently warned about the difficulties of translations into Spanish. After all, the Mapuche *Weltanschauung* is a complex philosophical system in which the concepts cannot be simply reduced in order to make them analogous to other systems of belief and thought. Once his explanation was finished, he posed questions to the participants in order to promote their learning. One of the course participants came from a different region than the teacher and knew the concepts, which were explained by other names. The participant frequently asked about the equivalence of concepts. From time to time the discussion took on the appearance of a debate between specialists. Equivalencies to the concepts were searched for between the speakers, and attempts were made to explore whether the concepts they proposed corresponded with one other. Each of the speakers used the words in a specific context and searched for phrases in Mapudungún which are expressed in daily situations or under special conditions, such as in the *Nguillatún*. The speakers attempted to reconstruct the contexts of communication in which the concepts are applied. The rest of the participants limited themselves to watching with fascination the linguistic proficiency which was being displayed in the room. The discussions lasted a few minutes and then the seminar continued as programmed.

Most of the participants had a basic knowledge of Mapudungún. Therefore, the *machi* repeatedly warned that a profound comprehension of the concepts was difficult. Concepts of space, territory, wisdom, and thought, among others, were presented in

---

[15] The *machi* is the main religious authority of the Mapuche who possesses knowledge of traditional medicine and carries out shamanistic rites. Generally, it is a man or a woman who enjoys a high status in Mapuche society.

the following sessions. The participants took notes and asked questions with interest. The seminar always took place during the week, at a time in which a large number of the inhabitants of the city were traveling back to their homes after work. The same participants attended each session. The portions of *sopaipillas* and *mate* tea provided at each session were enormous.

Conducting a seminar on the Mapuche worldview could seem paradoxical, but in an urban context, Mapuche spirituality and philosophy are forced to compete against other systems of thought, mainly against the westernized Judeo-Christian vision. However, there are still two important reasons to carry out this type of activities. The first one is the unequal experience which members of the organization have with Mapuche culture. Secondly, the diverse origins and therefore the mixed traditions of knowledge between the members turned these encounters into a place of confrontation and recognition of diverse traditions.

The regional variation of Mapuche society has led to a highly diverse group of different types of practices linked to spirituality. These differences are clearly crystallized in the case of *Nguillatún*. A *Nguillatún* is carried out by a community or a group within the community in accordance with a particular tradition. Although the ritual shares a structural base, each community has its particular way of performing it. Therefore, when a community invites others to participate in a *Nguillatún*, those present must humbly accept the procedures established by the *Nguillatufe*, who can be a *lonko*, a *machi*, or a respected person of the community who possesses deep knowledge of the tradition. The participation of different families, the type of prayer, the organization of the dances, the tempos, the incorporation of local elements into the offerings, the moments and methods of performing animal sacrifices, etc., all represent a complex group of elements which regulate a ritual during the course of at least two days and one night (the time must be clearly defined beforehand).

This situation is no different in the city. In fact, it is even more complex. The celebration of *Nguillatún* is organized and executed by Mapuche originating from a multiplicity of communities. This translates into a multiplicity of ways of performing the ritual. In Santiago, especially during the 1990s, at a time in which the ritual began to take place frequently in the city, in many of these celebrations the participants retired in the middle of the activities because they thought that the ritual was being carried out incorrectly, in which case taking part could be an offense to *Nguechén* (the Supreme Being). This assumption arises out of the confrontation between different variations of the ritual in which each person believes that his or her version is the correct one.

A sort of agreement has recently been achieved between some organizations in Santiago. Now, as is the case in the rural communities, whoever invites others to *Nguillatún* has the complete responsibility over the organization, and the invited participants must respect the way in which the ritual is executed. First, in order to achieve this, the organization who hosts the event must reach an internal agreement. The large organizations, or groups of them in a sector of the city, try to celebrate

Nguillatún at least once a year. This practice requires them to establish negotiation mechanisms which do not exist in traditional communities or whose dimension is at least not known to them.

Activities like a seminar on worldview serve the function of sharing and reaching agreements of knowledge regarding Mapuche culture. The formalization required by city life affects the form in which traditional knowledge is reproduced. Over the course of time, the specific negotiations which take place in Santiago to practice *Nguillatún* could end up producing a specific form of ritual. In fact, it is possible that the *Nguillatún* of Santiago acquires its own identity.

What is known as the *neo-comunidad* in Santiago is characterized by two things which distinguish it from the 'traditional' model. First, the extreme diversity of its members elucidates the wide regional variety of the Mapuche culture, which manifests itself in the existence of parallel traditions rather than in a search for a mixture or combination in praxis, as in the case of religious ceremonies. The existence of an organization—foundation, division, fusion, or disappearance—has a very unstable character, is short-lived, fragmented, and extremely dynamic.

Although the differences between community and neo-community are very clear, the urban organization is a type of association which has inherited the non-statist aspect of Mapuche society. Urban organizations maintain themselves like affiliated cells, affinity groups which are not capable of subsuming themselves under a major urban model. Despite the fact that a certain intellectual Mapuche sector and decision-makers in the political arena would like to see the formation of a major representative model for the Mapuche population in Santiago, the organizational landscape remains non-hierarchical, marked by this long-standing traditional trait in the Mapuche culture.

5.   Hip-Hop as an Instrument of *Warriache* Identity

The children of the migrants have been instrumental in constructing the urban Mapuche identity. Mapuche urban youth have had little exposure to traditional communities and consequently, they are searching for an urban youth identity to be affirmed by adults stemming from rural social backgrounds. For their part, they are seeking recognition as young Mapuche in an urban space shared with young Chileans. Their strategies of recognition are complex and not devoid of tensions.

To better describe this process, I will present a youth organization whose main activity is a hip-hop band. The following ethnographical account of a concert intends to outline relevant aspects of how Mapuche urban and youth identity is performed within an event which stages 'the indigenous' in an urban context.

* * * * *

In the first week of January 2006 a feast of solidarity, a '*peña*[16] with indigenous organizations' takes place at the Centro Cultural La Barraca in the center of the commune of La Florida in Santiago. The wooden shed, which is the main structure of the Cultural Center, was the scene of the first cultural events of opposition to the dictatorial regime in the *comuna* at the end of the eighties. The humble infrastructure of the Center was then an area of cultural resistance, which had a close link with grassroots organizations targeting the political left wing. At my arrival, the place is half empty. The stage is in the background and at the edge there are tables. On one side of the entrance gate is a kitchen, which is occupied by a group of women who fry *sopaipillas* and French fries and sell beer and beverages. Relatives and friends of the members of the band Wechekeche ñi Trawün are already placed at a table next to where the food and beverages are being sold. It is Saturday afternoon and from outside, the bustle of long lines of cars leaving and entering the nearby shopping centers can be heard. The shed is beginning to fill slowly, while a familiar and quiet atmosphere still dominates. *Sopaipillas* and one liter of beer in plastic cups are shared at the table. The three women of the band stand and go to the dressing room while the men tie their *trarilonko* on their heads with choreographic movements. We are all at the vast table to drink, to eat, and to greet friends and acquaintances who continue to arrive. Greetings in Spanish mixed with *mari mari Peñi, mari mari lamngen!* are heard. The presenter on the stage promotes the sale of *sopaipillas,* and, with some excitement, describes the full program of the evening. He promises entertainment for a couple of hours. Meanwhile the members of a band playing Andean music have gotten on the stage, armed with *quenas, zampoñas,* drums, guitar, and *charango.* They open with a piece of traditional Andean music. The drums and wind instruments light a bit more enthusiasm in the hall, which gradually fills. The bustle of people talking and the children playing at the free tables in the center of the hall delivers the impression that the public is more entertained by familiar conversation than by the music on the stage.

The women of the band return from the dressing rooms, wearing long black dresses and jewels, both in Mapuche traditional fashion. The hairstyles are also traditional. Without further preamble the band members, seven in total, approach the stage. The master of ceremonies and the sound technician converse briefly with the band. The musical director delivers a CD to the sound technician and explains the use of the recorded tracks. The instructions are simple and are accompanied by a list of songs that will be played. The master of ceremonies takes the microphone and introduces the band: "Our coming artists are Wechekeche ñi Trawün; they are a group of young Mapuche of La Florida who merge the music of their ancestral land with contemporary rhythms,"[17] repeating exactly the phrase that the musical director conveyed to him. Timid applause follows and the band begins its performance. The seven members are standing in line on the stage, only with microphones, without instruments; the music comes from the CD that sounds from the speakers.

---

[16] A *peña* is an event of folk music in the format of a café concert.
[17] All translations of song lyrics etc. into English are my own.

The first sample sounds from the speakers. It is a rhythmic base of a rhythm-and-blues style, and all sing the chorus: "Look in front of the opponent, feel proud of your race, follow your path, I am Mapuche and what is going on?!" The chorus is repeated twice, melodiously. Immediately a female singer attacks, rapping: "When we were children we did not know the legacy that we had in name and blood, the difference is present when all mocked us for carrying in our body—the history of our people." The chorus responds. The singer continues with more strength: "Separated from the rest, then came the day when we came together to talk about our ancestors between the differentiated, ignoring the meaning of what had reunited us—we realized that we were brothers and share a history" (chorus responds).

The name of the theme is "Proud," and it is a sort of introduction of the band. From the recorded base, two different sounds can be recognized: one recorded with synthesizers and another recorded with the sounds of traditional Mapuche instruments, such as the *kultrún*, a percussion instrument that makes—in this case—a hip-hop rhythmic pulse. The rapped texts explain that the Mapuche origin was discovered in the city, by young people who were born in Santiago. It recounts in a simple way how discrimination has been experienced, how mobbing at school for the mere fact of carrying a Mapuche surname has been endured. The discovery of a Mapuche origin is accompanied by an attitude of defense, of pride in its history of resistance, disclosed against the condition of historical oppression and updated daily. The message of the song is clear and strong.

Before proceeding to the next song, the musical director salutes the public in Spanish and Mapudungún. The second sampler starts ringing, announcing a *reggeatón* rhythm. The song is called "Wizards," and the joy and excitement of Caribbean rhythms are reinforced by the chorus that announces: "Here they are! Who arrived? The Mapuche with the gift, like magicians will defeat with our worldview." This is a standard *reggeatón*, a rhythmic base made for dancing, which has achieved great commercial success in recent years. The song is playful and fun. Without giving a break the performance continues with the start of the third song with chorus shouts: "Freedom, freedom, freedom to the Mapuche fight!" Immediately the strong rapping of a male singer dominates the stage. He gives a historical review of the Mapuche fight against the invaders and how it is expressed even at present, a situation which in recent years has escalated into violence and police repression. This song is a slogan for combat, street demonstration, or an inflaming assembly speech. Meanwhile, the public is following the performance closely; the songs are listened to with curiosity and respect. The mixture of sounds and visual elements is not easy to understand at first; it is not easy to circumscribe, to set up in a hermeneutic circle that immediately allows meaning to be ascribed to the whole. The space of the *peña* and its guests, the dress of the musicians, the sound of the samplers, and the rapped words align in a way that exceeds the standard classifications of popular folk or indigenous music.

The presentation continues with a *ranchera* song, a song with a simple melody, as is customary in this style. It narrates the story of a recent migrant Mapuche in Santiago:

For my work I came to *Warria* (city), long ago left my land, I am very sad, because I remember it in the midst of this great city, I am a baker, I travel every day, for as long as two hours to go to work, life is hard here in Santiago, where one must know how to fight, I met some *peñis* of an organization, with my brothers I feel better, we are all Mapuche and I am not alone anymore, with my people it is like being in my *lof* [family/home].

Although *ranchera* music has its origins in Mexico, it was appropriated by the Chilean rural culture in the middle of last century. Thus, its sound bears obvious associations with a peasant origin. Two more songs to go. The next is a *ragamuffin* sample type, a mixture of hip-hop and reggae, and the last song of the presentation mixes hip-hop with dancehall:

Young Mapuche we are many, the voice of my ancestors is what I hear, in this land colonized and misappropriated, the echo of the land is not silent now, but we live in the city with pride and scream! I am Mapuche, descendant of this people of great warriors … [chorus] I want to fly beyond the wind, I want to go back to where my people are, I want to stay with my ancestors, the land that *kalfulikán* [historical Mapuche warriors] step upon.

With this song, a gentle melody, beautiful and easy to follow, in perfect harmony with the poetry of the chorus, "I want to fly beyond the wind," the band ends its performance.

The audience applauds. Once at the table, the members of the band comment on details of the presentation—some errors in the timing, some segments of forgotten lyrics—but the overall assessment is positive. The musicians stay around the table which is filled with relatives and friends who greet them and invite them to continue the party with drinks and *sopaipillas* with chili.

The next show is a band playing Andean music. However, when they are introduced, the stage is empty. Suddenly from the gates twenty people in a symmetrical row formation, in short and coordinated steps, enter the hall. All are men, dressed in traditional clothes of the Aymara communities in the far north of Chile. The shed shudders at the sound of percussion and Andean pan-flutes. The group walks slowly to the center of the hall, which is unoccupied. It is a group of Andean carnival revelers; like a small military formation they should be following a virgin or a patron saint in pilgrimage between villages of the Andes, but here they just find their way to the middle of our shed. This music is different from that of the Andean group which played earlier. If the first had a folkloric character, popular and mass-oriented, this is the music of an Andean carnival, a religious-pagan activity with limited diffusion.

The audience stands up, following the rhythm with clapping hands. They attentively await the entry of the brass section that consists of trumpets, trombone, and tuba. The group has taken the center of the shed and does not move from there. Only then the shed looks crowded, a little over five hundred people; this *peña* is successful in terms of audience. The brass section blasts with enthusiasm, its power in short melodic figures inviting complicity with the pulse of the music. Someone explains the group of Aymara musicians comes from La Pintana, a nearby *comuna*. Immediately dance groups are formed by those who are familiar with the rhythms that are presented: *saya* and *huaino*. The spontaneous dancers reach the dozens; they manage the dances naturally. The Andean carnival music is dance music. It is music of movement, not contemplation. It is instrumental music with marked pulses. In the Atacama desert or Puna of Tarapacá, in the north of Chile, it is the music of religious celebrations or festivals linked to community work. In the villages of the Chilean highlands the combination of the monotony, duration, and strength of the sounds allows dancing in a kind of collective trance, in a very similar manner to techno-raves, in which the same musical principles are at work. I am surprised at how many of the participants among the guests participate in these dances. There are several dozen adults, youths, and children. The members of the Wechekeche, still dressed in their traditional Mapuche costumes, incorporate themselves into the collective choreographed movements. They are Mapuche dancing Aymara.

The hall has been transformed into a festival. After one hour of dancing the group withdraws in the same manner in which it entered. The audience has experienced real excitement. It is hard not to be carried away by the power of this music, and the participants of the *peña* showed no great resistance. While the group is making its exit, the music keeps on playing, as if the party is to continue elsewhere, as is usual in the Andean carnival and its three or four days of uninterrupted dancing and celebration. After the musicians have left the hall, the guests look exhausted. Everyone returns to their seats and demands beverages and beer. In the small kitchen, the half-dozen women struggling to supply the demand nearly collapse.

After a fifteen-minute break, the master of ceremonies climbs back onto the stage. It is obvious that he is happy about the concert's apparent success. Now he announces the final number: "Get ready because our next group will make you dance more than ever!" he encourages the audience. Behind him a small band with traditional *Rapa Nui* costumes has already found its place. Before he ends the introduction, the band interrupts him with sounds from guitars, ukuleles, and percussion. From the same entrance from which minutes earlier the Aymara group exited the hall, a group of dancers makes its appearance formed in four rows: twelve men and twelve women. They are unequivocally Polynesians of Rapa Nui, the island that by historical accident came under the administration of the Chilean state, and not of the French as would have been the logical geopolitical distribution of the empires of the 19th century.

Judging by their dress, composed of tiny sets made with palm fibers that leave much of the body exposed in the case of the men and the stomachs in the case of the women, they are clearly Polynesians. They are also unequivocally Polynesians because of their sensual movements, the pelvises of the men and hips of the women. If in the Chilean common perception, the Mapuche are seen as a tenacious and fighting culture, Rapa Nui represent a kind of sensuality nonexistent in Chilean society. The longing for the 'tropical rhythms' and the sensuality associated with them is taken by the national imagination through the exoticism of the Rapa Nui people and the pride of them being 'part' of the Chilean culture. An imagined exoticism is reinforced by the perceived beauty of its people, its paradise island landscapes, and the joy and sensuality of their dances.

The presentation of the Rapa Nui group is designed to affect the audience from its very beginning. Strength, speed, and showmanship prevail. The public quickly gets excited. The dances are well choreographed; the professionalism of the group is indisputable. The members of the musical section, who are on the stage, give explanations of the dances in a few words. They announce: "The next dance represents a day of fishing" or "This is a dance in which men should show their strength." After these brief introductions, sometimes mixed with shouts in Rapa Nui language, the band plays with great force.

No doubt the display of the bodies of the dancers plays an important role. All the men are tattooed with traditional motifs. The drawings make the display of their muscular torsos even more attractive. Women move their hips and their bellies in an attempt to capture the public attention, but, as in every good spectacle, the center of attention alternates between the men and women. At my table all stand to get a better view. Women make comments on the male dancers, and among men, comments on the female dancers can be heard. After thirty minutes of vibrant spectacle, accompanied by shouts and applause, a lady from the audience is invited to the stage. "The men will give her a dance of conquest," says the leader of the band on the microphone. A shy woman is pushed toward the center of the dance floor while the audience laughs. The woman is in the center, watching stunned as the twelve men jump around her, moving their hips, playing with a spear in one hand and shouting war cries to the accompanying music. The audience laughs with pleasure; the scene is charged with comic eroticism. One of the dancers, a warrior now in the act of conquest, has 'won' the contest over the woman, who receives a short dance as a prize, with movements of stalking her. The audience is in a kind of ecstasy. It is all very playful and contains a great sense of spectacle: rhythm and intensity. Then it is the turn of a young man, who will be hunted by the female dancers. With this sketch of seduction of a member of the audience, the production takes the unequivocal form of a show of entertaining, exotic dance, in which the codes are like those of a spectacle for tourism. The staging, marked by the speed of the show, the energy of the artists, and audience participation, is complemented professionally with the use of a sensuality that operates as 'wild exoticism,' which recalls the format of the great cabarets in Havana and Rio de Janeiro. The presentation ends with applause, whistles, and shouts of approval. The musicians are exhausted; with fresh sweat on their bodies they withdraw from dancing with joy and leave a trail of smiles and excitement. The evening has come to an end.

In a few minutes the shed will be emptied. The audience is exhausted after four hours of entertainment. Within these four hours, four very particular forms of presentation of the cultures which meet in Santiago were appreciated and celebrated. The following analysis will be centered on them.

* * * * *

The event described here can be understood as a staging of that which is 'indigenous' in the city. This is a '*peña* with urban indigenous organizations,' with representatives of the major ethnic groups in the country—Aymara, Mapuche, and Rapa Nui. These organizations have been invited to share their music and dance in front of a large audience of not necessarily indigenous origin. The music and dance of the Aymara, the Andean, and the Polynesian Rapa Nui are the most widespread ethnic cultural expressions among the Chilean population. The teaching of their dances has been integrated into the public education program as part of what is recognized as 'national folklore.' It is not so in the case of the Mapuche, whose musical expressions have remained restricted to a limited sphere within the Mapuche society.

At this event, cultural performances have been presented. 'Performance' can be understood as meaning a staging as a form of communication which expresses and disseminates cultural content. In this case, the staging of the urban ethnic groups is a presentation of music and dance that encapsulates forms and values shared by a group, including not only the music itself, but the whole behavior and its associated underlying concepts. They are presentations that have a beginning and an end, varying degrees of organization, an audience, and a place for specific staging. As Reinoso points out about musical performances: "[Musical performances] are not only reflections of culture, but thoughtful cultural forms, in which members of a group return to themselves and to the relationships, actions, symbols, codes, meanings, roles, status, social structures, ethical rules, and others components that constitute their public *selves*" (226, my translation, original emphasis).

To observe the performances as a social practice allows for a focus on the context in which it is being staged as a space of differentiation. The co-presence of these groups is only possible in the city, especially in Santiago (originally everyone inhabits very different parts of the Chilean territory). In this specific case, each ethnic group is trying to mark their differences, not only from the 'Chilean,' but also among themselves. I focus on two key aspects: The first is the ascription of each of the performances to a semantic field (a sociological musico-semantic field); the second key element is how one can identify the specificity of the Mapuche performance from this ascription.

A. Andean music group. They play a kind of music that was vigorously developed in Chile in the sixties. Back then it was called 'neo-folklore.' Neo-folklore made a link between an aesthetic balance based on research of the peasants and vernacular elements of popular music within a left-wing political project. Its relationship to the aesthetic co-narration of the social transformation of the sixties allowed its classification and transformation into a genre of popular and urban music. The performers and creators of this musical style—often called simply 'Latin American folklore'—merged sounds of other geographies of the continent and developed a brilliant time of musical creation. It is a version of the indigenous music made by the non-indigenous. The *peñas*, in fact, emerged as spaces to accommodate these sounds and aesthetics.

Today, for the younger generation, this type of institutional music corresponds to a canon of 'Andean folk music.' While this group is not part of an indigenous music collective, it also plays with the idea of a 'rescue of the roots'—in this case aimed at the Chilean *mestizo* population. In the context of the described activity, it fulfills the role of 'introduction to the original (indigenous) roots.'

B. Andean Carnival. This presentation is also part of the tradition of Andean music, but its major difference from the above-mentioned group is that their production and reception are limited to specific contexts, usually anchored in traditional communities in the Chilean Andes. The usual context for the production and reception of this music is within a festival marked with religious components. It is a performance that replicates forms of a religious festival outside a religious context. It presents a carnival form intrinsically linked to the Andean world. Hence its staging in Santiago is only possible in a context such as this; that is to say, in a prescribed event for 'indigenous cultures.'

C. Rapa Nui presentation. The dances staged by the Rapa Nui group would be inspired by ritual passages. Other dances narrate stories of everyday life on the island; hunting, fishing, competition among clans, and so on. The performance sets these dances, inspired by certain ritualism or by everyday life, in a form of theatrical entertainment performed with precision by a dance company. Elements such as the rhythm of the show—a very precise coordination between sketches—as well as a constant and successful communication with the public, endow the presentation with a show character, in the sense of modern entertainment. But there is also a particularly striking element that crosses the entire performance: the sensuality. There is a clear exploitation of gestures in the dance aimed toward creating an atmosphere of stereotypical sensuality; men as machos, and coquettish and fragile women. An exotic sensuality, playful and direct, is being staged. In the ethnographic description, I allude to the similarity between this performance and 'exotic shows' for tourist consumption. It could also be understood within the tradition of 'national ballets,' as introduced in the Soviet Union in the 1920s, resulting from an abstraction of traditional practices, stylized in a form of 'high culture,' which would permit overcoming local contexts of traditional production and consumption, and at the same time forge national identities.

In the performance of the Andean carnival, the public participation arises spontaneously; the audience feels free to dance with musicians. In the Rapa Nui case, audience participation is mediated and controlled by the artists. The final game of the presentation, when a member of the audience is invited on stage, consists precisely of establishing the difference, marking the distance between artists and the audience. For everyone who attends this event, Rapa Nui culture is also exotic and foreign, and the group exploits this element. In this case one can say that the specific context of the presentation is irrelevant. It is a performance which is liberated from an 'indigenous' context to be staged, in terms of performance, within international codes of folk dance companies, which allow decoding in a global space.

D. Mapuche performance. The first element that distinguishes the Mapuche performance from the others is the impossibility of defining it as having a folkloric character. The musical fusion, strongly supported by hip-hop, makes a fundamental distinction from the others. The staging is not meant to be understood as a repetition of traditional forms; the performance must be understood through the fusion with hip-hop. This allows us to identify three articulations that permit this kind of music and through which it establishes differences from the other performances.

First of all, a key element is that hip-hop belongs to a youth culture. In this sense, this performance is shaped as a separate discourse within adult Mapuche society, and, as a result, it is not meant to be 'Mapuche' as a whole. While the link with hip-hop makes clear its placement within a youth culture, it also makes evident the urban condition of its members. Secondly, the Mapuche performance rests on the strength of the rapped texts. The text is precisely what is central to hip-hop music (cf. Dimitriadis 23). While members of the band were dressed in traditional outfits—especially the women—and the songs incorporate the sound of traditional musical instruments, the structure of the performance is based on the texts as a means of communication of symbols, codes, roles, and the status of the collective. The songs mix Spanish and Mapudungún lyrics. Here there are other differences with the Rapa Nui group: although the group sings in Rapa Nui language, it is not out of an urgent need to transmit a message in their original language. Language plays a secondary role, as the performance's core is in the dances. In the Mapuche case there is a need for oral communication; the text, the rapped word, is at the heart of the message. It is in Spanish, but marks a difference with the Chilean in the untranslatability, the nature of the Other, when employing Mapudungún concepts. The third articulation is that the performance is far from a pastoral representation of the indigenous, aestheticized and contemplative; rather, it is a kind of political appeal, which calls attention to the status of oppressed people. The aim is to provoke its interlocutors through a call to fight against the powers of the *winka* culture, expressed in police repression in the ancestral territory as an answer to the legitimate historical claims. It is a call to ethnic consciousness. In this regard, hip-hop is used as a strategy, a language that has its own code of political expression.

The Mapuche performance indicates that the process of urban Mapuche ethnicity in Santiago is shaped by the second generation in a dynamic and complex way. The performance can no longer be reduced either to a stylized form, as it was in the first case, nor to a dislocated representation drawn out of an original space—as we noted with the representation of the Andean carnival, nor is it an exotic version of ethnicity, as in the representation of the Rapa Nui group. It is a hybrid, located at a node of currents in the construction of their ethnicity, where elements of the local (community-city relationship), the national (historical lawsuit between the state and the Chilean

Mapuche people), and the transnational (adoption of an aesthetic of a global order, i.e., hip-hop) intersect.

6. Towards an Urban Ethnicity of a Stateless Society

Mapuche migration to Santiago was a mass phenomenon, but had quite a hetero-geneous character. Each migrant started constructing his social networks out of rela-tionships with other Mapuche migrants, but primarily based on the relationships they had with the already established urban population. The lack of indigenous associations which organized and facilitated integration into the urban setting has its roots in Mapuche society's segmented character. Societies which never developed hierarchical structures have more of a tendency to disperse than to develop representative organiza-tions that delegate responsibility. This long-term tendency in Mapuche society mani-fested itself in the urban setting by impeding the construction of large networks based on acquiring an overall ethnic Mapuche identity. The modern migrant, stripped of his or her lineage or torn from his or her extended family—the latter of which is a structure which does not exist in urban life—gives birth to a social subject who is not privy to building associations. Even though a large majority of migrants share the same social elements, such as being employed in menial jobs, residing in poor neigh-borhoods, and being subjected to discrimination, the wide variety in urban integration strategies is a byproduct of individual rather than collective trajectories.

The Mapuche have still not constructed their own economic space in urban life. Unlike many other migrant groups, particularly those in the Andean region who have ethnically solidified based on economic structures, the case of the Mapuche reminds us of the Clastres discussion in respect to the lack of emphasis of stateless societies on the economic sphere (cf. 144). In effect, economic demands and initiatives play a marginal role, even with the present proliferation of urban organizations initiated and backed by indigenous politics. Indeed, the new organizational terrain places a higher priority on preserving cultural aspects and politically supported traditional communities.

The legacy of a segmented Mapuche society is therefore revealed in the new urban organizations. Current forms of organization are based, in fact, on a structure similar to associations of traditional lineage and are thus characterized by a fragmented and conflict-ridden organizational landscape. It is evident that the system of mutual aid which sustains an urban organization is much less stringent and thus weaker than in a traditional society. This leads to an urban organization subjected to dynamism and temporality, making it difficult to consolidate into a long-term neo-community.

We can posit that to a large extent, the difficulties in seeing (on the part of re-searchers), comprehending (on the part of Chilean society), and controlling (on the part of the Chilean state) the urban Mapuche stem from overlooking the reproduction of segmentary social qualities in urban Mapuche life.

The next generation of migrants represents a scenario of 'the Mapuche' caught between multiple identities. As described in the account above, they construct their difference using traditional means of urban ethnic expression through music. This does not simply involve the reproduction of traditional practices independent of their original context, but rather a practice which is juxtaposed with other symbolic universes circulating in the urban experience. The young Mapuche are exhibiting a complex interplay of knowledge gained from the indigenous experience in relation to identity, oscillating between the traditional and the urban, local and global, urban youth and urban Mapuche. This musical practice doubtlessly confirms the extremely dynamic character of acquiring a Mapuche identity.

This essay has excluded other relevant aspects in the analysis, such as religious practice, political discourse around acknowledge, or urban Santiago's overall receptiveness to migration. In any case, the points outlined in this essay suggest an observational model not only used to study urban Mapuche ethnicity, but also applicable to other social groups which have likewise been observed as not having fully developed an ethnic identity as an urban indigenous group.[18]

Works Cited

Abarca Cariman, Geraldine. *Rupturas y continuidades en la recreación de la cultura mapuche en Santiago de Chile*. La Paz: Plural Editores, 2005.

Ancán, José, and Margarita Calfío. *Retorno al país mapuche: Reflexiones sobre una utopía por construir*. Working Paper Series Ñuke Mapuförlaget 6 (2002). <http://www.mapuche.info/mapuint/ankalfio020300.pdf>.

Aravena, Andrea. "Los Mapuche-Warriache: Migración e identidad mapuche urbana en el Siglo XXI." *Colonización, resistencia y mestizaje en las Américas, Siglos XVI-XX*. Ed. Guillaume Boccara. Quito: Ediciones Abya-Yala, 2002. 350-81.

Bengoa, José. *La comunidad perdida: Ensayos sobre identidad y cultura: Los desafíos de la modernización en Chile*. Santiago: Ediciones Sur, 1996.

———, and Eduardo Valenzuela. *Economía mapuche: Pobreza y subsistencia en la sociedad mapuche contemporánea*. Santiago: PAS, 1984.

Caniuqueo, Sergio. "Siglo XX en Gulumapu: De la fragmentación de la Wallmapu a la unidad nacional mapuche, 1880 a 1979." *Escucha Winka!: Cuatro ensayos de historia nacional mapuche y un epílogo sobre el futuro Marimán*. Ed. Pablo Marimán, Sergio Caniuqueo, José Millalén, and Rodrigo Levil. Santiago: Lom, 2006. 129-217.

Clastres, Pierre. *Investigaciones en antropología política*. Barcelona: Gedisa, 1981.

Contreras Painemal, Carlos. "Los parlamentos." *Actas del Primer Congreso Internacional de Historia Mapuche*. Ed. Contreras Painemal. Siegen: self-published, 2002. 51-69.

---

[18] I would especially like to thank Ana Millaleo, Paul Paillafil, Manuel Lincovil, Jano Weichafe, Jeannette Cuiquiño, Angelina Huainopan, María Nahuelhuel, Omar Carrera, Marcela Lincovil, Andrés Millaleo, Soledad Tinao, Eugenio Paillalef, Eusebio Huechuñir, Julio Llancavil, Juan Huenuvil, Rosario Huenuvil, Ambrosio Ranimán, Mauricio Ñanco, the members of Wechekeche ñi Trawün, Lelfünche, and CONAPAN.

Cuminao, Clorinda. *El Gijatún en Santiago: Una forma de reconstrucción de la identidad mapuche*. Santiago: Universidad Academia de Humanismo Cristiano, 1998.

Dimitriadis, Greg. *Performing Identity/Performing Culture: HipHop as Text, Pedagogy, and Lived Practice*. New York: Peter Lang, 2001.

Faron, Louis. *Antüpaiñanko: Moral y ritual mapuche*. 1964. Santiago: Ediciones Mundo, 1997.

Foerster, Rolf, and Sonia Montecinos. *Organizaciones, líderes y contiendas mapuches (1900-1870)*. Santiago: Centro de estudios de la mujer, 1988.

Gissi, Nicolás. "¿De minoría étnica a minoría etno-nacional?: El pueblo mapuche, la sociedad chilena y el debate en torno a la autonomía." *América Indígena* 3 (2006): 35-56.

Golte, Jürgen. "Redes étnicas y globalización." *Revista de Sociología* 11.12 (1999): 55-79.

———, and Norma Adams. *Los caballos de troya de los invasores: Estrategias campesinas en la conquista de la Gran Lima*. Lima: IEP, 1987.

Han, Petrus. *Soziologie der Migration*. Stuttgart: Lucius & Lucius, 2005.

Huaiquilaf, Márcos. *Las Organizaciones sociales mapuche de la Región Metropolitana: Catastro, caracterización y demandas*. Santiago: CEDESCO, 1996.

Lincoqueo, José. "El genociodio, caballo de Troya de Mefistófeles (el demonio): Análisis jurídico acerca de los parlamentos." *Actas del Primer Congreso Internacional de Historia Mapuche*. Ed. Carlos Contreras Painemal. Siegen: self-published, 2003. 70-76.

MacDonald, John, and Leatrice MacDonald. "Chain Migration: Ethnic Neighbourhood Formation and Social Networks." *An Urban World*. Ed. Charles Tilly. Boston: Little, Brown, 1974. 215-62.

Martuccelli, Danilo. "Etnicidades modernas: Identidad y democracia." *Revisitar la etnicidad: Miradas cruzadas en torno a la diversidad*. Ed. Daniel Gutiérrez and Helene Balslev. Mexico: Siglo XXI, Colegio de Mexiquense, and Colegio de Sonora, 2008. 41-67.

Marimán, Pablo. "Los mapuches antes de la conquista militar chileno-argentina." *¡Escucha Winka! Cuatro ensayos de historia nacional mapuche y un epílogo sobre el futuro*. Ed. Marimán, Sergio Caniuqueo, José Millalén, and Rodrigo Levil. Santiago: Lom, 2006. 53-128.

Marimán, Pedro. "La diáspora mapuche: Una reflexión política." *Liwen* 4 (1997): 216-23.

Millaleo, Ana. *Multiplicación y multiplicidad de las organizaciones mapuche urbanas en la RM: ¿Incremento en la participación mapuche o fragmentación organizacional?* Santiago: Universidad ARCIS, 2006.

Montecinos, Sonia. "El mapuche urbano: Un ser invisible." *Revista Creces* 13 (1990): 30-48.

Paerregaard, Karsten. *Linking Separate Worlds: Urban Migrants and Rural Lives in Peru*. New York: Berg, 1997.

Reinoso, Carlos. *Antropología de la música de los géneros tribales a la globalización*. Buenos Aires: SB, 2006.

Saavedra, Alejandro. *Los Mapuche en la sociedad chilena actual*. Santiago: Lom, 2002.

———. *La cuestión mapuche*. Santiago: UNO-FAO-ICIRA, 1971.

Steinhauf, Andreas. *Integrationsnetze als Entwicklungsstrategie: Zur Dynamik sozialer Netzwerke im informellen Sektor Perus*. Münster: LIT, 1992.

Velasco, Laura. "Migraciones indígenas a las ciudades de México y Tijuana." *Papeles de Población* 52 (2007): 184-209.

Waqcuant, Loïc. *Urban Outcasts: A Comparative Sociology of Advanced Marginality*. Cambridge: Polity P, 2008.

Navigating Little Italy: Carceral Mobility in Martin Scorsese's *Mean Streets*[1]

ALEXANDRA GANSER

> Little Italy for me is in a sense a microcosm
> for something much, much larger.
> —Martin Scorsese (qtd. in Massood 77*)*

1. Introduction

In the context of his theory of the simulacrum as the real(ity) of postmodernity, Jean Baudrillard once said of the U.S.-American city that it "seems to have stepped right out of the movies" (56), and that it was hence with urban film that the analytical rapprochement to American urbanity should start. It can indeed be argued that iconic urban films, along with other visual cultural products, pre-structure the perception of New York City, Chicago, or Los Angeles; furthermore, and more importantly in the context of the nexus of urbanity and ethnicities, film uses the "participative distance" (Caviglia n.p.) of its spectators in order to enable them to vicariously and imaginative-ly experience off-limit ethnic neighborhoods—only think of Spike Lee's iconic con-structions of ghettoized African-American urbanity—and thus to acknowledge that cities are made of myriads of stories, some manifest in stone, some in social structure, and others in celluloid. In this view, urban screenscapes broaden our urban imaginaries without reducing urbanity to single grand narratives.

As a screenscape, the modern U.S.-American city has been articulated as a site of contesting social forces where difference must be addressed so that a complex social fabric might be navigated by its pluriethnic inhabitants. Set before the first waves of Italian immigration, Martin Scorsese's *Gangs of New York* (2002), for instance, imag-ines the gang wars between different ethnic groups as formative for the history not only of the city, but of the whole U.S.-American nation. In this essay, however, I will concentrate on another filmic enactment of Little Italy in Scorsese's oeuvre, *Mean Streets* (1973). Not only was *Mean Streets* Scorsese's first widely acknowledged

---

[1] This essay is an outcome of collaborative research with Karin Höpker (cf. her article in this volume). The theoretical similarities and duplicities between her contribution to this volume and my own are by no means unintentional. On the contrary, we hope that in this way, our articles demonstrate the usefulness of a spatial perspective on the ethnic-urban filmic imag-inary inspired by the writings of Michel de Certeau beyond the limited scope of a single case study. Parts of this essay have been published in an earlier version (cf. Ganser/Höpker).

feature film; it also marks a cornerstone of the Italian-American director's engagement with the production of Italian-Americanness, preceded by the little-known *Who's That Knocking at My Door?* (1965-68)[2] and continued by both semi-documentary and fictional films: *Italianamerican* (1974), *Goodfellas* (1990), *A Personal Journey with Martin Scorsese through American Movies* (1995), and *Il mio viaggio in Italia / My Journey to Italy* (1999). All of these works emphasize the importance of film for the formation of Italian-American identity and could hence be read as the cinematographic rendering of Baudrillard's statement from an Italian American point of view. This point of view is a crucial structuring element of *Mean Streets* and is translated by a variety of semi-documentary camera techniques, influenced by the French *nouvelle vague* and *cinéma vérité* styles and by Italian neorealism. On this cinematographic metalevel too, then, Scorsese tries to articulate a distinct transatlantic filmic language, doubling the immigration legacy of Italian Americans.

Mean Streets uses the claustrophobic script of its predecessor, *Who's That Knocking at My Door*, for an iconic New Hollywood staging of Italian-American characters who have a hard time navigating the dense fabric of their 'hood,' a territorial space that exceeds geographical boundaries and marks what Guy Debord has called the 'psychogeography' of its protagonists. However, the importance of *Mean Streets* exceeds that of articulating an Italian-American filmic vision and language, as on a general level it also reflects both the hopes and fears for the U.S. metropolis of the 1970s, torn between ethnic conflict and integration, between Robert Moses's plans for metropolitan purification and renewal and Jane Jacobs's visions of micro-level multiethnic harmony (cf. Caro; Jacobs; Sennett 439; Ganser/Höpker). In the following selective reading of *Mean Streets*, my focus will be the enactment of ethnic (im)-mobility in a film that communicates as the crux of a ghettoized ethnic urbanity what I term 'carceral mobility': confined by narrow geographical boundaries, the protagonists are "paradoxically liberated by the turmoil of the bars, tenements, and streets that make up their confines" (Kolker 168). This paradoxical version of mobility is structured by an often contradictory dialectics of inclusion and exclusion, of shelter and imprisonment, of safety and surveillance characteristic not only of Little Italy but of other ethnic neighborhoods as well.

2.   Carceral Mobility, Certalian Tactics, U.S.-American Mobilities

How does *Mean Streets* construct the carceral mobility of Little Italy, and how, in turn, does spatial confinement influence the screened development of the ethnic subject? What role does the specific history of Italian America play in this context? In order to answer these questions, Michel de Certeau's *The Practice of Everyday Life* provides a

---

[2]   As Lourdeaux notes, *Mean Streets* was in fact conceived as the third part of a trilogy, starting with *Jerusalem, Jerusalem* (a project Scorsese never realized) and continued by *Who's That Knocking at My Door?* (232).

vocabulary of mobile forms and itineraries as well as of resistant tactics versus hegemonic strategies that has influenced urban studies to a great extent for a few decades now. According to de Certeau, urban movement always contains an element of (re-) appropriation, a claim to space by the person who moves about, even if such a claim may only be momentary.[3] As Karin Höpker also argues in this volume, the present and presence relative to time and place will necessarily establish the individual as a (temporary) agent within a network, interconnected via spatial relations of proximity and distance and informed by codes of race, class, and gender.

De Certeau himself presents much less than a harmonious view of the socio-cultural realm, as he describes culture as a force field which "articulates conflicts" and "develops in an atmosphere of tensions, and often violence" (xvii). In the chapter "Walking in the City," de Certeau is mainly interested in the manifold practices of everyday mobility through which individual agents tactically reappropriate space; tactics, according to de Certeau, are applied from a position which has no place of its own as such and which is not visibly distinguishable in terms of a clear borderline.

This tactical mobility is also at work in *Mean Streets*, where protagonists do not behave according to the grand narrative of U.S.-American exceptionalist individualism and ascendant social mobility, but act as "loc[i] in which an incoherent (and often contradictory) plurality of … relational determinations interact" (de Certeau xi). The filmic vision counters the dominant U.S.-American narrative, in which mobility has been of special symbolic value for the formation of ideas and ideals of freedom and national identity (and thus constitutes an important element in the discourse of American exceptionalism). The ascription of a democratic, conflict-solving potential to social and geographical mobility constitutes a main topos in U.S.-American culture and literature, from slave narratives to Mark Twain and Walt Whitman, from Woody Guthrie to Jack Kerouac and the road movie. Yet U.S.-American cultural constructions of mobility, in their mainstream versions at least, often implicitly rest on the construction of the ethnic or gendered Other as immobile, as 'not free to move.' Arguably, literary and cultural narratives have had a crucial share in the process of forming a rhetoric of territorial expansion and limitless social mobility, which neglects those 'less central' stories of slavery, internment, marginalization, segregation, and exclusion from the grand narrative of American mobility. Correspondingly, the street or the road often acts as a shifting signifier in cultural narratives, immersed in a dialectics of

---

[3]   While de Certeau's theories have been criticized for their structuralist, sometimes dichotomous logics as well as for their representational, humanist approach, *The Practice of Everyday Life* and especially the much-anthologized chapter "Walking in the City" are still valued by urban theorists as a starting point for making sense of the urban everyday. It has to be noted that de Certeau differentiates between walking as a form of self-directed, tactical mobility and movement by railways or busses, which he considers passive. For a view of urban automobility building on and updating de Certeau, cf. Thrift.

geographical and social mobility *and* immobility within the larger context of ethnic, class, and gender differences.[4]

The dialectics of (im)mobility is also at work in de Certeau. He, too, develops a notion of "'traveling incarceration' in which human bodies are able to be ordered" (Thrift 44-45), but he only refers to traveling by train and bus where "the carriage is mobile, the passengers are immobile" at this point (Thrift 44-45; cf. de Certeau 111). For him, only the 'walked' street itself functions as an urban space that has the potential for moments of rupture in the socio-spatial structure and the monitored machinery of urbanity, a space where a vis-à-vis with the Other is possible on a shared street-level.[5] However, such encounters do not imply that social hierarchies are ever completely or permanently suspended. As is the case in *Mean Streets*, these hierarchies can even feed into a paradoxical carceral mobility of roads in closed circuit structuring an ethnic ghetto.

In the 1970s, Martin Scorsese brought the results of postwar urban development on screen and made them a subtext of popular perception: *Taxi Driver* (1976) is the most renowned outcome of this project (cf. Ganser/Höpker). Scorsese's *Mean Streets* addresses spatial practices of motion and interaction as a part of everyday itineraries, foregrounding the paradox of carceral mobility as a result of invisible but closely policed segregational cityscapes. The trajectories of Scorsese's protagonists move on "lignes d'erre" (de Certeau xviii), aberrant lines that navigate what de Certeau describes as "a jungle of functionality" and of "technocratically constructed, written, and functionalized space" (xviii).

3.   The Urban Villagers

How can we make sense of the cultural specificity of Scorsese's filmic articulation of Italian-Americanness through the concept of carceral mobility and the Certalian theoretization of the street? For one, *Mean Streets* is grounded in, though by no means reducible to, the historical experience of Italian immigration to urban America. In 1962, sociologist Herbert Gans published his classic study of the life of Italian Americans in Boston's West End, *The Urban Villagers: Group and Class in the Life of Italian-Americans*. With a focus especially on the second and third generations, Gans characterized Italian Americanization by fast acculturation (especially due to mass culture and the media)[6] on the one hand and slow assimilation on the other. The latter

---

[4]   Regarding gender, I have analyzed this dialectics more closely elsewhere (cf. Ganser 2009).

[5]   The similarity of this point in de Certeau's theorizing with Mikhail Bakhtin's conception of the chronotope of the road and its democratic potential are striking, but space does not permit a more detailed discussion here.

[6]   Scorsese's musical choices in the soundtrack would confirm this diagnosis; a number of classic Anglo-American soul and rock'n'roll songs by the Ronettes, the Shirelles, or the Rolling Stones are much more dominant in the film than Italian music, which appears mostly in association with the parent generation.

he understood as "the disappearance of the Italian social system" (35) that did not happen in America's Little Italies and subsequently led to what Fred Gardaphé calls the "trappings of Italianitá" (*Italy* 4): this continual social "Italianness" becomes an obstacle to entering American mainstream culture, as it "becomes a closet with all the claustrophobia that small spaces encourage" (Gardaphé, *Italy* 159). The pervasiveness and durability of the social system, built on strong kinship ties among extended families, religious conformism, strong social cohesion, and nostalgia for the past, is what led Gans to the seemingly paradoxical title that characterizes Italian Americans as "Urban Villagers" who had successfully transferred socio-economic structures of Italian villages to New York, Boston, and other American cities. Contemporary commentators like Gardaphé are hesitant to call this transferral a success, however; Michael Viscusi, for instance, terms Little Italy "a captive market of eternal exiles, who could neither enter the order of English America nor return to Italy" (64-65).

Historically, a main factor that accounts for the durability of the Italian ways of social life—besides the upholding of family values and religious and cultural traditions—functioned on a territorial basis: *campanilismo* or "village-mindedness" (Glazer/Moynihan 186) referred to the fact that America's Little Italies were uniformly ordered according to regional provenience of the Italian immigrants, who stuck to their village of origin and distrusted *forestieri*, the 'strangers' outside one's own extended family; Little Italy was thus by no means a homogeneous whole (cf. Maffi 109, 116; Glazer/Moynihan 184) but rather, as Richard Sennett calls it, an "ethnic palimpsest" (440). Scorsese's own neighborhood of New York's Elizabeth Street, for instance, was almost exclusively inhabited by Italians from around Palermo; as he himself commented, even as a third-generation Italian American he often was confused as a child as to whether he lived in America or Italy (qtd. in Blake 153). "Although the nation he was in might have been a matter of some confusion to the young Scorsese," Richard Blake comments, "the neighborhood was not":

> In fact, so precise were the boundaries of this world that in his documentary film *Italianamerican* (1974), his father … makes a clear distinction between their street and the Neapolitan settlement two blocks over on Mulberry Street. Although outsiders may speak of New York and New Yorkers of Little Italy …, the residents view their area as a federation of even smaller enclaves, each with its own personality. (153-54)

The resulting tightness of social control within any Italian-American neighborhood can be viewed as a consequence of these tightly-knit federations, even though it might have been more lenient in comparison with other ethnic ghettos like Chinatown, as Maffi argues (cf. 112). *Mean Streets* presents a conclusion that differs from Gans's sociological study, however. Gans writes:

> In view of the severity of social control, it would be easy to caricature peer group life as a prison for its members. To the outsider, the concern with social control and self-control might indeed seem oppressive. But he must also take into account that there is little desire for voluntary nonconformity, and consequently, little need to require involuntary conformity. Nor do people seem to be troubled by fears about the breakdown of self-control, or about the possibility that they may be suspected of misdeeds. Although these

potentialities do lurk under the surface, they do not usually disturb the positive tenor of group relations. (88)

Scorsese chooses to focus on this very issue: what happens when adolescent Italian-American males, well integrated into a socially cohesive community, are "troubled by fears about the breakdown of self-control, or about the possibility that they may be suspected of misdeeds"? What happens when the lurking potentialities come to the surface and do disturb "the positive tenor of group relations"? In this manner, *Mean Streets* tests the boundaries of the Italian-American urban social system and asks its audience to evaluate the price the ethnic/ized individual pays for its sustenance: violence, self-denial, and loss of mobility. In this way, the film presents us with a rather bleak critical evaluation of this system.

Tight social cohesion on the inside and strong rejection of the non-Italian-American world certainly also account for spatial segregation or ghettoization, which has functioned, from an 'inside' perspective, as both shelter from a discriminatory outside (manifest also in the violation of Italian Americans' civil liberties and the detention of Italian Americans as both 'Reds' and fascists up to the Cold War; cf. Gardaphé, *Italy* 24-26) and a guarantee for cultural continuity. The street was a distinct site of negotiating Italian American masculinity and cultural identity, as "the male's corner hangout, the streets, and the stag environments in which he spent his spare-time as a young man were not respected by the American climate of opinion" (208).[7] An earlier major sociological study on Italian American life by William Foote Whyte is tellingly named *Street Corner Society*. The street as a central site of performing Italian-American masculinity and identity functioned as a territorial marker for the carceral mobility of the enclave, providing 'home turf' while simultaneously inhibiting movement:

> Movement could be dangerous when crossing the street meant entering a neighborhood patrolled by a hostile group. Consequently, Little Italies across the country became stages for the public display of manhood as Italian-American men protected their home turf from invasion, and these neighborhoods were breeding grounds for street gangs. (Gardaphé, *Wise Guys* 18)

Where Gans speaks about Italian-American mobility, he differentiates between individual and group mobility on the one hand (referring to the social unit that is undertaking to change itself) and internal and external mobility on the other in his chapter "Obstacles to Change: The Pattern of Social Mobility" (217-25). For the discussion of *Mean Streets*, the most interesting interplay is that between internal mobility, exemplified by the upwardly mobile protagonist Charlie, and external mobility, a moving-out of the community that potentially breaks up groups and social structures and thus is often perceived as a threat to Italian-American cultural continuity: "The

---

[7] Cf. also Maffi 75-78, who characterizes the streets of the Lower East Side as "a vital source of inspiration and apprenticeship" where "amid yearnings and traumas, discoveries and obsessions, ... the difficult process of reinventing one's identity [as an Italian American] began" (78).

rejection of external mobility is largely a rejection of middle-class elements in the outside world" (219), the mainstream American society associated with suburban life, college attendance, careerism, and different 'tastes' (cf. 219). This rejection, Gans argues, is based on feelings of "inferiority, and consciousness of some real—and some imagined—deficiencies" (221). While internal mobility might change the behavior of the group but will not threaten it as such, external mobility has therefore been frequently punished by expulsion from the group and was thus almost nonexistent among Bostonian West Enders around 1960. In Gans's study, "people who have moved away from the group are described as renegades or deserters" (221).[8] Similarly, *Mean Streets* highlights the harsh and violent form this ostracization may take, emphasizing the potential personal and collective tragedies to follow.

In representations of American Little Italies, both Michael Viscusi (cf. 65) and Fred Gardaphé (cf. *Italy* 151) note, nostalgia and death are major themes that are related to the fact that as ethnic enclaves, Little Italies have become increasingly smaller in the course of the 20th century. As long as Americans of Italian descent occupied the area, the histories and stories of immigration and cultural identity did not die; but when Italian Americans moved out and other Americans moved into the neighborhoods, oral culture was turned into cultural products like literature, film, photography, and museums to provide Italian Americans with a sense of ethnic identity and tradition (cf. Gardaphé, *Italy* 151). The ambiguity of Little Italy as both refuge and closet continued to structure many of these narratives (cf. Gardaphé, *Italy* 159), as *Mean Streets* perfectly demonstrates. In that way,

> Little Italies can be studied as instances of the *precarious pluridimensionality* of the nation in the twentieth century. If they move beyond the origin, immigrant enclaves also resist the location, the structure hosting them, the nation of nations of which they are a part. With respect to one or with respect to the other, as a non-territorial extension or as an internal component, they are always somehow centrifugal, never quite coincide with the political units (or unities) which purport to enclose them or to define them. (Loriggio 21, original emphasis)

---

[8] Italian-American housing patterns are not always as stable as in Gans's object of study, Boston's West End. Binder and Reimers, for instance, name a number of Italian-American residential areas in 1970s' New York, many of them emerging in the wake of U.S.-American suburbanization: Brooklyn's Canarsie, Red Hook, Bensonhurst, and Cobble Hill neighborhoods or parts of Staten Island (cf. 205). Earlier, upwardly mobile Italian Americans had settled in East Harlem or Yorkville, for instance (cf. Maffi 108). Unsurprisingly, it has often been class mobility that resulted in geographical mobility as well (cf. Sennett 452), but one should also remember working-class forms of mobility such as seasonal mobility before 1900 (cf. Maffi 111-12) and those Italian Americans moving to the margins of New York in search of semirural areas where one could grow vegetables and raise goats (cf. Glazer/Moynihan 187).

4.   The Mean Streets of Little Italy

The bleak appearance of New York in the early 1970s is a central issue in *Mean Streets*, a film I read as symptomatic in its dystopian vision of a number of urban filmic discourses at the time. Martin Scorsese and the New York School of filmmakers were especially investigative of the seemingly incoherent street ramblings of disenfranchised men (and much fewer women)[9] whose lives were confined by narrow geographical boundaries in ethnic enclaves like that of Little Italy. Drawing heavily on the French *nouvelle vague* and *cinéma vérité*, *Mean Streets* foregrounds film syntax and constructs an episodic, elliptical narrative with the plot less important than the themes. It articulates a specific ethnic milieu as a dilapidated, quotidian diegetic world or what has been termed a sociological "simulation of the Lower East Side" (Grist 65). Historically, *Mean Streets* is also significant because it was the first feature film to depict Little Italy from a distinct insider perspective (cf. Taubin 15).

The film portrays the lives of small-time crooks, focusing on Charlie Cappa, Jr. (Harvey Keitel), the well-dressed nephew of the local 'mafia' *padrone*, who dreams of his own Italian restaurant,[10] and his friend Johnny Boy (Robert De Niro), a crazy trickster-conman[11] constantly taunting the hood's loan sharks, or, in sociologist Herbert Gans's terms, one of those schizophrenic characters that have historically functioned as a source of entertainment for the neighborhood (15). Gans distinguishes between action-seekers and routine-seekers in his study of Italian-American life in Boston around 1960, and Johnny and Charlie seem in fact to embody the prototypes of each.[12] Charlie is torn between street life on the one hand and social aspiration paired with a

---

[9] As Paula Massood notes, women usually have little agency in Scorsese's films, although they often signify movement. In *Mean Streets*, Teresa (Amy Robinson) is the only one who seriously plans to move out of Little Italy, and Charlie projects his desires of border-crossing onto the bodies of women like Teresa and Diane (Jeannie Bell), an African-American stripper (cf. 82).

[10] The problematics of stereotyping via the mafia theme in the representation of Italian Americans has brought forth a plethora of scholarly studies. With respect to film, cf. esp. Cavallero; Tamburri; Hostert/Tamburri; Bondanella.

[11] Fred Gardaphé has argued that the Italian-American wiseguy is in fact a continuation of the archetypal trickster figure (cf. *Wise Guys*, 3-9). Like Hermes, the trickster figure of Greek mythology, Johnny Boy "begins to represent a power against familial collectivism and for acquisitive individualism" (7) and stands for "chaos and change ..., disorder to a system" (8). He overlooks, however, that traditional trickster figures ultimately function to reestablish harmony and to ensure the continuation of the social system.

[12] Gans characterizes them as follows: "Routine-seekers are more likely to be regular churchgoers, to live by the ethical norms of the religion, and to favour moderation in all pursuits. They will accept the authority of the more powerful as long as it is wielded equitably ... . The action-seeker ... is belligerent in the presence of authority, and is certain that government is always exploitative and corrupt" (30).

strong religiosity on the other.[13] He sees his faith tested in the form of Johnny Boy and Teresa (Amy Robinson), Johnny Boy's cousin and Charlie's secret girlfriend, both of whom are outcasts of the *famiglia*; through them, he seeks penitence for what he perceives as his sinfulness but finally reaps violent physical punishment by associating with two 'untouchables.' As Francesco Caviglia states, Scorsese's portrait of Italian-American men enacts a nostalgic vision of old-fashioned Italians translated onto American cityscapes, a vision "that is the American dream plus more archaic Catholic overtones, with sins that have to be atoned for somewhere, and suffering as a way to redemption" (n.p.).[14] Old-fashioned Italian ideas about masculinity and family here function as integral parts in constructing a shared memory of immigration, a "foundation myth" (Caviglia n.p.) from which Italian-American cultural narratives can take off. On a similar note, Fred Gardaphé sees Scorsese's visual explorations as resting on a self-fashioned mythology of Italian-American life that contrapuntally accompanied the process of assimilation (cf. *Italy* 37).

In the initial sequences, the jump-cut high-angle shots of Little Italy's Mulberry Street at night, illuminated by the feast of San Gennaro[15] in a view from above, place it as an "insignificant enclave within the dark mass of Manhattan" (Grist 73). These images stand in opposition to the shots of the feast taken in the streets, which create a crowded shabbiness, but also a vibrant, energetic atmosphere of heterogeneity (Grist 73). As the 8mm shots expand into a full-screen frame, the camera sinks into the street and begins the filmic narrative. A coherent, totalizing view from outside is no longer possible as the viewer is now absorbed by a bilingual ethnic community of semi- or illegal economies, pool-hall fights, card games, money collecting, and movies. By a cacophonous sound mix and documentary filmic devices such as hand-held cameras and the integration of fictional home movies, the spectators are spatially entrapped with the characters in a sub-cultural environment seemingly homogeneous and 'authentic,' despite its being shot only partially in Little Italy (cf. Grist 73; Massood 79).

---

[13] The coupling of a heightened religiosity among Italian Americans since the 1940s and a simultaneously rising Italian middle class is analyzed, for New York, by Glazer/Moynihan (cf. 203). Their observations revolve around the fact that Catholic churches gave upwardly mobile Italians the opportunity to show off their success in public.

[14] Caviglia names four characteristics typical of Scorsese's construction of Italian-American masculinity: self-denial, moral and amoral familism, violent jealousy, and a hierarchical, hostile outside world. Regarding familism, he notes how "there is nothing unusual or wrong in the family itself—at least not worse than in other ethnic groups: the problem lies in relations to the external world" (n.p.). While this is generally irrefutable, I would argue that Charlie's relationship with Teresa, who is denied normality by the inside rather than the outside world, complicates this dichotomous analysis. On Scorsese's filmic constructions of masculinity, cf. also Gardaphé, *Wise Guys*; Nicholls.

[15] A feast celebrated in Little Italy every September for the patron saint of Naples. According to popular legend, the blood of San Gennaro liquefies and turns bright red during the time of the feast (cf. Grossvogel 69). The importance of religious *festas* for early Italian American culture is noted by Binder/Reimers (cf. 147) and Maffi (cf. 113-14).

These filmic techniques, producing documentary effects, are deeply colored by the characters' perspective, yet always "allude to a material presence, a factual existence" (Kolker 165). The ambiguity of narrative actuality and potentiality (the alternative filmic reality suggested by the use of 8mm reels) thus generated not only foregoes closure, but ultimately also suspends the fiction of the scopic—in de Certeau equivalent to the figure of the World Trade Center—as that which renders urban complexity readable. Thus the film resists turning opaque mobility into a simplified, transparent filmic text.

The film starts with home movie scenes that seem to depict a future fantasized by its protagonist: we see Charlie at the baptizing party of his imaginary child, with Johnny Boy as the godfather[16] and Teresa as his wife. The sequence is interrupted by what is apparently Charlie's voiceover (but is spoken by Scorsese himself rather than Harvey Keitel) immediately after he wakes up in his bed. To the soundtrack of the Ronettes's "Be My Baby," an ironic comment on the immaturity of the protagonists to be introduced (cf. Gardaphé, *Wise Men* 69), Charlie's opening words imply that although this subculture of Little Italy might oppose hegemonic lawfulness, it also creates a strict, regulative socio-economic system of its own: "You don't pay for your sins in church: you pay in the streets and at home. The rest is bullshit and you know it." Charlie draws a parallel between doing penance in the street as well as at home, foreshadowing the theme of conflicting private-public configurations. While the Super 8 reels of the opening sequence unite Charlie's domestic bliss with Teresa and his street career, the plot opens analeptically and ends with the three main characters as only potential survivors of a 'mafia' attack. Scorsese thus leaves it to the viewer to decide whether these reels document Charlie's actual future or merely visualize his (utopian) dreams and hopes—as *pars pro toto*, Charlie's future might stand for the future of ethnic urban life in general.

In the film, the main characters appear as random parts of unpredictable events. When Charlie is in the streets, for example, no matter how central he is to the narrative moment, he is composed in the frame as one figure among many, standing off-center, next to a building, other people moving by him (cf. Kolker 168). Similarly, the outcast Johnny Boy exemplifies a misfit who, eluding disciplinary measures from the inside, employs a guerrilla tactic reliant on moments of opportunity as well as on the spatial blind spots of urban order and control. Charlie knows the risks involved in taunting prescribed rules and is determined to save Johnny Boy in an attempt to unite the private and the public—his religious fervor and personal loyalty as well as his street credibility. Yet Johnny Boy is a lost cause, overrating his abilities and unable to control himself, a main concern of Italian-American action-seeking adolescents, according to Gans (87), mainly for fear of losing attachment to one's group (a fear that Johnny Boy shows in his pleas with Charlie to help him). Finally, he, Charlie, and Teresa are

---

[16] On the familial standing of the godparent in Italian-American culture and his/her importance for upholding, affirming, and extending family relationships, cf. Gans 74.

punished, shot during their attempt to escape Little Italy—it remains unclear who, if any of them, survives.[17] In the end,

> [t]he film's concluding moments suggest that border crossing is dangerous, whether it's a literal emigration from the neighborhood or a more figurative departure from one's upbringing and traditions. It cannot be forgotten that Charlie's uncle warns Charlie away from the deviance that Johnny Boy and Teresa represent. (Massod 83)

"Mean streets": in the American metropolis, the street is an integral part of the 'hood,' a communal, ethnically marked space travelled routinely and circularly by its inhabitants. Those in motion always return to the same locations, leaving the impression that they are drawn into the ethnic enclave by centripetal social forces; thus, "[c]ars offer little promise of escape to a world beyond Little Italy" (Blake 171). That *Mean Streets* comes to a brutal end at the very moment the main characters try to escape from their tightly-knit segregated community by crossing Brooklyn Bridge by car is not a coincidence, but a punishment for their transgression, their attempted escape: Charlie pays for his sins in the streets, and the film comes full circle.[18] Brooklyn Bridge, as a symbol of the expansion of modern New York, loses its force and expansion is foreclosed.[19] The cityscape has shrunk into an ethnic enclave, a mixture of the carceral (referring to seclusion from outside) and the gated community (referring to seclusion from inside), for Charlie, Johnny Boy, and Teresa. At the same time, the film's conclusion narrates "the breakdown of the third-generation Italian-American family and the failure of its traditional culture, particularly the Church, to maintain its integrative function" (D'Acierno, qtd. in Gardaphé, *Wise Guys* 76). Again, one can thus discern a strong nostalgic element in the film's construction of Little Italy and its inhabitants; yet this nostalgia is not the same as regret or romanticization (which is formally evaded by Scorsese's realist, semi-documentary cinematography).

The specific spatiality of *Mean Streets* is made up by "a mosaic of locations within an extremely small geographic area," each of which "reveals a facet of the constricted, claustrophobic world of the main character" (Blake 170); its tragedy, as Martin Seeßlen has observed, is thus not that the main characters fall prey to inner-city violence, but that they cannot cross the ghetto border, within which they must continue to exist (cf. 77).

The clash of differing cultural versions of public and private spheres is embodied by Charlie, who suffers from the disintegration of conflicting values (an element

---

[17] Teresa's crime, for which she is symbolically punished in the accident, is perhaps simply her aspiration to leave Little Italy and move uptown.

[18] Lourdeaux discerns a multicultural conflict within Charlie, noting that *Mean Streets* shows an Irish-Catholic, individualist, institutional understanding of penance, law, and order (due to the fact that even in Little Italy it was Irish priests who reigned the parishes) that acts as a counterpoint to Italian ideas of responsibility and family (cf. 228, 241).

[19] For the symbolic dimension of Brooklyn Bridge in the context of the modernist city, cf. Trachtenberg; Shiel 166.

typical of film noir, cf. Siegel 149).[20] A second or third-generation immigrant, he is torn between romantic love (his feelings for Teresa) and the reality of his Italian-American patriarchal *famiglia*, a sphere that traditionally encompasses both 'private' affairs and local economics and politics.[21] As Glazer and Moynihan have argued, the early immigrants brought with them a strong sense of family, which served "both to advance and to limit them" (182). It is for the sake of family conformism that Charlie denies his feelings for Teresa and asks her not to speak of an official relationship, as his boss/uncle, the local don Giovanni Cappa (Cesare Danova), interprets her epilepsy as mental deficiency; the values and judgments of the *famiglia* thus pervade the bedroom. For different reasons, Charlie and Johnny Boy's attempt at breaking free of ethnic patriarchy entails breaking laws and the temporary disruption of the neighborhood, a structure Lourdeaux finds typical of Scorsese's filmic oeuvre (cf. 218).

The second conflict, related to the first, is that between religious duties and the everyday demands of secular society that Charlie tries to retranslate into the religious domain. The restless camera and bustling urban atmosphere resonate with these cultural tensions, as the city presents the characters with two conflicting apparatuses of interpellation, producing subjectivities that reflect this collision and are unable to escape the rules of either. The most satisfying resolution of the resulting tensions, suggested by Glazer and Moynihan, is some form of worldly success that is admired by one's family and the friends of one's childhood (cf. 194). They thus read Charlie's ambition, which indirectly also lures him away from Little Italy, as an attempt to solve the tension between individual strivings and community demands; crime is interpreted as a consequence of the desire for upward mobility coupled with a lack of access to professional labor (197).

In *Mean Streets*, Scorsese mixes documentary conventions and European realist cinematography and expressionism (e.g., the use of intense colors and glaring neon lights) to create a distinct 'street imagery' characteristic of a transatlantic vision of American-Italianness and Italian-Americanness. Yet, while *Mean Streets* emphasizes a reality of an ethnic enclave in both its violence and community aspects, it ultimately remains dystopian in its insistence on Little Italy as a modern continuation of what Ed Soja, following Mike Davis, has termed the 'carceral archipelago' (cf. 298-322). The street as a place of encounter and negotiation has turned into the closed circuit of the ghetto and has thus lost its democratic potential. This dystopian vision of the city as a desolate battleground responds to the worsening conditions of inner cities in the 1970s, to racial conflict, rising crime, urban dilapidation, and financial ruin. In the aftermath of the 1960s and in the context of a paradigm shift from modern to postmodern urbanity, Los Angeles had become the archetypal, expansive postmodern city in the cultural imaginary, while 'modernist' New York remained as either a dystopian pro-

---

[20] On the influence of film noir on Scorsese's *Mean Streets*, cf. Martin, chapter 3.

[21] Cf. the reasons Gans gives for the importance of the family as a social and economic unit in the history of Italian immigration in America (211).

jection, or, in fewer instances, an object of nostalgia (e.g., in the films of Woody Allen). Scorsese's work of that time reflects a sensitivity for an atmosphere of contestation and tension, highlighting the threat of ethnic immobility to stifle the utopian vision of a nation defined crucially by the freedom of social and spatial mobility as an ethnically integrative force.

5. Conclusion

New York, endowed with a model character of the modern city and suspended between European and a radically different West Coast urbanity, has been cinematographically represented as both a utopian and dystopian ethnic site since the late 20th century. Depicting rites of passage in an urban jungle, *Mean Streets* shows as a leitmotif the problematic dynamics between the wish for both mobility and belonging. Scorsese counters the romantic view of the gangster presented by *Mean Street*'s most influential predecessor, Francis Ford Coppola's *Godfather* (1972), by using a semi-documentary cinematography and provoking a striking sense of realism, thus emphasizing "the reality of the documentary rather than the romanticism of fictional drama" (Gardaphé, *Wise Men* 68).

Rather than romanticizing traditional Italian-American masculinity in a dramatic plot, the film opts for the visualization of the multidimensional tensions concerning Italian-American urbanite males at a time in which the future of the multicultural metropolis in the U.S. was at a watershed: between adolescence and adulthood, the religious and the economic, Irish, Italian, and American cultural elements, the parent and peer generations, homosociality and heterosexual relations, the public and the private, stasis and mobility. Scorsese portrays a "destructive patriarchy," "young men who gradually destroy themselves while trying to fit their ethnic family values to the Anglo-American success ethic" (Lourdeaux 229): "a superstitious, insensitive patriarchy that has no use for either an ill young woman or a clever hellion" (Lourdeaux 245). In a reading of *Mean Streets* and *Gangs of New York* that focuses on ethnicity and urban space, Paula Massood also emphasizes the interconnected themes of ethnicity and the maintenance of literal and figurative borders in both of these films, which thus become narratives "that are at one and the same time about local and national mythologies" (77) revolving around Italian-American identity and the myth of the melting pot, clearly debunked in *Mean Streets*.

As I have argued in this essay, *Mean Streets* enacts the paradox of carceral mobility in its effects on three young Italian-American characters, who are all trapped, for different reasons, within the confines of their ethnic neighborhood. Their tactical appropriations of urban space, in Certalian fashion, are only momentarily, fleetingly successful before the surveillance system of the 'mean streets' of Little Italy polices the boundaries of territorial norms. Ultimately, the film engages with opacities and criss-crossing movements and seeks to trace the turns and meanderings of those 'less central' spatial stories and itineraries that arguably 'make' U.S.-American 'EthniCities,' but its ultimate evaluation of non-conformist tactics vs. institutional, systemic strategies of control emphasizes the strength of the latter over the potential of the former.

Works Cited

Bakhtin, Mikhail. "Forms of Time and of the Chronotope of the Novel." *The Dialogic Imagination: Four Essays*. Trans. Caryl Emerson and Michael Holquist. Austin: U of Texas P, 1981. 84-256.

Baudrillard, Jean. *America*. London: Verso, 1988.

Binder, Frederick M., and David M. Reimers. *All Nations under Heaven: An Ethnic and Racial History of New York City*. New York: Columbia UP, 1995.

Blake, Richard A. *Street Smart: The New York of Lumet, Allen, Scorsese, and Lee*. Lexington: UP of Kentucky, 2005.

Bondanella, Peter. *Hollywood Italians: Dagos, Palookas, Romeos, Wise Guys, and Sopranos*. New York: Continuum, 2004.

Caro, Robert A. *The Power Broker: Robert Moses and the Fall of New York*. New York: Knopf, 1974.

Cavallero, Jonathan J. "Gangsters, Fessos, Tricksters, and Sopranos: The Historical Roots of Italian American Stereotype Anxiety." *Journal of Popular Film & Television* 32.2 (2004): 50-63.

Caviglia, Francesco. "Looking for Male Italian Adulthood, Old Style." *P.O.V. 12: Comparing American and European Cinema*. <http://pov.imv.au.dk/Issue_12/section_1/artc4A.html>.

de Certeau, Michel. *The Practice of Everyday Life*. 1984. Trans. Steven Rendall. Berkeley: U of California P, 1988.

Gans, Herbert J. *The Urban Villagers: Group and Class in the Life of Italian-Americans*. New York: Free P of Glencoe, 1962.

Ganser, Alexandra. *Roads of Her Own: Gendered Space and Mobility in American Women's Road Narratives, 1970-2000*. Amsterdam: Rodopi, 2009.

————, and Karin Höpker. "Cruises and Crusades: Productions of Urban Space in *Taxi Driver* and *Mean Streets*." *Conformism, Non-Conformism, and Anti-Conformism in American Culture*. Ed. Antonis Balasopoulos, Gesa Mackenthun, and Theodora Tsimpouki. Heidelberg: Winter, 2008. 237-57.

Gardaphé, Fred L. *Leaving Little Italy: Essaying Italian American Culture*. Albany: State U of New York P, 2004.

————. *From Wise Guys to Wise Men: The Gangster and Italian American Masculinities*. New York: Routledge, 2006.

Glazer, Nathan, and Daniel Patrick Moynihan. *Beyond the Melting Pot: The Negroes, Puerto Ricans, Jews, Italians, and Irish of New York City*. Cambridge, MA: MIT P, 1963.

Grist, Leighton. *The Films of Martin Scorsese, 1963-77: Authorship and Context*. New York: St. Martin's P, 2000.

Grossvogel, David I. *Scenes in the City: Film Visions of Manhattan Before 9/11*. New York et al.: Lang, 2003.

Hostert, Anna Camaiti, and Anthony Julian Tamburri, eds. *Screening Ethnicity: Cinematographic Representations of Italian Americans in the United States*. Boca Raton: Bordighera P, 2002.

Jacobs, Jane. *The Death and Life of Great American Cities*. 1961. New York: Random House, 1993.

Kolker, Robert Phillip. *A Cinema of Loneliness*. New York and Oxford: Oxford UP, [2]1998.

Loriggio, Francesco. "Introduction." *Social Pluralism and Literary History: The Literature of the Italian Emigration*. Ed. Loriggio. Toronto: Guernica, 1996. 7-28.

Lourdeaux, Lee. *Italian and Irish Filmmakers in America: Ford, Capra, Coppola, and Scorsese*. Philadelphia: Temple UP, 1990.

Maffi, Mario. *Gateway to the Promised Land: Ethnic Cultures on New York's Lower East Side*. Amsterdam: Rodopi, 1994.

Martin, Richard. *Mean Streets and Raging Bulls: The Legacy of Film Noir in Contemporary American Cinema*. Lanham: Scarecrow P, 1997.

Massood, Paula. "From *Mean Streets* to the *Gangs of New York*: Ethnicity and Urban Space in the Films of Martin Scorsese." *City That Never Sleeps: New York and the Filmic Imagination*. Ed. Murray Pomerance. New Brunswick: Rutgers UP, 2007. 77-89.

Nicholls, Mark. *Scorsese's Men: Melancholia and the Mob*. Melbourne: Pluto P, 2004.

Seeßlen, Georg. *Martin Scorsese*. Berlin: Bertz, 2003.

Sennett, Richard. *Flesh and Stone: The Body and the City in Western Civilization*. New York: W.W. Norton, 1994.

Shiel, Mark. "A Nostalgia for Modernity: New York, Los Angeles, and American Cinema in the 1970s." *Screening the City*. Ed. Shiel and Tony Fitzmaurice. London and New York: Verso, 2003. 160-79.

Siegel, Allan. "After the Sixties: Changing Paradigms in the Representation of Urban Space." *Screening the City*. Ed. Mark Shiel and Tony Fitzmaurice. London and New York: Verso, 2003. 137-59.

Soja, Edward W. *Postmetropolis: Critical Studies of Cities and Regions*. Malden: Blackwell, 2000.

Taubin, Amy. *Taxi Driver*. London: BFI, 2000.

Tamburri, Anthony Julian. "Italian Americans and the Media: Cinema, Video, Television." *Giornalismo e letteratura: simposio tra due mondi; atti del Simposio internazionale su Giornalismo e Letteratura tenuto a Roma presso la Facoltà di Scienze della Comunicazione Sociale dell'Università Pontificia Salesiana il 18 novembre 2005*. Ed. Giuseppe Costa. Caltanissetta: Sciascia, 2005. 305-23.

Thrift, Nigel. "*Driving* in the City." *Theory, Culture and Society* 21.1 (2004): 41-59.

Trachtenberg, Alan. *Brooklyn Bridge: Fact and Symbol*. Chicago: U of Chicago P, 1979.

Viscusi, Robert. "Making Italy Little." *Social Pluralism and Literary History: The Literature of the Italian Emigration*. Ed. Francesco Loriggio. Toronto: Guernica, 1996. 61-90.

Whyte, William Foote. *Street Corner Society: The Social Structure of an Italian Slum.* 1955. Chicago: U of Chicago P, [4]1993.

Filmography

Manhattan. Dir. Woody Allen. United Artists, 1979.

Mean Streets. Dir. Martin Scorsese. Warner Brothers, 1973.

Who's That Knocking at My Door? Dir. Martin Scorsese. Trimod Films, 1965-8.

The Cab and the City: Chance Encounters and Certalian Perspectives in Jim Jarmusch's *Night on Earth*[1]

KARIN HÖPKER

1. Introduction: Urbanity and the Quotidian

The city, for sociologists, geographers, and philosophers alike, has been thought of as host and place of culmination of both a society's utopian and dystopian tendencies. The city condenses and throws into sharp relief, it accumulates and concentrates. Consequently, the city often serves as a seismographic device to read a society's pertinent motions, indicative of its "best of times" and "worst of times" (Dickens 3). Host to a plenitude of contradictory forces and interests, the city is at the center of struggles for power and control, while, at the same time, its complexity and particular materiality seem to endow it with a capacity for recalcitrance and an obdurate resistance to becoming subject to any singular force. Henry Lefebvre, for instance, perceives the city as a "differential space" (52) of encounter capable of evading the homogenizing forces of a dominant culture; similarly, Marxist geographer David Harvey envisions an interesting spatial exceptionalism:

> The logic of capital accumulation and class privilege, though hegemonic, can never control every nuance of urbanization (let alone the discursive and imaginary space with which thinking about the city is always associated); the intensifying contradictions of contemporary urbanization, even for the privileged …, create all sorts of interstitial spaces in which liberatory and emancipatory possibilities can flourish. (Harvey, "New Urbanism" 3)

As a screenscape, the modern American city has been articulated as a site of contesting social forces by numerous writers and filmmakers throughout the 20th century. It opens up a potential for confronting difference and has thus become the locale and subject of many cultural productions, where differences must be addressed and where (post)modern inhabitants struggle to navigate its complex social fabric. Clearly, at the center of current debates lies the question whether the city's heteroclite spatial

---

[1] This essay has developed from joint research and a collaborative paper presented at the ZiF Bielefeld with Alexandra Ganser (cf. her article in this volume and also Ganser/Höpker). Although my present essay goes beyond my earlier observations, the theoretical similarities and duplicities between our contributions to this volume are intended. We thus hope to demonstrate the broad range of fruitful applications that a critical spatial perspective based on concepts of Michel de Certeau might yield for readings of an ethnic-urban filmic imaginary, and are grateful to the editors of this volume for granting us the opportunity to do so.

structure, its division along faultlines of race and class into enclaves and exclaves, fortresses and carceral archipelagoes, will lead to zoned forms of homogenization. Both urban theory and discourses of cultural production speculate whether, ultimately, this process will result in a segregated conformity or whether, as suggested by Lefebvre and Harvey, the constant processes of restructuring may, repeatedly if temporarily, open up spaces of transience and subversion.

More recent trends in cultural and urban studies have developed new perspectives on these urban phenomena and reject top-down organizational approaches along with the traditional privileging of macro- over micro-level studies. The constant negotiations and sometimes violent struggles of social forces along the faultlines of, above all, race and class may not be best assessed from a theoretical bird's-eye perspective. Instead, a street-level observation of everyday practices is more fruitful to understanding the specificities of a prototypical and yet peculiar U.S.-American city like New York or Los Angeles. In his work *L'invention du quotidien* (Vol. 1: *Arts de faire*, 1980), which I will refer to in its widely received 1984 translation by Steven F. Rendall, *The Practice of Everyday Life*, Michel de Certeau generated a framework for an analysis of the micro-level and the quotidian which provides a vocabulary of mobile forms and itineraries, of small tactics versus overall strategies. In the following, I will employ terms from this Certalian framework to discuss how filmic forms of the urban imagination stage such scenarios in ways that reflect both the hopes and the fears for the late-20th-century American metropolis. As I will argue, Jim Jarmusch's *Night on Earth* has become iconic in its depiction of an American cityscape from the vantage point of the car window and provides for a new perspective on the dense fabric of postmodern urbanity and the inhabitants who navigate it.

Read in conjunction with Michel de Certeau, driving through the city, be it in a cab or a private car, operates within a grammar of spatial interaction, a system of moving about and interacting within the urban social grid. Any trip through the cityscape must contain an element of (re)appropriation, a claiming of space by the person who moves about; even if such a claim may only be fleeting and temporal. This present and presence relative to time and place establishes the individual as an agent within a network of spatial relations, interconnected via relations of proximity and distance, and informed by codes of race, class, and gender. De Certeau focuses on the operations and manifold practices through which individual agents or consumers reappropriate space produced by specific socio-cultural techniques. The rules, the internal logic of the operations, which according to a Certalian framework must necessarily remain fragmentary and relative to situations, will be investigated. Since these rules never manifest themselves in ideologies or institutional structures but can only be insinuated and concealed, they may precisely surface only as spatial narratives. Filmic cultural productions may narrate such patterns and become a vehicle to such motions of insinuation and concealment; they can sound out how individual agency may manifest itself in highly diverse urban settings and how individual operations may be foregrounded from the assumed passivity of urban inhabitants (without suggesting modernist forms of exceptionalist individualism as a consequence). Protagonists come to the fore not primarily as singular individuals, but, according to de Certeau, "as the locus in which an incoherent (and often contradictory) plurality of … relational determinations interact" (xi). Confronted, for instance, with urban spaces heavily inscribed by strategies of urban planning, zoning, and segregation, or by a closely regulated space like the taxi cab, an investigative Certalian interest must lie in the uses of such spaces—not in the abstract phenomenon of spatial re-formation but in individual and collective acts of appropriation and making habitable. In the case of a cab, these acts constitute a series of individual encounters which adhere to the framework of social roles and rules regulating the use of such a cab. Simultaneously, these acts also consist of tactics which render possible propitious signatures of actual encounters that suggest openings and moments of permeability in the clear divides of driver and fare and the particular orders of demarcated hierarchies. Ways of moving through urban spaces in everyday itineraries thus become acts of a *poiesis* underneath and within the more obvious systems of production which seeks to reduce its recipients to the passivity of consumers and to census-transparent groups of biopolitical subjects. To look at such forms not in terms of an anthropological gaze but as a witness to forms of a filmically constructed urban imaginary may be a crucial device, which makes this difference between intended and appropriated consumption more gaugeable to perception. That which is not generated as part of the productive apparatus but as a making-do form of an inventive but provisional *bricolage* is highlighted by the intentional acts of filmic imagination and *mise-en-scène*.

De Certeau himself has a far from naively utopian view of the socio-cultural realm; he describes culture as a force field which "articulates conflicts" and "develops in an atmosphere of tensions, and often violence" (xvii). Here temporary contracts, alliances, and compromises may develop in ways which render the quotidian highly political. Hence, to sound out social practices of interaction in and through forms of cultural production may itself become an investment in movements of the tactical kind.

In the following analysis, I foreground characteristic figures of spatiality and movement in an ethnically inscribed cityscape, which have since become iconic to our perception of specific forms of American urbanism. Jim Jarmusch's *Night on Earth* (1991) addresses spatial practices of motion and interaction as a part of everyday itineraries. Jarmusch's film attempts to utilize the peculiar, half-public, semi-permeable moving space of the taxi cab to narrate a street-level urban imaginary that focuses on the characteristically metropolitan and urban rather than solely on the historically specific aspects of the U.S.-American city. In his view of urban interaction and everyday chance encounters, Jarmusch seeks to connect the serial with the accidental, the regulated with the transgressive, and the global with the local. The figure of the cab is used to envision and narrate complex cityscapes and individual attempts to navigate the multiple and intersecting lines of the public and the private, of interiority and exteriority, and of inclusion and exclusion. Where Jarmusch's film depicts a rhetoric of the quotidian in images and dialogue, the trajectories of his protagonists nevertheless seem to move on "lignes d'erre," on aberrant lines (de Certeau xviii), but they seem capable of establishing tactics that remain without permanent or visible place but adaptable enough to grant an amount of sustained mobility.

2. Jim Jarmusch: Propitious Moments

Throughout his career as an independent filmmaker, Jim Jarmusch has honed an anthropologist's gaze, which, however, does not aim at the quasi-documentary and its claims for social reflection. Instead, it develops a dense visual fabric of thick description which approaches the everyday of a rich and heterogeneous American imaginary. In almost 30 years he has made films like *Down by Law* (1986), *Dead Man* (1995), *Ghost Dog* (1999), or *Broken Flowers* (2005) that address core subjects of U.S.-American society neither via the abstract theoretical or philosophical, nor by directly evoking the grand narratives of American mythology. His films provide trains of images which in all their density stage an encounter with their subjects on an eye-level perspective without becoming flatly socio-realistic or identificatory. As *Night on Earth* serves best to demonstrate, his filmic gaze has been trained by a close look at the quotidian and the particular of the American city- and screenscape, and the likeness of his scenarios becomes all the more striking through the fact that his imagery and narratives tend to foreground their intertextual and artifactual character in an understated way.

Jarmusch shows the city as a living fabric, formed not only through its built space but by its inhabitants, as a dense social fabric interwoven with boundaries and trajectories of human action, as an invisible ordering system that establishes fault-lines of race, class, and gender. His cities are full of David Harvey's "intensifying contradictions" that may create "interstitial spaces" ("New Urbanism" 3) and surprising moments of vis-à-vis human encounters beyond the compressing forces of exclusion and ghettoization. While *Night on Earth* acknowledges the repressive forces of implicit zoning that inform the city—when the first episode leads us across Los Angeles into plutocratic Beverly Hills, or when the New York episode renders visible ethnic divides—, it also pays heed to those forces which are dynamically at work in ways traverse to these boundaries. Literally zooming in on the zoned grid of the metropolis, down to the street-level and into the itineraries of the cities' inhabitants, the film locates moments when categories and orders are destabilized and create contact zones between individuals of disparate groups, or when unlikely encounters within a framework of the usual and unspectacular simply happen.

Combining these unlikely elements with the familiarity of common, everyday situations, Jarmusch's film connects the spatial with the temporal to form what might best be described by the Certalian figure of the propitious. For, in his reflections on tactics, de Certeau imagines a moment when a vis-à-vis with the other seems possible on the shared street-level (cf. xix). Movement renders possible a chance encounter, and to him it is specifically the city which holds the potential for confronting not sameness but an otherness which may be engaged in conjunctural operations without necessitating a utopian suspension of a repressive order or a further dissolution of differing socio-cultural and historical contexts in universalisms.

Clearly, the unexpected encounter with a potential outsider or newcomer is a much-used topos within filmic representations and itineraries of metropolitan life. The occurrence of the strange and heteroclite opens up a momentary and fleeting rupture within the institutionalized homogeneity of the Cartesian grid and the monitored machinery of functioning urbanity. But Jarmusch foregrounds the common space of the taxi and the brief period of its journey across the urban fabric as he seeks to highlight the structural commonalities across specificity and accidental peculiarity of the singular encounter. This interest and tactical agenda is not only observable on the level of content and filmic diegesis but has repercussions that traverse Jarmusch's work.

3.   The Construction of Space: The Cab and the City

A characteristic of Jarmusch's oeuvre is the method of working 'from the inside out,' starting with specific actors in mind and letting the film develop from an idea of specific characters and a collection of notes (cf. Hertzberg vii-viii). This method (or alleged absence thereof) becomes particularly evident in the production process of *Night on Earth*, which was not preceded by long-term planning. It was a spontaneous project Jarmusch engaged in after *Mystery Train* (1989) when the financing efforts for his following film (*Dead Man*, 1995) seemed to have reached an impasse.

Evolving from the idea of a short film centered around Isaach de Bankolé as cab driver and Béatrice Dalle as blind passenger, *Night on Earth* establishes notions of the fleeting moment and the incidental as its subject matter, but it also incorporates ideas of coincidence, the fleeting but propitious as parts of its own myth of origin: "So it was all a little accidental" (Jarmusch, qtd. in Mauer 158). Jarmusch's claims to have written the script within eight days aside, driven by frustration with the faltering project of *Dead Man*, brevity of form and episodic structure clearly have become a poetic principle in *Night on Earth*. While Jarmusch himself likens his episodic work to poetry—"I consider myself a minor poet who writes fairly small poems. … I'd rather make a movie about a guy walking his dog than about the emperor of China" (qtd. in Hertzberg 92)—Roman Mauer in his 2006 monograph *Jim Jarmusch: Filme zum anderen Amerika* draws a connection between *Night on Earth* and the modern form of the short story, ranging from Anton Chekhov to Sherwood Anderson in terms of its demands for considerations of the life-like and for credibility in the choice of subject matter. According to Anderson, it is the open and fragmentary form of the short story that best reflects actual experience, for "[life] is a complex delicate thing. … There are no plot stories in life" (qtd. in Rideout 566)—a quotation which points to an even more significant connection: Similar to Anderson, Jarmusch generates his subject matter from the realm of the quotidian, creating situations which are familiar and yet peculiar enough to hold the viewer's interest.

Stylistically, *Night on Earth* already shows developments in Jim Jarmusch's film-making which render his earlier demands for reduced, minimalistic structures and his well-known "skepticism about camera-movement and non-diegetic music" (Hertzberg ix) less rigorous. Compared with earlier films such as *Stranger Than Paradise*, *Night on Earth* is also much more dialogue-oriented. Interestingly enough, Jarmusch describes that as a necessary consequence of his choice of locale:

> Because we're in an enclosed space, I didn't have much room for characters to express themselves physically or in moments where there is no dialogue as I could in *Stranger Than Paradise*. That's what I like most about that film: the moments between dialogue when you understand what's happening without them saying anything. If you think about taking a taxi, it's something insignificant in your daily life: in a film when someone takes a taxi, you see them get in, then there's a cut, then you see them get out. So in a way the content of this film is made up of things that would usually be taken out …: the moments between what we think of as significant. (Jarmusch, qtd. in Keogh 106)

Obviously, the choice of the taxi's restricted interiority as setting and the spatial construction of the taxi-scenario as a fundamentally interstitial urban space put a strong emphasis on spatial demarcation as such, on boundaries of inclusion and exclusion that are to be negotiated within the ethnically heterogeneous city. *Night on Earth* presents its audience with an array of shots of the cities and the protagonists, a dense fabric of gazes, which range from exterior shots of the cab to interior shots of the protagonists. It alternates between shots into the cab from the outside, shots of the exterior streets from inside that take the perspective of a passenger, and perspectives interior to the cab, filming not only drivers and passengers but mimicking glances through the back mirror. Thus, depicting the city functions through an assembly of seemingly chance images and glimpses and aims at generating a mood or atmosphere characteristic of the particular city rather than at representing it in more explicit ways:

> This is not merely a question of depicting a city's topography or architecture, or even of highlighting a particular aspect of its social life (the racial melting pot and aggressive conversational manners of New York, for instance, or the presence of African immigrants in Paris, or the influence of the Catholic Church in Rome), but of playing variations on the way the cities have been represented in the movies. (Andrew 156)

The spatial reduction, imposed by centering the narrative around taxi journeys, creates visual constraint. In my reading of Jarmusch, this is a chosen and intentional constraint, not simply a side-effect of the technical difficulties of filming within and around a taxicab that might produce a certain amount of stereotypical images of the city. The images of *Night on Earth* are iconic rather than stereotypical; they evoke recognition by the viewer and thus serve the narrative economy and visual density of the episodes. More importantly, the visual aesthetics directly relate to the spatial construction and mobility and thus become curiously self-reflexive: the 'flatness' of the images (in a Jamesonian use of the term, cf. Jameson 60) creates a visual effect specific to the type of movement—to cruise through an urban environment in a car often creates a sense of filmic experience, when the images of the exterior city seem to move and flicker across the screen of the window panes. At the same time, Jarmusch utilizes the 'flatness' of the image to resist or at least discourage allegorical readings of the city—it is not the modernist city, through which the *flâneur* may walk at leisure, and not the complex system of signs and symbols behind which a viewer and reader may find a deeper meaning. Instead, *Night on Earth* insists on a certain degree of 'face-value' and *Unhintergehbarkeit* of the iconic image. The street-level perspectives of the passing cabs are part of the everyday itinerary and of the quotidian; they neither penetrate nor do they assume the authority of implying deeper symbolic meaning. Flatness implies not only a reduction, but the impermeability of the surface image. It thus grants a certain openness to the individual episodes and the kaleidoscopic view of the global city as such, as well as a distinctive resistance to depicting alterity as transparent.

As a film that evolves around the fleeting moment and the urban interstitial, the taxi-film has virtually no generic precedents to Jarmusch's *Night on Earth*. It is not a film of trains, busses, or airplanes, of small social gatherings or groups and their dynamics, but a film of the individual and her loneliness, granting a brief glimpse of a stranger's life (cf. Kilb 219). Here, the trip functions not as a connecting device between two narrative segments but to draw attention to this interstitial moment itself. Even a film like Scorsese's *Taxi Driver* (1976) focuses not on taxi driving but uses it as an illustrative if generic social scenario to relate stories in which the taxi situation itself is marginal.[2] The limitations of the miniature interiorities of taxicabs as movie sets impose a "kind of artistic straitjacket, both technically and esthetically" (Pall H13). This is even more so since Jarmusch "scorns the use of sound stages" and also had no budget for cutting sections of numerous cars open and towing them on a flatbed trailer (cf. Pall H16).

The moment of meeting consists of a short verbal exchange, a gesture, a glance, and yet these fleeting moments seem to contain an entire story. Jarmusch's reductive aesthetics contribute to the effect of a low-key density often said to be strongly influenced by Danish filmmaker Carl Theodor Dreyer, whose minimalist narrative style and symbolic techniques Jarmusch had worked with since *Stranger Than Paradise* (cf. Schindler 78). And yet critics like *The New Republic*'s Stanley Kauffmann have lamented the alleged co-optation of Jarmusch by Hollywood cinema, complaining that Frederick Elmes (who among other projects also filmed David Lynch's *Eraserhead*

---

[2]   What the taxi as a specific form of urban mobility is meant to illustrate and how this element changes throughout the history of American feature film is a different subject. The semi-public situation of the cab traditionally ranges between the social settings of public transport (often signaling scenarios of the under-privileged or anonymous urban crowds), of driving one's own car across the cityscape (as, for instance, a symbol of independence and modern mobility), and of being chauffeured. Thinking of film noir as an example of a typically urban genre, the hard-boiled detectives of the West Coast tend to rely on their own cars but frequently make use of cabs for spontaneous pursuits and preferably anonymous tailing; these purposes create brief moments of complicity with otherwise faceless cab drivers as the 'common man' who assists the case for 'a little extra.'

and *Wild at Heart*) "shot this film in excellent color, from the late afternoon of L.A. to the wintry dawn in Helsinki. But what's a Jarmusch film doing in excellent color?" (Kauffmann 32).

4. Driver and Fare: Encountering the Other

Formative to *Night on Earth* is what Geoff Andrew calls "the anthology structure of separate stories" (153), a series of five episodes connected through the taxi as a topos, but with apparent shifts not only in geography but in the parameters that inform the various urban encounters. The parallelism of the temporal setting for each episode is emphasized by its corresponding visual introduction. Each begins with a tracking shot of a clock and zooming in on a dot marking the geographic location of the respective city on a map, or rather, globe. What follows is a brief sequence of iconic images of the city, static shots of everyday sights (bridges, diners, squares, neon lights, phones) that are nevertheless characteristic of the location.

While the first episode of *Night on Earth*, the L.A. episode starring Winona Ryder and Gena Rowlands, implicitly negotiates issues of class and age, the second episode, set in New York, foregrounds ethnicity as a theme. Displaying an openly episodical structure, the five segments of the film are devoted to the cities of Los Angeles, New York, Paris, Rome, and Helsinki. And yet, while the images are to a certain extent iconically characteristic of the cities and the individual storylines derive part of their humor from the recognizability of setting and inhabitants, the film nevertheless refrains from overplaying the culturally stereotypical. Instead, the individual narratives are strongly shaped by aspects of their contingence, which forges an inter-connectivity between the otherwise unconnected episodes. Thus, the theme of each segment, with dialogues shot respectively in English, French, Italian, and Finnish, is not necessarily attached to the city (pitting, for instance, a clichéd notion of urbanity of West Coast L.A. against East Coast New York, or New World against Old World), but instead, the curious arbitrariness of the stories suggests a certain amount of cosmo-politan interchangeability between cities, despite the culturally specific encoding.

The motif of the global—suggested already by the title and the first images of Earth from outer space which are repeated within each episode—interconnects the five segments through the specific topos of the taxi cab: The situation is inscribed by a peculiar relationship of interiority and exteriority, private and public. More than a setting, the city renders itself visually present as it runs by, as it were, on the 'screen' of the car windows. The interior is socially closely circumscribed by 'rules' of inter-action between driver and fare, parameters of an economic situation of service, which is by no means as strictly and mono-dimensionally shaped as one might expect. Quite on the contrary, driver-fare relations are imprinted by a complex situation of service and empowerment, rendering the cab driver economically dependent on his passengers, while the sheer number of fares distributes this power to an extent which also grants a certain amount of independence. In addition, the passenger is also the one in need of transportation, temporarily dependent on the driver as the one who grants access and mobility.

In the second episode of *Night on Earth*, the implications of this mutual dependency are explored in ways which render visible the urban texture of latent segregation. The New York episode ties in with the leitmotif of vision, visibility, and blindness that runs through the entire film[3] by depicting protagonist Yoyo (played by Giancarlo Esposito) as an 'invisible man.' Unable to hail a cab to Brooklyn despite his openly displayed cash and social status of a confident, fashion-conscious member of the Brooklyn middle class, the protagonist is introduced, with emphasis on his ethnic background, as standing on the other side of some unspecified 'color line.'

When finally a cab stops, its driver turns out to be the East German Helmut Grokenberger (played by a memorable Armin Mueller-Stahl), a former circus clown from Dresden, who not only has limited command of the English language and would as such not be unusual for a stereotypical Manhattan cab driver, but he also has difficulties driving an automatic and no idea of how to reach their destination. In the following exchange, after brief negotiations, a switch of seats takes place, temporarily suspending the traditional roles of driver and fare. The evolving conversation between Yoyo and Helmut derives its humor, similar to the other episodes, from a confrontation and subsequent subversion of cultural stereotypes, contrasting for instance Helmut's hyperbolic immigrant naïveté and heavy German accent with Yoyo's cool display of the street- and fashion-savvy Brooklynite. When Helmut tries to bridge their evident difference by emphasizing similarities, his observation on their "same hats" is indignantly rejected by Yoyo, who refuses to have his fashionable headgear which he calls "fresh" and "the hype" compared to Helmut's NVA-issue fake fur Chapka.

This sets the tune for an ensuing dialogue based on patterns of comparison, which unwittingly emphasize the similarities in their differences. While Yoyo in his native urbanite confidence makes fun of the stranger's name, claiming "Helmut" was like calling your child "lampshade," he reacts piqued at Helmut's comment on the potential semantic ambivalence of his own name connoting a toy, claiming that this "has nothing to do with it." Yet, across the differences and the distance of an obvious imbalance in the distribution of means and knowledge, the halting dialogue negotiating the confrontation of ethnic and social differences remains sympathetic. It is interrupted and structured by the introduction of external factors like the city entering into the interiority of the cab via shots of the cityscape or the pickup of an additional passenger. Helmut, clearly demarcated as 'the stranger' even within the bounds of his own cab, mainly reacts with a sense of astonishment and wonder to the new impressions of the city, its sights and inhabitants. He stares at the Brooklyn Bridge with the same fascination he displays for Yoyo's sister-in-law Angela (played by Rosie Pérez), a mixture of street-smart beauty and high-flaring Nuyorican temper. Yoyo's and Angela's clear sense of belonging, a mixture of pride and love-hate

---

[3]   As Andrew points out, there are also night-blindness in L.A., a blind female passenger in Paris, and sunglasses at night in Rome (154-55).

relationship to their Brooklyn neighborhood, thus becomes contrasted with Helmut's stance as outsider, which they treat with the friendly casualness of driving advice, directions for the return to Manhattan (which he fails to heed), and the humorous and stereotypical "learn some English." When, at the end of the New York episode, Helmut drives lost and erratically through the streets of Brooklyn, his overwhelmed admiration is not directed at the iconic sights and glamorous promises Manhattan is traditionally depicted to hold for the newcomer and immigrant. His disbelieving "New York. I'm in New York" is instead filled with a curious sense of wonder at the heterogeneous metropolis, where a chance encounter with the unexpected Other may grant a glimpse into other lives, a moment of dialogue which, even in its miscommunication, may momentarily suspend the grids of social order and interactional boundaries and open up the unlikely possibilities of the propitious moment. The utopian potential is less one of promise and new order, but presents itself, here as in the other four stories, as part of everyday itineraries and a poetics of the quotidian.

Thus, the seemingly generic space of the cab, a microform of what Marc Augé calls "non-places" (cf. 75-76), is endowed with qualities of what Marie Louise Pratt describes as 'contact zones': "social spaces where cultures meet, clash, and grapple with each other, often in contexts of highly asymmetrical relations of power" (33). The micro-space of the taxi constitutes itself as a space between social poles of tension and asymmetrical power relations—the anonymous service-relation between driver and paying customer regulates but sometimes conflicts with the intimate spatial proximity of the car's confined interior; the static and passive interiority is contrasted with an experience of exterior mobility, granted by the function of transportation across urban space (cf. Mauer 159-60). Jarmusch's taxi situations explore the peculiarities of this space; they stage a moment of encounter in which dialogues and interaction perforate the membrane of urban anonymity between the closely circumscribed social roles of driver and fare. Protagonists step out of their roles and become visible to each other as individuals with personal stories, making possible a moment of recognition of the other in an actual vis-à-vis encounter, and yet the intimacy of, for instance, the confessional scenario (Rome) does rely heavily on the anonymity of the temporal situation, after which the participants part, in all likelihood, never to meet again.

5.   Mapping the Metropolis

Especially the American cities Los Angeles and New York have traditionally been considered, each in its own way, a model of the modern city. They each represent both utopian and dystopian elements as their cityscapes are suspended between a seemingly European and a radically different American urbanity.[4] The filmic constructions of

---

[4]   For a more extensive discussion of dystopian representations of Los Angeles as a highly mediated city, cf. my chapter on real-and-imagined spaces, in which I use the early 1990s "*Chinatown*"-controversy involving Mike Davis, Ed Soja, Derek Gregory, and Rosalyn Deutsche to illustrate the peculiar featuring of L.A. as urban critics' favorite dystopia (23-28).

urban experience, which are in many ways generically American in their heterogeneity and post-immigrant genealogy, offer a new perspective on an urbanity on the verge of change: they are caught between ideals of modernist metropolitanism and the not-yet postmodern, between post-war urban renewal and conservationist concerns, between the estrangement of disinherited city dwellers, the aggressive propagation of suburban single-family housing as the American middle-class ideal, and efforts toward affordable urban housing as part of community building.

Although de Certeau's depiction of New York (or, more specifically, Manhattan) in the street-walking chapter of *Practices of Everyday Life* seems greatly to differ from Jarmusch's visual *mises-en-scène* and emplotments of individual experience, his concepts provide a productive framework for an analysis of such real-and-imagined spaces. By juxtaposing de Certeau's tropes of urban experience with Jarmusch's 1990s vision, I intend to forge a descriptive framework which profits from de Certeau's potential to analyze spatial structures of the quotidian; by a selective reading of spaces and spatial movement in *Night on Earth*, by investigating the patterns which the protagonists 'write' onto the street maps, I aim to devise a spatial hermeneutics which uses de Certeau's grammatology of urban movement and involvement in daily urban practices. This hermeneutics does not seek to construct a voyeur's "texturology," subscribing to "the fiction of knowledge … related to this lust to be a viewpoint and nothing more" (de Certeau 92), but a 'migrational' and 'planetary' one, which engages with opacities and criss-crossing movements, which seeks to trace the turns and meanderings of spatial stories and itineraries without projecting onto them authorial fantasies of the linear.

As *New York Times* film critic Vincent Canby pointed out in his review,

> [t]he first image in *Night on Earth* … is important: that of universal darkness in the center of which is a rotating sphere of brilliant blue overlaid by wisps of white.
>
> As the camera approaches, the wisps of white turn into cloud formations so beloved by forecasters as "weather systems." Familiar oceans and seas appear, also land masses that are as yet undivided by and unclaimed for by national aspiration. (C1)

Thus, *Night on Earth* refers to a reality of the global city as already perceived through a (culturally and historically specific) tradition of filmic representation, a perspective on the city already shaped by film, filtering the images of the cityscape through previous shots and views. The respective city is an intertextual construct, but no less real since that very realization shaped our viewing habits, for Jarmusch is far from any sort of lament of a loss of the real for the hyperreal. Quite on the contrary, *Night on Earth* loses none of its atmospheric density nor any of its interest as a filmic negotiation of a glocalized cityscape when it stresses its constructedness and artifactual character instead of representational notions of depicting social reality. Despite his evident and professed admiration for those filmic qualities he sees in the works of Scorsese or Cassavetes, such as realistic strength or credibility of characters (cf. Keogh 108), Jarmusch's own brand of realism does reflect its own constructedness. When in the opening sequences the Earth is shown from a distance, the camera zooming in shows us very literally a 'global' vision, for what the zoom renders visible is not an overall image of Earth but a second-degree representation. What we see is a topographic map, an old-fashioned globe. Zooming in reveals the material structure of its surface, the slight welt where its seams overlap and are glued together. Thus, the materiality of the medium is foregrounded through a *mise-en-abyme* and the visual representation of space is no longer deceptively transparent. The actual vision of the globe as a whole, a dream of mankind ever since the introduction of the cartographic grid and the Mercatorian system of projection (cf., e.g., Schneider 64-65) is reflected as historical and necessarily based on a construction.[5]

In *Night on Earth*, the visible materiality of the map functions as a self-reflexive commentary on a narrative which offers the audience both a global and a local perspective. The visual frame narrative embedding the episodes only superficially takes the god's eye-view of a traditional omniscient observer. For the outer-space perspective, zooming in on cities of one's choice, into the individual lives and itineraries of an everyday street-level interaction, must remain a fiction, a fictive yet, as I would argue, necessary act of imagination. Or, as Michael Hardt and Kathi Weeks write:

> How can we do justice to both the phenomenological richness of individual existence and the immensity and complexity of the global world system to which life is bound? How can we conceive the connections among the most intimate local dimensions of subjective experience and the abstract and impersonal forces of a global system? (22)

6.   *Night on Earth*: Imagining the Planetary

As I have shown so far, one of Jarmusch's greatest achievements is the way in which he manages to present the ordinary and quotidian to the viewer as a matter of human interest, as an aesthetically interesting construction, and as an ever-changing perspective on urban existence. What may easily be read as an entertaining and slightly absurd comedy of miscommunication and oddly timed connections is also an understated and unobtrusive commentary on the contemporary western metropolis, for "the flickers of humanity in those taxis are soon dulled by time, sex, race, language and money" (Travers 111). There is a trait in Jarmusch's filmic work that might be called an "epistemological modesty" (Suárez 4). It is the acknowledgement that what can be known (and, within filmic logic, rendered visible) is always limited and thus includes only a small portion of lives, situations, scenarios encountered. Indeed, film would become ideologically dubious, if it were to suggest it could procure the totality and panoptic possibilities of a CCTV from a god's-eye perspective.

And yet, as I have argued above, *Night on Earth* is not free from a utopian impulse in an attempt to render the transnational metropolis more imaginable. This effort to think across borders without making claims to totality or a controlling and

---

[5]   For a fascinating and more detailed account of cartography and digital imaging, cf. Serres xxxi.

projective gaze, heedless of difference and alterity, might best be described as an effort not towards an imagination of the 'global,' but, as Gayatry Spivak suggests, as a move towards the 'planetary.' For, as she suggests in chapter three of *Death of a Disclipline*, it is the 'planet' that can overwrite the 'globe': Whereas the globe and globalization signify an overall imposition of similar systems of exchange within a "gridwork of electronic capital" (72), Spivak's notion of the 'planetary' rejects homogeneity as a necessary consequence of comprehensive transnational thinking and embraces human alterity (cf. 101-02).

Night on Earth is programmatic for Jarmusch's filmic enterprise beyond the specificity of the urban locale in that it does venture to address a transnational notion of the city on a larger, more encompassing scale. The title already suggests such an endeavor in a deadpan manner, and the period of a night from dusk (Los Angeles) to dawn (Helsinki) sets the geographic limits through time zones. And yet its images do not harness the cartographic grid of global information systems which suggests panoptic visibility within a computer-simulated globe: "The globe is on our computers. No one lives there. It allows us to think we can aim to control it. The planet is in the species of alterity, belonging to another system; and yet we inhabit it, on loan" (Spivak 72).

In keeping with this view, Jarmusch's spatial poetics, as I argued above, rely on their visible constructedness—an interpretation that cannot only be supported by the imagery, but also by the particular soundtrack. When Tom Waits sings "Back in the Good Old World" and "On the Other Side of the World," the songs function as a pro- and epilogue to *Night on Earth* and as a commentary on the depiction of 'world' not so much as a totalitarian vision of the global, but, as the initial segments of an 'outer space' camera shot suggest, as an alternative view of the 'planetary.'

The scratchy harmonies of the gypsy waltz sung by his trademark raspy voice are suggestive of a transcultural and deeply hybrid dimension that evades the ominous *mélange* of the generic segment of record store 'World Music.' Its form and lyrics caricature and run transverse to songs of imagined globality which have long entered the collective cultural encyclopedia of U.S.-American mythology, such as, most notoriously, "It's a Small World (after all)." Written by the Sherman Brothers in 1964, the song accompanies the ride of the same name in Disneyland (cf. Smith 354). The cheerfully polyglot stanzas and simple counterpoint harmonies become uncannily tenacious—mainly due to their mere repetitiveness from which the audience literally cannot escape during the railed ride in open box-cars.[6] Its well-known infantile lyrics rely heavily on the alleged universalism of human emotions in a world within which geographic separation is the biggest obstacle. The song's second stanza constructs a metaphoric globality that can be read as characteristic of a disneyfied global paradigm: "There is just one moon and one golden sun / And a smile means friendship to

---

[6] Apart from the direct exposure of taking the ride at Disneyworld, this may best be experienced in the 1964 *Wonderful World of Color* clip "Disneyland Goes to the World's Fair," in which Walt Disney himself narrates his introduction of the new ride "It's a Small World."

everyone. / Though the mountains divide / And the oceans are wide / It's a small small world." Even if the intertextual connection was not intended, the popular evocation of global imagery is directly countered in Tom Waits's opening lyrics to "Back in the Good Old World": "When I was a boy, the moon was a pearl the sun a yellow gold. / But when I was a man, the wind blew cold the hills were upside down" (Original Motion Picture Soundtrack).

The soundtrack runs contrary to generic expectations, just as Jarmusch's shots of cityscapes may be iconic and recognizable for each city but have little in common with Disney's imaginations of a global locale, let alone with the distinctly non-urban scenario of *Main Street*, U.S.A. as core of the all-American town.[7] The corporate consumer vision of the global as an imagined space consists of a cleverly engineered mixture of stereotypical scenarios which combine the all-too-familiar with enough of the exotic to be able to claim a pedagogical and informational interest. Jarmusch, on the other hand, not only uses but caricatures and subverts images of cultural stereo-types, either by way of excess and exaggeration (most apparent in the Rome and Helsinki episodes) or by foregrounding the intertextuality of his own work, highlighting his filmic quotes and samples. As I previously pointed out, Jarmusch's films always retain a certain amount of opacity; they render visible their artifactuality and their contextuality within a filmic universe of urban images and stories instead of making claims for authenticity and transparency of representation. Thus, *Night on Earth* remains at a participating distance from its subjects and preserves a sense of alterity without presenting the Other as beyond all imagination:

> If we imagine ourselves as planetary subjects rather than global agents, planetary crea-tures rather than global entities, alterity remains underived from us; it is not our dialec-tical negation, it contains us as much as it flings us away. And thus to think of it is already to transgress, for, in spite of our forays into what we metaphorize, differently, as outer and inner space, what is above and beyond our own reach is not continuous with it as it is not, indeed, specifically discontinuous. (Spivak 73)

Night on Earth manages to provide a *tertium comparationis* via its temporal figuration of the propitious moment and the basic spatial situation of the taxicab. Human en-counters become comparable and partially accessible beyond their individual par-ticularity without leveling the intersecting boundaries of race and class, age and gender. The film preserves alterity without abandoning all hope for envisioning 'humanity' as part and parcel of the contemporary metropolis, and thus, in its neither naïve nor overtly pedagogic but undeniably utopian implications, may be read as an attempt towards what Spivak came to demand as a 'planetary ethics.'

---

[7] For an interesting exploration of the global Disneyfication of space and the 'imagineering' of the nostalgic, cf. Chung.

Works Cited

Andrew, Geoff. "Jim Jarmusch." Andrew. *Stranger Than Paradise: Maverick Film-Makers in Recent American Cinema*. London: Prion, 1998. 135-164.

Augé, Marc. *Non-Places: Introduction to an Anthropology of Supermodernity*. Trans. John Howe. New York: Verso, 1995.

Brüggemeyer, Maik. "Tourist im eigenen Land." *Rolling Stone* 176 (2009): 57-63.

Canby, Vincent. "Urban Life Seen From a Taxi Seat." *New York Times* 4 Oct. 1991: C1& C8.

Chung, Chuihua. "Disney Space." *Project on the City: Harvard Design School Guide to Shopping*. Ed. Jeffrey Inaba, Rem Koolhaas, and Sze Tyung Leong. Köln: Taschen, 2001. 270-98.

de Certeau, Michel. *The Practice of Everyday Life*. 1984. Trans. Steven Rendall. Berkeley: U of California P, 1988.

Dickens, Charles. *A Tale of Two Cities*. New York: Dodd, Mead & Co., 1985.

Ganser, Alexandra, and Karin Höpker. "Cruises and Crusades: Productions of Urban Space in *Taxi Driver* and *Mean Streets*." *Conformism, Non-Conformism, and Anti-Conformism in American Culture*. Ed. Antonis Balasopoulos, Gesa Mackenthun, and Theodora Tsimpouki. Heidelberg: Winter, 2008. 237-57.

Hardt, Michael, and Kathi Weeks. "Introduction." *The Jameson Reader*. Ed. Hardt and Weeks. Malden: Blackwell, 2000. 1-29.

Harvey, David. *Justice, Nature and the Geography of Difference*. Oxford: Blackwell, 1996.

———. "The New Urbanism and the Communitarian Trap." *Harvard Design Magazine* 1 (1997): 1-3.

Hertzberg, Ludvig. "Introduction." *Jim Jarmusch: Interviews*. Ed. Hertzberg. Jackson: UP of Mississippi, 2001. vii-x.

Höpker, Karin. *No Maps for These Territories: Cities, Spaces, and Archaeologies of the Future in William Gibson*. Amsterdam and New York: Rodopi, 2011.

Hommels, Annique. *Unbuilding Cities: Obduracy in Urban Sociotechnical Change*. Boston: MIT P, 2008.

Jameson, Fredric. *Postmodernism, or, The Cultural Logic of Late Capitalism*. 1991. Durham: Duke UP, 2003.

Kauffmann, Stanley. "On Films: Around the Globe." *The New Republic* 18 May 1992: 32.

Keogh, Peter. "Home and Away." *Jim Jarmusch: Interviews*. Ed. Ludvig Hertzberg. Jackson: UP of Mississippi, 2001. 104-10 [first published in *Sight and Sound* 2.4 (1992): 8-9].

Kilb, Andreas. "Night on Earth." *Jim Jarmusch*. Ed. Rolf Aurich and Stefan Reinecke. Berlin: Bertz, 2001. 213-26.

Lefebvre, Henri. *The Production of Space*. Trans. Donald Nicholson-Smith. 1974. Malden: Blackwell, 1991.

Maurer, Roman. *Jim Jarmusch: Filme zum anderen Amerika*. Mainz: Bender, 2006.

Pall, Ellen. "'Night on Earth': Was Filming Inside a Cab a Deadly Trap?" *New York Times* 7 June 1992: H13 & 16.

Pratt, Mary Louise. "Arts of the Contact Zone." *Profession* 91 (1991): 33-40.

Rideout, Walter B. *Sherwood Anderson: A Writer in America.* Vol 1. Madison: U of Wisconsin P, 2006.

Schindler, Oliver. *Jim Jarmusch: Independent-auteur der achtziger Jahre.* Hamburg and Alfeld: Coppi, 2000.

Schneider, Ute. *Die Macht der Karten: Eine Geschichte der Kartographie vom Mittelalter bis heute.* Darmstadt: Wissenschaftliche Buchgesellschaft, 2004.

Serres, Michel. "Vorwort." *Thesaurus der exakten Wissenschaften.* Ed. Serres and Nayla Farouki. Trans. Michael and Ulrike Bischoff. Frankfurt/M.: Zweitausendeins, 2001. ix-xxxix.

————, and Nayla Farouki, eds. *Thesaurus der exakten Wissenschaften.* Trans. Michael and Ulrike Bischoff. Frankfurt/M.: Zweitausendeins, 2001.

Smith, Dave. *Disney A to Z: The Official Encyclopedia.* New York: Disney, [3]2006.

Spivak, Gayatri Chakravorty. "Chapter 3: Planetarity." Spivak. *Death of a Discipline.* New York: Columbia UP, 2003. 71-102.

Stockhammer, Robert. *Kartierung der Erde: Macht und Lust in Karten und Literatur.* München: Fink, 2007.

Travers, Peter. "When Worlds Collide in a Taxicab." *Rolling Stone* 630 (1992): 111-12.

Filmography

Night on Earth. Dir. Jim Jarmusch. JVC et al., 1991.

Discography

Waits, Tom, and Kathleen Brennan. *Night on Earth: Original Soundtrack Recording.* Polygram Records, 1992.

City of Germs: Biological Identities and Ethnic Cultures in the Metropolis

RÜDIGER KUNOW

> Infection in the sentence breeds
> —Emily Dickinson[1]
>
> Berlin ist größtenteils unsichtbar
> —Alfred Döblin

> New York City [during the Bicentennial] had hosted the greatest party ever known. The guests had come from all over the world ... . This was the part the epidemiologists would later note when they stayed up late at night and the conversation drifted toward where it had started and when. They would remember that glorious night in New York Harbor, all those sailors, and recall: From all over the world they came to New York. (qtd. in Wald 239)

This quote is taken from Randy Shilts's bestselling report on the HIV/AIDS crisis in the United States. It is useful as an introduction because it strikes a note to which I will return repeatedly in my paper: the city as a city of germs, the city as a diseased milieu in which people, in addition to their social and cultural identities, acquire also a biological identity. And this identity is particularly important when we figure outsiders, strangers, ethnic minorities into the picture. Their presence in the city is undesired to begin with, but it can cause even more apprehension once their biological identity comes into the picture. Strangers, ethnic or social Others can, as the Shilts quote indicates, attain a presumed microbiological agency, they can be seen as *carriers*, more or less unwitting movers of dangerous biological material. This issue of biological identity is all the more important since diseases have in many cultures been constructed as 'imports.' For instance, the names given to syphilis—the French disease, the Italian disease, etc.—offer ample evidence that illnesses, and especially contagious diseases, carry with them an index of foreignness. As a matter of fact, for long periods of Western history, disease was the only way in which urban populations experienced such foreignness.

In this context it is certainly no accident that contagious diseases, such as the plague, cholera, yellow fever, are, in medical parlance designated as communicable diseases, diseases transmitted through contact between people. There is a *double*

---

[1]   Poem # 1261: "A Word dropped careless on a Page / May stimulate an eye / When folded in perpetual seam / The Wrinkled Maker Lie / Infection in the sentence breeds / We may inhale Despair / At distances of Centuries / From the malaria."

entendre in the term 'communication,' an obvious semiotic reference which we are all familiar with and which we use, and a less well-known biomedical sense which I will highlight in my argument. Incidentally, the term 'culture' likewise has an equally often neglected biological dimension at the semantic root of the word.

There exists ample historical evidence to prove that the city, particularly the big city, the metropolis, is an almost ideal *contact zone*, not only for people but also for germs, it is a veritable melting pot, but as Priscilla Wald has suggested, a "melting pot … of microbes" (Wald 51). In this zone of intense biological traffic the spread of pathogenic materials can proceed much more effectively than in remote areas of casual, rare contact such as the countryside. Mary Louise Pratt's concept of the 'contact zone,' which has figured prominently in the Cultural Studies debates, could be usefully re-read in terms of biological contacts in the urban spaces. Thus, when she speaks about "the spatial and temporal co-presence of subjects previously separated by geographic and historical disjuncture and whose trajectories now intersect ... often within radically asymmetrical relations of power" (6-7), this describes quite accurately the situation in city spaces where one encounters, sometimes with alarming frequency, unfamiliar people who bring with them materials visible and invisible and which may or may not transform both residents and newcomers.

This samples in a roundabout way the compass of my present inquiry for which the somewhat ostentatious title of my paper serves as shorthand. This title contains an echo. In 1971 Toni Tanner published a seminal study called *City of Words* in which he presents a nuanced argument about the inherently unstable relationship between the city of words in which writers live and the social world, "between the provinces of words and things, and the problematical position of man [sic], who participates in both" (21).

My own argument today is not altogether different from his. I am likewise interested in the relation between what Tanner calls "lexical playfields" (33) and the urban fields, but these urban fields are in the present context anything but playful. Communities afflicted by a communicable disease are communities under hermeneutic stress, under a pressing need to make sense of what is happening to them. Ethnic minorities are involved in this sense-making to a degree that far exceeds their 'objective' presence in numbers. I will return to this later in my paper. Communicable diseases have in past and present often been the impetus for developing new forms of communication. In various cultures and historical contexts the presence of an epidemic illness in a city has acted as a catalyst for new modes of representation, from Thucydides and Sophocles, via Boccaccio and Defoe to the AIDS narratives of our time.

Communicable diseases possess great representational significance—representation here understood in both its semiotic and political sense. I regard communicable diseases, in classical Cultural Studies manner, as biomedical 'facts' that are socially and culturally constructed and, given the danger vested in these diseases, this construction process proceeds under great emotional and cognitive strain. Therefore, what is at stake in these 'disease constructs' is not their truthfulness, their representation of the medical 'facts' as seen at a given moment in history. What matters just as much is a representation of another kind, the representation they produce of a community—an urban community—in crisis. "[C]ommunicability configure[s] community" (Wald 12). What matters is the vocabulary used in this process of fashioning an imaginary community, the stories told about the how, why, wherefore, and especially the where-from of the communicable disease. I read communicable diseases as offering both, cognitive strain and cognitive gain: Epidemics do not only challenge our capacity of understanding, they also produce understanding, for example by making visible the otherwise invisible interactions between people in the urban manifold.[2] The HIV/AIDS epidemic in the 1980s, for example, made 'visible' unacknowledged or unobserved forms of sexual contact, and it also made visible the ways in which the United States defined the compass of "we the people."

Furthermore, epidemics and the socio-cultural responses to them follow a certain 'dramaturgy' with beginnings, twists and turns, and, hopefully, a happy ending. A prominent part of this dramaturgy is the military response model. Diseases are routinely fought, germs are perceived as invaders, even silent invaders against whom "legions" of medical experts fight in hopes of finding "a magic bullet," etc. (Weidling, qtd. in Slack 14, 15). Furthermore, there is the outbreak scenario, the real or imagined 'beginning' of a disease, a beginning that is often associated with certain persons, the mythic Patient Zero, in the case of the HIV/AIDS epidemic, the Canadian flight atten-dant who allegedly brought the disease 'out of Africa' to the unwitting gay community in the United States. There is also the medical detective story, featuring the lone ranger hero in his laboratory pitted against a hysterical public and a cynical bureaucracy.

Also, I hope to show how communicable diseases are central for the ways a city as "the site of juxtaposed ethnicities" (LiPuma/Koeble 160) forges individual and collective identities.[3] The ethnic city "cannot be known by its internal coherence and thus its closure and territorialization. Its residents do not therefore become part of the city by becoming part of a community" (Welsch 198), but they can become part of a biological community, not in terms of essentialized racial or ethnic identity, but as sharing the same ecosystem.

Thus, in my argument, I will attempt to develop a triangulation between ethnicity, epidemic illness, and the city. And I hope to show that not only will certain structural characteristics of cities explain the emergence of epidemic illnesses, but, inversely, also certain features of epidemics can serve to explain ways of life in the city. The triangu-lation I propose between ethnicity, illness, and urbanism is not only theoretically challenging, it is also historically plausible. After all, what Victoria Harden has called

---

[2] "HIV makes sex visible; it shows that people's desires are not bound either by the social sanction of marriage or the social classifications of race, gender, and sexuality, and it dem-onstrates the indifference of those desires, like the virus through which they are manifest, to national boundaries as well" (Wald 240).

[3] "Microbes do not just represent social bonds; they create and enforce them" (Wald 120); "The gradual acceptance of the dangers of microbes and healthy carriers as facts of life altered their representational significance" (124).

the "heroic decade of bacteriological discovery" (9)—the age of Pasteur and Koch[4]—
was the heroic period also of colonization and also the not-so-heroic high time of mass
immigration and accelerated urbanization.

My paper is organized in three parts: in the first section, "Cities of Germs," I will
deal with a historic example which shows the interrelation in the urban crucible of
epidemics and ethnicities; in the second section under the title "Urban Disease Imaginaries" I will develop the proposition that communicable diseases generate a genuinely urban imaginary, an imaginary in which the city as a public sphere and as a way of
life is configured or re-configured around the notion of the ethnic communicability, of
the ethnic other as the embodiment of a biological threat. In the concluding section
under the title "Medical Urbanism: Epidemics, Bare Life, and the Public Sphere," I
will try to explore the relationship between communicable diseases and urban communities, also with an eye toward the theoretical challenges this brings to our understanding of the city and of urban life.

1.   Cities of Germs

In this chapter I propose to view cities not so much as urban landscapes but as ecosystems. Such an ecosystem is characterized by the fact that great numbers of people
must share the same relatively circumscribed environment and are thus vulnerable to
undesired biomedical contact. It is no surprise, therefore, that visions of the city as a
cauldron of contagion can be found in cultural archives all over the world. Such
visions of the urban as breeding grounds for all kinds of diseases were more often than
not inflected by the association of such diseases with socially undesired elements of
the population. Ethnic minorities in particular were continually and iteratively identified with contagious diseases. They also figured prominently in origin stories of such
diseases.

On December 12, 1899, five deaths in the Chinatown section of Honolulu, on the
island of Oahu, Hawaii, were attributed to the bubonic plague. At that time, more than
half of Honolulu's population (of 30,000) was made up of Asians living in a crowded
tenement district. As these tenements showed unsanitary living conditions to the
inspectors of the all-white city Board of Health, a hysterical public opinion began to
blame the coming of the Black Death to the paradisiacal Pacific island on the Chinese
immigrant population, and not on the conditions under which they were made to live.
Visions of Oahu as hotbed of infection were spreading faster than the disease itself. The
government called in the National Guard. They immediately disinfected all Chinese,
herded them into railroad cars as temporary shelters and after that burned down all

---

[4]   Louis Pasteur (1822-1895) discovered the role of bacteria in fermentation processes, found
      vaccine for anthrax, rabies, and swine erysipelas; Robert Koch (1843-1910) discovered the
      bacteriological processes causing cholera and tuberculosis; Nobel Prize for Medicine in
      1905.

their homes. It is perhaps a small irony that the fire went out of control and burned down other city sections, including the house of the fire department (cf. Wisniewski 9).

This example is instructive in a number of ways. It shows how the emergence of an epidemic in a city causes not only a medical emergency but also a cognitive one. People needed to make sense of what was going on around them, and this very fast, before the disease could infect greater parts of the city's population. In such an emergency, questions of disease control and questions of community formation and belonging became inextricably interwoven. The plague, while in itself invisible, thus made visible the tenuous and complicated relations of immigrant quarters with the rest of the city. What was mostly overlooked in 1899 and continues to be overlooked to this very day is the fact that the outbreak of the plague in Honolulu would not have occurred had it not been for the network of trade and service in which Hawaii, just recently annexed by the United States, was implicated. The Chinese had been 'imported' to the island to work on the sugar plantations, plantations that were owned by Americans. So this particular incident can also be read as bringing to light the otherwise invisible fabric of personal mobility and an emerging global connectivity. *What made people wealthy could also make them ill.*

The case of Honolulu may not be particularly well-known, but it is by no means an exception, especially not at that historical juncture when the new and prestigious field of bacteriology entered the international scene. Bacteriology not only made possible a new disease construct, one which made the containment of certain diseases more feasible, but it invested the newly found biomedical processes with a decidedly Euramerican point of view. Medical historian Philipp Sarasin has shown how bacteriology very quickly became a "master metaphor" in Western thought (15), however, a master metaphor with decidedly sinister implications at home and abroad: Those infectious pathogens which invade our bodies from outside and make it sick became, by a catachrestic "sleight of hand, synonymous with the strangers that were presumably their carriers" (16). The identification of diseases with certain population segments invests the usual insider-outsider dichotomy with added urgencies. Outsiders are not just others but others that bring something with them, something that is unseen, unknown and undesirable. This construction of the infectious Other worked itself out also in the colonial empires of the West. Here the colonized people—"half devil, and half child," in Rudyard Kipling's (in)famous words—were seen as enacting their childish selves by failing to measure up to the standards of sanitation and hygiene achieved by the 'white man,' whereas their devilish side manifested itself when they transmitted to the colonizers all sorts of diseases which then added to the "White Man's burden." The German word "Fremdkörper" and the terrible uses to which it has been put represents yet another example of this same sinister identification of the Other with communicable diseases. I will return to this issue later.

As time went on, this notion of the 'infectious Other' became an integral part of a thought complex which I would like to call 'phobic urbanism' or perhaps better, and less dramatically, 'medical urbanism.' In the wake of new 'scientific' thought, and vested with the authority of such modern science, medical urbanism became centrally important for a city's "project of self-totalization" (LiPuma 175), for the ways a city reproduced itself socially, culturally, and of course also politically. Not only did this urbanism bring about a new mapping of urban spaces around the dualism of purity and danger, it also contained an element of performativity configured around the Other as itinerant carrier of invisible and infectious biological material. He/she does not just embody the dark sides of city life, but carries with him/her and into the city a perceived lack of discipline and control and an undesired dose of contact with the unknown. No wonder, then, that at the end of the 19th century the new mobility within urban spaces of single women quickly came to be conceived as a health threat: They might infect the family father and thus bring blight into the bourgeois nuclear family.

As biomedical considerations of health or rather health hazards came to play a critical role in the discourses of urbanism, they fashion something I want to call 'a vocabulary of non-belonging,' a glossary in which, as my Dickinson epigraph suggests, infection breeds and produces disease constructs which impact people far beyond the original infliction, or, in Dickinson's words: "Infection in the sentence breeds / We may inhale Despair / At distances of Centuries / From the Malaria." It is to this kind of interpretive work performed by discursive constructions of disease that I will now turn in my next section.

2.   Urban Disease Imaginaries

My prime example in this section is the 1793 epidemic of yellow fever in Philadelphia, PA, then the capital of the newly independent United States. Yellow fever had been at that time a globe-trotting disease (cf. Wald 30) which had broken out intermittently in harbor cities all over the world. It had also been ravaging the coastal towns of America almost from the beginning of European settlement on. Concerning the etiology of this disease, two conflicting theories were in competition with one another: one was the miasma theory, according to which the fever was caused by exhalation of vaporous effluvia from stagnant water in the city. This 'localist' theory of infection constituted the medical orthodoxy at that time. It was challenged by a 'traveling theory' in a sense not quite adumbrated by Edward Said, a theory based on the recognition of the transnational mobility of communicable diseases. Its adherents argued that the fever had been imported to Philadelphia by French refugees and their slaves who had recently escaped from the revolutionary uprising on Haiti headed by Toussaint l'Ouverture. This "outbreak narrative" (Wald 26 et passim) brought with it its own distinct containment strategy, the demand that the United States break off all relations with Haiti and other places, in order to keep the revolutionary "contagions"—this was the word they used—from Europe and the American hemisphere from infecting the young republic. This latter theory found support mainly among those Philadelphians whose Republican political persuasions made them wish the U.S. should mind its own business, whereas the supporters of the opposite camp, many of them Hamiltonians, had their own trade interests in mind when they suggested that such isolationism would stymie the country's promising economic growth. This early instance of the classic U.S.-American dichotomy between Internationalism and Isolationism shows how intimately the representation given to microbiotic processes is linked to questions of what the meaning of 'America' is or should be (cf. Berlant).

The Philadelphia epidemic is important for the present inquiry because it produced and continues to produce a wide variety of disease constructs, which in their different ways use the disease to reflect on this very same question—what is the meaning of 'America?' My first example, almost contemporaneous with the event itself, is Charles Brockden Brown's *Arthur Mervyn, or Memoirs of the Year 1793* (1799). Brockden Brown's (1771-1810) fiction, self-advertised as "a faithful sketch of the condition of this metropolis during that calamitous period" (1), is one of the first genuinely 'U.S.-American' novels. It is resourced by the discursive archives of the Gothic romance, particularly Godwin and Richardson, a Gothicism which allows Brown to develop what might be called 'a disease aesthetic' organized around the cognitive strain which the epidemic inflicts and which is particularly geared to convey the invisible and inexplicable modes of infection:

> As I approached the door of which I was in search, a vapour, infectious and deadly, assailed my senses. ... I felt as if I had inhaled a poisonous and subtle fluid, whose power instantly bereft my stomach of all vigor. Some fatal influence appeared to seize upon my vitals; and the work of corrosion and decomposition to be busily begun. (137)

It would be interesting to trace in more detail the contours of this Gothicism inflected by biomedicine and read it against some of Poe's texts of urban life, but this would extend beyond the capacities of this paper, thus I will turn to the medical urbanism in *Arthur Mervyn* and the interpretive work it performs.

I want to begin by noting that Brocken Brown, like Defoe before him in his *Journal of the Plague Year* (1722), anchors his representation of the city and the disease afflicting it through the figure of a participant observer, or, as Brown calls him in his Preface, a "moral observer" (1), Dr. Stevens. Stevens not only mediates on the plot level between the eponymous figure of Arthur Merwyn and the city, he also metadiegetically registers the representational challenge which the *sujet* of a medicalized urbanism presented. Only by mustering all the powers of his mind can he dwell on what he calls "the theatre of disasters" (132) in a way that is helpful to his patients and enlightening to the reader: "During this season of pestilence, my opportunities of observation had been numerous and I had not suffered them to pass unimproved" (208).

Speaking of observations, much of the representation of city life in this novel is organized less around the medical aspects of the disease or its victims than around the civic dimension of disease. This civic dimension manifests itself as a phobic dynamism which wraps the city in fear and causes the fictional characters, as the narrative voice observes, to be "haunted by a melancholy bordering upon madness ... [and] sleepless panics" (124). On the other hand, Arthur Merwyn, a young man of 18, enters the narrative as an outsider whose home is in the countryside. He becomes the Patient

Zero of the narrative whose experiences capture all the issues Brockden Brown wants
to bring up in his novel. Originally, Arthur does not even know that a yellow fever
epidemic has broken out in Philadelphia; he decides to go to the city because he wants
to clear himself of allegations of embezzlement and arrives at the very moment when
many others, among them the city elite, are leaving. He is soon stricken with yellow
fever but befriended and finally cured by Dr. Stevens. My reading of this not-so-
exciting novel is less concerned with the various twists and turns of the plot through
which the author attempts to convey the dramatic nature of the disease. I am interested
instead in the ways the novel portrays Philadelphia as a city in which a communicable
disease communicates civic disorder. In the process, the capital city is scripted less as
a stable urban whole than as a highly confusing maze composed of invisible and in-
tangible contacts between people whose 'real' identity is uncertain. What totality then
emerges is made up of bonds, the involuntary biological bonds established by the
infectious disease and the voluntary bonds of "compassion" and "charity"—values
explicitly mentioned by Brown in his Preface.

Another way of saying the same thing would be to note that the people who inhabit
this urban space and circulate within it do not become parts of the urban totality simply
by virtue of their being in the metropolis. Rather, the city of Philadelphia is, at least in
part, an invisible city in the sense suggested by my Döblin epigraph, a disease(d)
environment in the grip of a communicable illness whose *modus operandi* remains
invisible and inscrutable. From almost the very beginning of the text, yellow fever,
here called "pestilence," is a powerful presence redefining citizenship in biological
terms, and in the process it simultaneously redefines who in the city of brotherly love
is in fact making up the professed brotherhood. As Boccaccio before him had done in
the *Decamerone* (1349-51), Brown repeatedly dwells on the socially divisive nature of
the pestilence; many people leave the city; people in need are refused access to safe
places, etc. (132). The anti-urban bent which Toni Morrison and others have noticed in
early American writing here uses the communicable disease to register the failure of
fashioning a community of shared responsibility. In the words of the text,

> [t]he city … was involved in confusion and panick, for a pestilential disease had begun
> its destructive progress. Magistrates and citizens were flying to the country. The
> numbers of the sick multiplied beyond all example; even in the pest-affected cities of
> the Levant. … The usual occupations and amusements of life were at an end. Terror had
> exterminated all the sentiments of nature. Wives were deserted by husbands, and
> children by parents. … The consternation of others had destroyed their understanding.
> (122)

In this way, Brown's novel constantly negotiates the line between public and private.
The personal is certainly becoming political here, because the epidemic, by calling the
physician to his civic duties, configures an ideal community, composed not of self-
seeking individualism but of communal responsibility. What made people sick can
also make them develop "a more perfect union." Thus Dr. Stevens explains: "I was
sustained, not by my concern for safety, and a belief in exemption from this malady …
but by a belief that this was as eligible an avenue to death as any other; and that life is

a trivial sacrifice in the cause of duty" (157). It is this personal commitment which develops and persists among the dissolution of all civic commitments that ultimately contains the disease. The repeated references in the novel to the unselfish care provided by individuals like Dr. Stevens are expressions of Brown's belief that "the response of individual sensibility to the trials of existence, was at the heart of fiction" (qtd. in *Arthur Mervyn* 11).

In this way, Brown's novel dwells on both, the cognitive strain caused by the epidemic *and* the cognitive gain: the latter afforded by the "lessons of justice and humanity" provided by this experience, lessons which Brown repeatedly highlights in his Preface to the novel. In this way, the novel is more than a disease narrative; it is also a narrative of healing, in which the emergence of an ethos of individual responsibility practiced by some people can serve as a cure for both the corporeal and the moral malaise caused by the fever epidemic afflicting the whole city. Brown was a firm believer in the use of U.S.-American materials for a new national literature, and within this frame his first novel can be read as a biopolitical tale of sorts, a tale in which the capital city of Philadelphia becomes an example and exemplar for what Brown hoped 'America' as a whole would become.

Philadelphia as example and exemplar—this is an issue which also emerges in the fictions of African-American writer John Edgar Wideman. Wideman uses the Philadelphia yellow fever epidemic as historical donné in two of his fictions. In the 1989 short story "Fever" he is concerned with the ways in which 'race' signified as 18th century Philadelphians sought to make sense of the yellow fever epidemic.

His novel *Cattle Killing* (1996) is intended as a revision of the earlier text in which, as Wideman stated, he "didn't get it right" (Lynch 2). *Cattle Killing* returns to Philadelphia, this time through the figure of an African-American itinerant preacher in search of a mysterious woman in a city that is violently split between black and white, healthy and infected people. In both texts, the Philadelphia epidemic figures as an early instance of the troubled relationship between the races in America. While in Brockden Brown's novel an occasional "faithful black" (153) ministering to the needs of the ill was a marginal figure at best, Wideman's two fictions are centrally organized around the presence of African Americans at the heart of the epidemic, as victims, as nurses, and as alleged carriers of the disease.

"Fever" takes us right to the heart of the public debate in 1793 about the causes and consequences of the epidemic. This debate played out in the newspapers of the time and also in two publications which function as intertexts for Wideman's own narrative. One of them is Matthew Carey's *A Short Account of the Malignant Fever Lately Prevalent in Philadelphia* which appeared the same year. In this text Carey, a Philadelphia printer and labor leader, distributes praise and blame along racial lines. While he pays tribute to white Philadelphians, he criticizes the city's African-American population for taking advantage of the disease. As whites were sometimes "abandoned to the care of negro[es]," these did not really minister to the needs of the afflicted; "the vilest of the blacks," Carey notes, "were even detected in plundering the houses of the sick" (qtd. in Lynch 782). Carey's racial polemic represents African Americans only in the idiom of non-belonging, of de-realizing their presence during the disease.

Carey's account was almost immediately challenged by a counter-narrative authored by two former slaves, Richard Allen and Absalom Jones. Their *Narrative of the Proceedings of the Black People, During the Late Awful Calamity in Philadelphia 1793: And a Refutation of Some Censures, Thrown Upon Them in Some Late Publications* (1794) offers a record of the civil services performed by African Americans during the epidemic, services which the authors insist were rendered at great personal risk and which did not receive much acknowledgment, even less gratitude from the white majority among the city's population. As they write African Americans back into the historical narrative of the yellow fever epidemic, their text is in its turn written into a fictional narrative. Actually, Wideman draws both texts into his own, by making Allen one of the central characters of "Fever," and by offering a mock dedication to Carey, "who fled Philadelphia in its hour of need and upon his return published a libelous account of the behavior of black nurses and undertakers, thereby injuring all people of my race" (127).

The 1793 epidemic, for Wideman, anticipates the racial antagonism that has continued to exist in America today. He explicitly links this antagonism to the coerced mobility of the slaves who were not only brought to America against their will but who were also accused by white Americans of bringing with them fever and other contagious diseases. As the fictional Allen says,

> "They say the rat's nest from Santo Domingo brought the fever, Frenchmen and their black slaves fleeing black insurrection. Those who have seen Barbados' distemper say our fever is its twin born in the tropical climate of the hellish Indies." (132)

Allegations of this kind were frequently made at that time, even by well-intentioned people. As Lisa Lynch has shown, the African slave as 'infectious Other' figured prominently also in Abolitionist texts which "used the fear of disease to promote anxiety about the slave trade" (Wald 781). Among the discursive maneuvers used in such texts was the motif of the slave "ships, which like the curse / Of vile Pandora's box, bring forth disease" (Wald 781). Thus, the fever is seen as traveling on the very same routes along which the slave trade flourished.

Epidemics are shockwaves of mobility, past and present. Communicable diseases have long been 'global players' *avant la lettre*. Not only have these diseases faithfully followed the routes of trade and information, they have demonstrated with a forcefulness uniquely their own the artificiality, the porousness, and tenuousness of political, social, and cultural borders even while they routinely offered occasions for reasserting these borderlines. This brings me back to Wideman's story.

As with Brockden Brown's novel, one can detect at certain moments of the narrative the contours of a disease aesthetic. One example is a scene in which the narrative voice delivers a tale of the actual process of the transmission of pathogens, a process which was inaccessible to him as to his contemporaries and which is therefore completely imaginary. The scene is on board a slave ship during the Middle Passage:

"In the darkness he can't see her, barely feels her touch on his fevered skin. Sweat thick as oil, but she doesn't mind, straddles him, settles down to do her work. She enters him and draws his blood up to her belly" (130). Medical infection is here taking place in the moment of contact between a male slave and a mosquito, scripted as female. This is a gendered, perhaps even sexist image for what is going on during the infection with a communicable disease.

Wideman further shows how the accident of bodily pigmentation, the contingencies contained in what is called 'race,' determine the civic status of people: "First they blamed us ... We were proclaimed carriers of the fever and treated as pariahs, but when it became expedient to command our services to nurse the sick and bury the dead, the previous allegations were no longer mentioned" (140). But even these services do not lead to the acceptance of the African Americans as full citizens: "wave after wave of white immigrants have come to the city and made their fortune, yet the road to such success has been barred for blacks" (Lynch 784). In this way, yellow fever as depicted by Wideman is less a medical than a civic emergency, an emergency, moreover, for which the text provides no healing. Instead, the civic subject position assigned to African Americans can be read as an instance of what Foucault called "bio-politics," a "technique ... of power present at every level of the social body ... [which] also acted as factors of segregation and social hierarchization ... guaranteeing relations of domination and effects of hegemony" (141).

In his narrative Wideman repeatedly shows how the explanations given for the disease outbreak are located within competing orders of knowledge. In the passage from which I quoted above, the narrator pits the 'white explanation' and its racist identification of contagion with blacks against alternative Africanist knowledge:

> They say the rat's nest from Santo Domingo brought the fever. ... I know better. I hear the drum, the forest's heartbeat, the pulse of the sea ... to explain the fever we need no boatloads of refugees ragged and wracked with filling fevers ... We have bred the affliction within our breasts. ... Fever descends when the waters that connect us are clogged with filth. ... fever is a drought consuming us from within ... Fever grows in the secret places in our hearts, when one of us decided to sell one of us to another. (132)

White medicine, allegedly the most advanced form of dealing with contagious diseases, falls drastically short when it comes to grasping that other equally contagious disease, slavery. This is the central point Wideman is making throughout the story "Fever," i.e., that the form of biomedical citizenship which evolved during the epidemic anticipates the racist notion of second-class citizenship that would run through U.S. history. His narrative then is not, like *Arthur Mervyn*, a story of individual and communal healing—rather, it is a narrative of an interactive communal disease, one that reveals "the corporeal contingencies of [the] civic status" (Anderson 5) of African Americans. In this way Wideman's "Fever" continues to chart the contours of black urbanism, a project he began in *Philadelphia Fire* (1991).

I now turn to my second example, another historical context. In the period from 1896 to 1914, the Indian subcontinent was visited by a series of communicable diseases, some of which assumed pandemic proportions and killed more than 8 million people. This pandemic had international and intercultural ramifications. Not only did such illnesses represent in the mind of many British people, in India and back home, the backwardness of their colony; inversely, for many Indians the first hesitant, then massive intervention by the colonizers stood for their callous disregard for India and her traditions. And on an international scale, the epidemics entered into the rivalries between the European powers during the period of Imperialism. After all, as Rajnarayan Chandavarkar and others have demonstrated, Great Britain significantly lagged behind France and Germany in that prestigious new science, bacteriology (cf. Arnold 143ff.; Chandravarkar). Like the Philadelphia yellow fever epidemic, this pandemic has been heavily textualized, for example by Indian writer Amitav Ghosh in his novel *The Calcutta Chromosome* (1995) and also in theoretical writings, especially those inspired by the Subaltern School and its concern with Colonialism.

In 1898 the pandemic hit especially hard the city of Kolkata, then Calcutta, the metropolitan center of the Bengal province. In the history of this pandemic, the city spaces developed into a veritable urban contact zone in which the dichotomies usually associated with local caste practices were crosshatched with the imperial gaze (cf. Arnold 131) to establish biomedical notions of the 'infectious Other.' Thus, during the course of the pandemic, the city and its population came to be configured around a complex system of binary opposites: Indian vernacular healing[5] vs. Western 'scientific' medicine, native 'apathy' vs. colonial paternalism, family-oriented crisis management vs. governmental intervention, etc.

The Kolkata epidemic, like those hitting Philadelphia or Honolulu, brought into broad daylight the otherwise invisible fabric of ideological and material connectivities without which the outbreak would not have occurred and which in turn determined the response by those in power to the disease. As the death rates rose precipitously, the British became alarmed by the prospect that the pandemic might substantially harm the commercial future of the 'jewel' of their empire and that it might harm their own people. Here again, the mechanism of 'what makes you wealthy can also make you sick' played itself out with particular forcefulness, as also the supposed superiority of the colonizer was at stake. Thus, some British administrators regarded the plague as a golden opportunity to clean up (qtd. in Arnold 217)—in more ways than one—their backward and superstitious colony. Said one official: "I consider that plague operations … present some of the best opportunities for riveting our rule in India" and "also for showing the superiority of our Western science and thoroughness" (qtd. in Arnold 214).

So the British brought an impressive array of the best Western medical experts to Kolkata. Together with the colonial government, "the most drastic [measures] that had ever been taken to stamp out an epidemic" (qtd. in Arnold 207) were set in motion. And the British went about their work with great zeal, conducting veritable 'search and destroy missions' into the urban 'jungle' of Kolkata. They isolated suspicious homes,

---

[5]   Cf. Swami Vivekananda's "Plague Manifesto" (written in Bengali); <http://www.rama-krishnavivekananda/volume~9/writings~prose~and~poems>.

subjected suspect individuals to public search, dug up the ground and destroyed whole sections of 'native' neighborhoods. These measures redrew the lines between the public and the private, dragged what was most intimate into the limelight of public attention, an attention, moreover, that was the colonizer's gaze. Unfortunately for both colonizers and colonized, all these measures were pretty much in vain. There was at that time no remedy for the bubonic plague and the British 'scientific' measures were as effective or ineffective as those proposed by native healers or outright quacks.

So, in looking back at the pandemic from a historical perspective, what is striking is the degree to which the British reaction to the plague was grounded less in medical fact than in culturalist assumptions about the Indians, whose "weak and puny constitutions" (as one colonial official described them) made them particularly susceptible to the ravages of the plague. In a way, it was "their disease," which they, i.e., the Indians, had brought upon themselves by—in the words of another official—by their "racial characteristics and innate prejudices" (qtd. in Arnold 220). In the system of colonial governance, the Indian colonial subjects were doubly coded: as infectious Others they required strict control, while as victims of the disease they fell under the purview of the enlightened colonialist white man's burden to extend the gift of Western healing to them while their illness ratified his superiority.

This multiple coding of the diseased Other is a central point also in Amitav Ghosh's novel *The Calcutta Chromosome*. The novel's epigraph establishes a reference to Sir Ronald Ross who won the 1902 Nobel Prize for Medicine for his discovery of the manner in which malaria is transmitted by mosquitoes. Ross was a member of the Indian Medical Service, the service which had so singularly failed in containing the cholera epidemic in Calcutta. I have spoken above of the "heroic decade of bacteriological discovery" (Harden 9)—*The Calcutta Chromosome* clearly debunks the heroism of scientific discovery by making Ross the more or less unwitting tool of a group of underground native scientists who were themselves trying to discover another form of transmission, i.e., the transmission of genetic information, the so-called "Calcutta Chromosome" (109). The novel develops the theme of transmission of biomaterial on a number of levels. Chief among them is a narrative, produced by a highly unreliable narrator, about the city of Calcutta as the site of major discoveries in biomedicine, one secret, the other well-known: Ross's findings about the transmission of malaria.

Ross's 'discovery' took place in a Kolkata laboratory and the text takes us—in true global fiction manner—from New York to present-day Kolkata and from there to the colonial city at the high time of Colonialism—and of bacteriological discovery. In a multi-layered narrative that one reviewer described as "a Pynchonesque web of conspiracy and cosmic connection" (Milani n.p.), the author mixes medical mystery tale with colonial science fiction. Ghosh repeatedly insists on the link between colonialism and communicable disease. "Remember," says a fictional character who is a medical sleuth trying to disentangle the various plots and counter-plots that surrounded Ross's alleged discovery, "remember," he says this was the century when old Mother Europe was settling all the Last Unknowns. ... And this was just about the time that the new sciences were beginning to make a splash in Europe. Malaria went right to the top of the research agenda ... everywhere except England. ... No sir: the Empire did everything it could to get in his [Ronald Ross's] way. (56-57)

In a related way, Paul Gilroy sees at work in the crisis response by colonial govern- ance not so much considerations of public health than of public order in the colonial metropolis: "colonial government contributed to the manifestation of bare life ... under the supervision of administrative and managerial systems that operated by the rules of raciology [with its] necessary reliance on divisions *within* humankind" (48-49; emphasis added). I will return to the theme of bare life in my conclusion.

Repeatedly, the text shows the callousness of British colonial governance toward malaria (cf. 93); this callousness extends to medical officers who use 'natives' as more or less unwitting medical guinea-pigs (cf. 72, 74, 90), but *The Calcutta Chromosome* does not exhaust itself in simple anti-colonialist polemics. Perhaps it would be more accurate to say that the narrative 'provincializes Europe.' Dipesh Chakrabarty, from whom I have borrowed this phrase, argues that Colonialism's most effective operation consisted in suggesting to the colonized a "'waiting room' version" (9) of historical development in which the colonized people were on the way to Modernity, under the guidance of the colonizers, but not yet on the same level of economic, political, and intellectual sophistication. Against this vision of the world-historical path to progress, the narrative pits its own counter-historical narrative and presents a counter-history of scientific progress by offering us "the other team" (104) composed of Indians who practice "counterscience" (106). They are not part of the comprador elite envisioned by Macauley in his vision of India, they are "fringe people" (106), or in critical parlance, subalterns, led by a cleaning woman who works for the English in the famous Ross laboratory. She may be a witch, a high priestess or a goddess, in any case, Westerners "can't ever know her, or her motives" (253), the subaltern agency manifesting itself in a project seeking to discover a new principle of information transmission which does not involve sexual reproduction: "when your body fails you, you leave it, you migrate— you or at least a matching symptomatology of your self. You begin all over again, another body, another beginning" (109). This vision clearly owes something to the Hindu belief in successive reincarnations, but it can also be read as a non-Western model of the life sciences, a colonial science fiction.

That this model is being developed in a British laboratory in Calcutta (141) unbeknownst to the British is more than a colonial or postcolonial irony. The city, "whose vocation is excess," is a fitting location, for scientific pursuit as well as for the fictional narrative. The greater part of the city, it seems, is invisible, composed of a veritable maze of imperceptible connections, "where all law, natural and human, is held in capricious suspension, that which is hidden has no need of words to give it life" (25). No wonder, then, that the medical sleuth who tries to find the real truth about Sir Robert Ross's discovery is lost in this place, and the novel withholds from us any conclusive knowledge about whether the whole plot he claims to have uncovered is 'real' or the figment of his imagination or a feverish mind, a mind infected by malaria.

In this way, Ghosh in this novel poses two forms of "medicalized nativism" (Alan Kraut's term)—"the fear of contamination from the foreign-born" (3)—against each other.

As I hope to have shown in this section, narrativizations of communicable diseases, while offering cultural constructs of biological 'facts,' do not exhaust their interpretive work in the field of biomedicine. Rather, these narrativizations are centrally about the *civic meaning of disease.*

Communicable diseases configure communities, but they do so under the inauspicious auspices of what Chris Shilling has called "body anxiety" (35); anxieties that manifest themselves in individual phobias and collective hysterias, and for both the urban spaces provide a vast echo chamber.

3.   Medical Urbanism: Epidemics, Bare Life, and the Public Sphere

In this paper I have tried to sketch the contours of a medicalized urbanism. Such a concept ties with some recent reversals in urban theory, especially those that suggest a changeover from a center-oriented to a relations-based understanding of the city. An example of this changeover is the work of Ludger Pries, who in the Simmel tradition of urban sociology views the city in terms of a 'leaky container' which allows people and material into the circumscribed urban spaces from where, inversely, other people and material leak out. How this 'leaky container' concept can be further developed in ways that bring in biological identity and infection can be shown by turning to Edward LiPuma and Thomas Koeble's 2002 essay "Cultures of Circulation and the Urban Imaginary." Using Miami, Florida as example the authors develop a notion of the cityscape as a porous space, through which people and objects, many of whom are originating elsewhere, are constantly "circulating at different speeds and with different degrees of rootedness or attachment" (157). Such a city cannot very easily know itself; it lacks the means for a core identity formation. Whatever sense of wholeness nonetheless accrues to such a city is then something made, not found, something LiPuma and Koeble call an 'urban imaginary.' Such an imaginary in their view "achieve[s] a certain perspectival totality through the creative (performative) production of an urban imaginary—an imaginary that is a necessary reification in the sense that … it is the necessary appearance of the circulatory object that it conceals" (157). Disease narratives can be read as instances of an urban imaginary, an imaginary, however, that is invested with a sense of personal and civic crisis.

The concept of medical urbanism can be situated within a long history of thought in which the city, in addition to its spatial identity, is invested with a biological identity, too, an identity which relied on the presumed analogy of the city to the human body. Richard Sennett has shown in more detail than I can present here how urban life and especially diversity found their representation through this analogy which, during the 17th and 18th centuries had performed a similar consolidating function for the emerging nation state. In the context of an evolving modernity, the body as concept metaphor for the city anchors its representation in the organic vision of a *totum simul*, the perfect fit between the increasingly diverse composite parts of the urban manifold: for example, "planners wanted the city in its very design to function like a healthy human body" (Sennett, qtd. in Urry 13).

Interestingly enough, the city-body analogy was pursued also with regard to the infectious body. The Chicago School of Urban Sociology, particularly Robert E. Park and Louis Wirth, found in the processes of biological transmission from body to body a way to express how social interactions in city spaces functioned. Park, for one, was convinced that "human society is organized on two levels, the biotic and the cultural" (Wald 127), and the former could be used to explain processes going on in the latter realm.

Thus, his answer to the question of "[h]ow does a mere collection of individuals succeed in acting in a corporate and consistent way?" (Wald 133) is organized around a principle that Park called "social contagion" or "the invisible contagion of the public" (Wald 133). Contagion became even more important as an explanatory concept, as Park and others were looking for a way to describe what they called "the assimilation cycle," the processes through which immigrants became Americans. In this context, the immigrant city became, for Park, a "moral region" (Wald 141), in which the immigrant went through a process of 'generative infection' (my term), or in Park's words, "a process of interpenetration and fusion in which persons and groups acquire the memories, sentiments, and attitudes of other [i.e., American] persons or groups" (Wald 139). Social contagion was for Park and his colleagues a way to imagine an Americanization that proceeded without coercion, an insinuation rather than a direct persuasion.

Epidemic diseases mark the moment when bare life enters the city. They are powerful reminders of the existence within urban spaces of what Judith Butler has called "the precariousness of life" (142). A body in the grips of the plague, malaria, cholera, or HIV/AIDS is not only a body whose very claim to life hangs in the balance, it is a body that makes normative claims concerning the principles and norms that guide urban life. Between the emergence of an epidemic and the communal response to it, a space opens up that is a space of representation, representation here understood in both its semiotic *and* its political meaning. This is the moment also when the *epistemological obligations* of a discipline such as Cultural Studies become indistinguishable from its *ethical obligations*, when cultural critique of the (mis)representations of certain marginalized groups of the urban population expands into a political critique of their (non)representation in the political domain.

Thus I want to return one more time to Butler and her argument that the precariousness of life, while a human universal, "functions differently, to target and manage certain populations, to derealize the humanity of subjects who might potentially belong to a community" (142).[6] Whenever one uses the term 'bare life' these days, a red flag pops up with the name Agamben written on it. His arguments on naked life and politics are circulating widely, perhaps beyond their deserts, and I do not want to rehearse them here.[7] I am less interested in states of exception than in states of rule, and in this context, bare life as represented in the guise of the 'infectious Other' is the name for a site where biopolitics and geopolitics intersect within urban spaces.

The entry of bare life into the public sphere is a deeply ambivalent process. Whenever public health becomes a matter of public concern, as it does in moments of communicable diseases, then the line separating the private from the public is being redrawn in a way that inserts what is most private into what Benhabib has called "discursive public space" (*Situating* 89), into the ongoing conversation within demo-cratic societies about the norms and values governing public life in the city. Considera-tions of 'life' and the 'body' are taken from what Hannah Arendt called "the shadowy interior of the household" (38) into the public domain. This is no small matter. After all, questions of the needs of the body, of reproduction, of care for the sick and elderly, have in many different cultures not only been relegated to the realm of the private, they have defined the very essence of privacy. This was one of the reasons why the population of Kolkata resented so much the intrusive medical operations launched by the British.

What is at stake in the public debate is nothing less than "the co-implication of private and public autonomy" (Habermas 420). The debate about HIV/AIDS has demonstrated how crucial the public conversation or non-conversation about a conta-gious disease can be for the afflicted and for the overall direction a society will take in questions of ethics and the social fabric. Seyla Benhabib has shown how crucial the public space is for the emergence of a deliberative democracy and for defining "the principles and practices of incorporating aliens and strangers, immigrants and new-comers, refugees and asylum seekers, into existing polities" (*Rights* 1).

Against this background, the discursive production of disease through narratives, films, or other media must be seen as part and parcel of the processes of discursive will formation in the public sphere. Inserting questions of bare life into the public domain is all the more important today, because in "the chill of globalization" (Gilroy 142), as many state-supported care-giving institutions have been dismantled, the public sphere of modern democracies is perhaps the only place left where the persistence of precarious life can be shored up.

---

[6] Accounts inspired by the ethos and methodology of Cultural Studies usually see ethnicity as importation of fixed, often counter-hegemonic identities into the demarcated city space—people with biological as well as cultural identities situated in the unstable porous urban spaces—"bodies of individual persons become metamorphosed into specimens of the ethnic [or national] category for which they are supposed to stand" (Malkki 88, qtd. in Appadurai 309).

[7] For a succinct critique of Agamben, cf. Bernstein.

Works Cited

Anderson, Warwick. *Colonial Pathologies: American Tropical Medicine, Race, and Hygiene in the Philippines*. Durham: Duke UP, 2006.

Appadurai, Arjun. "Dead Certainty: Ethnic Violence in the Era of Globalization." *Globalization and Identity: Dialectics of Flow and Closure*. Ed. Birgit Meyer and Peter Geschiere. Oxford: Blackwell, 1999. 305-24.

Arendt, Hannah. *The Human Condition*. 1958. Chicago: U of Chicago P, 1998.

Arnold, David. *The New Cambridge History of India. Vol. 5: Science, Technology and Medicine in Colonial India*. Cambridge: Cambridge UP, 2000.

Benhabib, Seyla. *The Rights of Others: Aliens, Residents, and Citizens*. Cambridge: Cambridge UP, 2004.

———. *Situating the Self: Gender, Community and Postmodernism in Contemporary Ethics*. Cambridge: Polity P, 1992.

Berlant, Lauren. *The Queen of America goes to Washington City*. Durham: Duke UP, 1997.

Bernstein, J.M. "Intact and Fragmented Bodies: Versions of Ethics 'after Auschwitz.'" *New German Critique* 33.1 (2006): 31-52.

Brown, Charles Brockden. *Arthur Merwyn or Memoirs of the Year 1793*. Ed. with an Introduction by Warner Berthoff. New York: Holt, Rinehart and Winston, 1962.

Butler, Judith. *Precarious Life: The Powers of Mourning and Violence*. 2004. London: Verso, 2006.

———. "How Can I Deny That These Hands and This Body Are Mine?" *Qui Parle* 11.1 (1997): 1-20.

Chandravarkar, Rajnarayan. "Plague Panic and Epidemic Politics in India, 1896-1914." *Epidemics and Ideas: Essays on the Historical Perception of Pestilence*. Ed. Terence Ranger and Paul Slack. Cambridge: Cambridge UP, 1992. 203-40.

Chakrabarty, Dipesh. *Provincializing Europe: Postcolonial Thought and Historical Difference*. With a new Preface by the Author. 2000. Princeton: Princeton UP, 2008.

Foucault, Michel. *The History of Sexuality. Vol. 1: An Introduction*. Trans. Robert Hurley. 1978. New York: Vintage, 1990.

Ghosh, Amitav. *The Calcutta Chromosome: A Novel of Fevers, Delirium and Discovery*. 1995. New York: Perennial, 1997.

Gilroy, Paul. *Postcolonial Melancholia*. New York: Columbia UP, 2005.

Habermas, Jürgen. *Between Facts and Norms: Contributions to a Discourse Theory of Law and Democracy*. Cambridge, MA: MIT P, 1998.

Harden, Victoria. *Inventing the NIH: Federal Biomedical Research Policy, 1887-1937*. Baltimore: Johns Hopkins UP, 1986.

Kraut, Alan. *Silent Travelers: Germs, Genes and the "Immigrant Menace."* Baltimore: Johns Hopkins UP, 1994.

LiPuma, Edward, and Thomas Koeble. "Cultures of Circulation and the Urban Imaginary: Miami as Example and Exemplar." *Public Culture* 17.1 (2002): 153-79.

Lynch, Lisa. "The Fever Next Time: The Race of Disease and the Disease of Racism in John Edgar Wideman." *American Literary History* 14.4 (2002): 776-804.

Milani, Abbas. "Reincarnation for Self-Improvement." [Review of Amitav Ghosh. *The Calcutta Chromosome.*] *The San Francisco Chronicle* 26 Oct. 1997. <http://www.sfgate.com/cgibin/article.cgi?file=/chronicle/archive/1997/10/26/RV55421.DTL>.

Morrison, Toni. "City Limits, Village Values: Concepts of the Neighborhood in Black Fiction." *Literature and the American Urban Experience: Essays on the City and Literature.* Ed. Michael C. Jaye and Ann Chalmers Watts. Manchester: Manchester UP, 1981. 35-43.

Pratt, Mary Louise. *Imperial Eyes: Travel Writing and Transculturation.* London: Routledge, 1992.

Pries, Ludger. *Die Transnationalisierung der sozialen Welt.* Frankfurt/M.: Suhrkamp, 2008.

Sarasin, Philipp. *"Anthrax": Bioterror als Phantasma.* Frankfurt/M.: Suhrkamp, 2004.

Shilling, Chris. *The Body and Social Theory.* London: Sage, 1993.

Simmel, Georg. "The Metropolis and Mental Life" (1903); "The Stranger" (1908). Rpt. in *The Sociology of Georg Simmel.* Trans. Kurt Wolff. New York: Free P, 1950. 402-08.

Slack, Paul. "Introduction." *Epidemics and Ideas: Essays on the Historical Perception of Pestilence.* Ed. Terence O. Ranger and Slack. Cambridge: Cambridge UP, 1992. 1-20.

Tanner, Tony. *City of Words: A Study of American Fiction in the Mid-Twentieth Century.* 1971. London: Cape, 1976.

Urry, John. *Mobilities.* Cambridge: Polity P, 2007.

Swami Vivekananda. "Plague Manifesto" (originally in Bengali). <http://www.ramakrishna-vivekananda/volume~9/writings~prose~and~poems>.

Wald, Priscilla. *Contagious: Cultures, Carriers and the Outbreak Narrative.* Durham: Duke UP, 2008.

Welsch, Wolfgang. "Transculturality: The Puzzling Form of Cultures Today." *Spaces of Culture: City, Nation, World.* Ed. Mike Featherstone and Scott Lash. London: Sage, 1999. 194-213.

Wideman, John Edgar. "Fever." Wideman. *Fever and Other Stories.* New York: Holt, 1989. 127-61.

———. *The Cattle Killing.* 1996. London: Picador, 1997.

Wisniewski, Richard A. *Hawaii: The Territorial Years, 1900-1959.* Honolulu: Pacific Basin, 1984.

III. PRECARIOUS IDENTITIES

ETHNIC SELVES & COMMUNITIES
AND THE CHALLENGE OF THE CITY

Metropolitan Cultures and Religious Identities in the Urban Periphery of São Paulo

PAULO BARRERA RIVERA

1. Introduction

The core issue of this essay is the analysis of the identities produced by religions in the social context of urban agglomerations, specifically in the urban periphery and the slum. The metropolis can be recognized by its pluralism, diversity, and mixed traditions, cultures, accents, customs, and religious forms that originate from different regions. It is necessary to use the plural and to take note of the multiplicity when metropolitan cultures are the focus: cultures rather than culture. Since the metropolis is so heterogeneous, we should ask whether religions, which are important factors in the production of identities, are able to foster lasting identities in such environments. As a rule of thumb, religions need clearly limited frontiers, in spite of the fact that the city is the place where borders can be easily transgressed. This essay aims to analyze these issues in the context of the specific realities of the urban periphery and takes into consideration the information collected in field research conducted in a slum in the city of São Bernardo do Campo in São Paulo.

I would like to start by pointing out that even though the slum has been studied for a long time, the study of religion in the slum has only recently begun in any systematic way. Yet, since more scholars have turned their interest to the religious practices in these regions, nowadays it is possible to regard the urban periphery as a research field for religions.

After pointing out the recent study perspectives about religion in the urban periphery, we shall discuss the main features of the Latin American urbanization processes that brought about such enormous urban peripheries. Later, we shall look at the main social and economic factors that make up the urban peripheries in Brazil, especially in São Paulo and Rio de Janeiro. In the final sections, the link between social and religious identities will be analyzed based on empirical information acquired from field observations in a slum in São Bernardo do Campo named 'Areião.' This essay shows preliminary conclusions of the project group "REPAL: Religion and urban periphery in Latin America."[1]

---

[1] I am very grateful to the editors for inviting me to the ZiF in Bielefeld to debate the initial results of our research in the workshop *EthniCities: Metropolitan Cultures and Ethnic Identities in the Americas.*

2.   Periphery and Religion: The Most Common Research Perspectives

Usually, there are five perspectives that should be carefully considered in the study of religions in the urban periphery of Latin American cities. These perspectives are characterized by the following research foci: social inequalities, violence, local power, vulnerability and social nets, and migration. All of these issues are crucial not only for the comprehension of the reality in the periphery, but also to explain the role of religions in this social context.

Traditionally, scholars in the sociology of religion have shown the importance of studying religion in the context of the social and economic reality and the individuals involved. The important relation between social inequalities and religious practices can be confirmed by the comparative study of religions in areas such as the urban periphery and the central regions. The studies regarding this issue are broad, especially those on São Paulo (cf. Avritzer) and Rio de Janeiro (cf. Leite).

Over the last decade, studies have shown that the Pentecostal churches, by turning them into 'brothers,' have been able to welcome people who have been involved in drug dealing, which is the main source of violence in the periphery, along with family violence and other crimes. This integration into a group keeps these people away from violent practices and turns them into engaged and highly committed participants in the religious activities of the church. Therefore, even domestic violence shows a sharp decrease after conversion, although the initiative to join a congregation usually comes from wives, followed later by the abusive spouses (cf. Machado).

The concept of 'local power' also has to be taken into consideration when studying the periphery. Local power consists of a spontaneous initiative of organizations inside the community, which cooperate in order to solve specific problems regarding health, transportation, and infrastructure in general without intervention by any official power, that is to say, by the government (cf. Marques, "Elementos"; Torres). Field research has shown meaningful participation of Pentecostals in local power, even though previous studies until recently overlooked this important presence. This topic will be further discussed later in the article.

Since official government participation is scarce and individuals are left devoid of proper education, housing, and basic resources for living, they engage in 'social nets' (cf. Whyte; Sampson/Groves), the religious net being the most important one (cf. Lavalle/Castello). Social nets provide residents a way to cope with their social vulnerability. It is important to remark that religious nets did not draw the attention of scholars studying social nets who (wrongly) assumed that the Pentecostals' participation in the nets was meaningless. It is important to note, however, that Pentecostals do in fact play an active role in these social nets.

The Pentecostal churches concentrate a large number of migrants who usually come from the north and northeast and have an Afro-Brazilian profile. The beginning of a slum generally coincides with a wave of migration. Therefore the growth of Pentecostalism in the periphery and the periphery growth are parallel processes along with migration (cf. Barrera). However, this phenomenon has not been sufficiently acknowledged by scholars. It will be developed in more detail while taking the role of Pentecostalism in the slum into consideration.

3. World Urban Population and Latin America

It is mandatory to compare the characteristics of urban growth in Latin America to urbanization in industrialized Europe, especially in the course of the 20th century, when Latin American countries entered the process of industrialization. Unequal urban growth can be observed between the 1920s and 1980s. While the population multiplied by 2.5 in industrialized countries, in poor ones it multiplied by a factor of 6 (cf. Oliveira). Thus, the phenomenon of urbanization was not at all homogeneous. The growth was more 'out of control' in the poor countries in Latin America (cf. table 1).

Year	World	Latin America
1970	37.4%	59%
1980	41.5%	65%
1990	46%	72%

Table 1: World urban population vs. Latin America
(CELADE/CEPAL, *Boletín Demográfico* 66, 2000).

The relation between urban population and industrialization is remarkable. The urbanization in Europe was progressive and followed the pace of technological revolutions and industrialization. Unlike in Europe, urbanization in Latin America was faster and more recent. The urban population in Latin America reached 390 million people in 2000, making this the most urbanized region of the world (cf. CEPAL, 2000). The following table shows the percentage of urban population of some countries in Latin America in 2000:

Uruguay	93.1%	Peru	73.5%
Argentina	90.6%	Bolivia	68.2%
Venezuela	88.8%	Ecuador	65.8%
Chile	86.9%	Panama	59.5%
Cuba	81.9%	El Salvador	57.8%
Brazil	81.7%	Nicaragua	56.7%
Colombia	76.6%	Costa Rica	52.3%
Mexico	77.2%	Guatemala	39.9%

Table 2: Urban population of selected Latin American countries
(CELADE/CEPAL, *Boletín Demográfico* 66, 2000).

4. Urbanization and Poverty in Latin America

Urbanization and poverty issues are clearly linked in the Latin American societies of the 20th and 21st centuries. Before the rise of the big cities, the countryside was most severely affected by the shortage of resources. The accelerated urbanization in the second half of the 20th century changed the geographical scenario of poverty. Although the rural communities remained poor, the lack of basic resources grew in the cities. The following illustration (fig. 1) shows the direct relation between urbanization and the growth of poverty in the last three decades of the 20th century. Therefore, it is possible to claim that the more urbanized Latin America has become, the more it was affected by poverty.

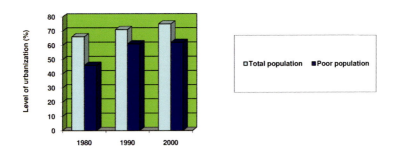

Fig. 1: Urbanization and the growth of poverty
(CELADE/CEPAL, *Boletín Demográfico* 66, 2000).

5.   Urban Periphery in Brazil

Brazil is the Latin American country where the parallel growth of poverty and urbanization happened most rapidly and most dramatically. Between the 1940s and the 1990s, the Brazilian urban population boomed from 12 million (31% of the total population) to 138 million (81%). This rapid urbanization went hand in hand with an actual geographical reconfiguration of poverty, with poverty belts expanding dramatically. This phenomenon was common in every country in Latin America. Industrialization and urbanization caused new poverty issues before the previous ones had been resolved. The new urban poverty was added to the traditional concentration of rural poverty hitherto located in the north and northeast. In a few words, the poverty expanded from the country to the periphery of the cities. The metropolitan regions of São Paulo and Rio de Janeiro played the most important role in the process of the concentration of poverty in the cities. In the 1990s, the metropolitan regions of São Paulo and Rio de Janeiro accounted for more than 50% of the total poor metropolitan population of the country (cf. Seabra). Thus, the big cities and their peripheries are a result of urban modernity.

The urbanization process in Brazil cannot be studied without considering São Paulo's role in the growth of the periphery. During the industrialization process, it was the destination of 50% of the migration flow, creating a large peripheral belt where the biggest slums are located today. Rio de Janeiro went through a similar process. The studies on slums in Rio de Janeiro reveal a century of slums (cf. Zaluar/Alvito; Valladares).

The 20th century is marked by the emergence of big cities all over Latin America, such as São Paulo, Mexico City, and Buenos Aires, to name but a few of the main examples of urban growth. Although these cities are synonyms of modernity in Latin America, they are also the nuclei of social inequalities in the respective countries. Consequently, the periphery, the slum, is a result of modernity. Ironically, those regions which concentrate great political and economic power also present peripheral spaces with shortages or a lack of basic infrastructure and presence of governmental power. Wealth and poverty are produced simultaneously in the modern city. This is arguably one of the main characteristics of the modern global society.

According to the main studies in the area, a broad concept of 'periphery' comprises poverty, a lack of means for physical survival, shortages of income and work, a lack of suitable physical infrastructure and proper housing sites, inadequacy or absence of social policies, violence, and a non-guarantee of basic citizenship rights. Other ways to define the periphery regard the high level of vulnerability and the human development rate (cf. Marques, "Elementos"), or the concept of 'urban frontier,' which means high demographic growth rates and limited accessibility of public services.

However, the geographical aspect is not enough to define the periphery. As a rule of thumb, the population occupying the outskirts usually comprises the people most strongly affected by economic and social marginalization. Yet, there are also richer people who decide to live far from downtown in condominiums, looking for safety, leisure opportunities, etc., creating spatial segregation with high walls (cf. Caldeira). Thus, the lack of resources is not enough to define 'periphery' either, not even when slums are in focus. There is a lot of social, cultural, and economic creativity. The residents do not merely survive; they live, produce, and reproduce, economically and culturally speaking. Religions are part of this socially and culturally dynamic movement, consisting mainly of Pentecostal churches, which are an important part of the slum landscape.

6. The Periphery in the 'ABC Paulista'

Even though plenty of socially unequal neighborhoods are found in the 'ABC Paulista'—the region bordering on São Paulo including, among others, the communities of Santo André, São Bernardo do Campo, and São Caetano do Sul—, there is an equal amount of religious evangelical groups present in all of them. The existent inequality allows us to picture the segregation in two ways: first, as a physical and geographical one and, second, as a socio-economic one which results in difficulties in having basic needs attended.

The neighborhoods of São Bernardo, Santo André, São Caetano do Sul, Diadema, and Ribeirão Pires are rated among those with the highest crime rates in Brazil. Moreover, according to official rates, São Paulo itself ranks among the highest figures. The homicide ratio for 100,000 inhabitants was 61.9 in 1998; one year later it increased to 68.8, whereas in Rio de Janeiro it remained at 64.7 (cf. Baierl; de Souza).

The Pentecostal leadership capacity to integrate newly converted members into the 'brother' community is well-known. According to Sampson and Groves, there is a link between disorganization and crime: Low participation in neighborhood associations, clubs, and religious organizations results in higher criminality. The Pentecostal churches can be considered sites of social organization in the periphery. Recent research has shown the important role of religious membership in slums in Rio de Janeiro (cf. Zaluar/Alvito).

The 'Grand ABC' has a large concentration of slums. According to the studies performed by the Paulista Company of Metropolitan Planning (cf. Baierl), which analyzed 39 cities, including the capital, the region accounts for 20% of the total area of slums of the metropolitan region of São Paulo, which has a total of 60.7 km^2, out of which 12 are in the 'Grand ABC.' Out of the 39 cities surveyed, São Bernardo at 5 km^2 ranks third in the geographical expansion of slum area. Diadema, in contrast, has 2.2 km^2 and is also among the cities with large slum areas. One third of its population lives in such areas.

Who are the believers in the Pentecostal churches in the periphery? Why do they join the churches? How do urban modernity and secular society affect the lives of the Pentecostal believers? These issues are discussed based on the field observation of a specific neighborhood, its worship services, and the social, economic, and cultural conditions of its believers. Montanhão was the chosen neighborhood due to its having the lowest social economic rates in São Bernardo city.

7.   Pentecostalism in the Periphery

São Paulo city forms the center of Brazilian industrialization and has played an important role in the accumulation and capitalization process since the 1930s. In this process, São Paulo was also the main destination of rural migration to the cities. In 1970, São Paulo accounted for 58% of the industry in the country. Nonetheless, since the 1980s, the industry in São Paulo has been unable to employ all the migrant labor force that continued to arrive in the city. The periphery and unemployment growth were boosted due to this fact.

Scholars have emphasized the fact that the fastest growing religion in the last decades has been Pentecostalism, which primarily grows among the poorest. There is a wide range of Pentecostal churches in the São Bernardo periphery; a virtual Pentecostal pluralism is offered to the people. Nevertheless, the choice of one of the Pentecostal churches is based on religious and non-religious reasons.

Crime, violence, and fear have become very evident in Brazilian cities since the 1980s (cf. Caldeira). These issues have been an important part of public concern since 2000; they have sparked city, state, and federal policies and have led to significant initiatives in society. The National Public Security Plan launched by the federal government in 2000 and the Social Programs Follow-Up Plan to Prevent Violence, linked to the government since 2001, may be mentioned here. There are state plans as well, such as Viva Rio or the Santo André More Equal project, among others. The recognition of higher crime rates, not only as reported by the media but also as shown by data available at several research centers, turned the violence issue into a major element to be analyzed when looking at contemporary Brazilian reality (cf. Sento-Sé).

Violence, as an individual or group practice (civilian, police, or military) or as a consequence of social inequalities, can be considered a consolidated historical procedure turned against the poor. The dialogue with the so-called 'local power' is inevitable sooner or later, since without it no project aiming at the prevention of violence would be effective. 'Local power' shall be defined as the set of initiatives, more or less spontaneous, more or less institutionalized, and more or less political, which achieves some efficiency level regarding the local problems of decision making. It is built from the daily reality of the people, object of and subject to violence. Since the churches are part of this daily life, they play an important role in the local power dynamics. While public security policies depend on election periods, change of government, etc., the local power is constantly present. The Pentecostal churches participate in the local social nets that inhibit or neutralize the rise of violence rates. As we will see, the Pentecostal view concerning the causes of and solutions to the violence problem is not a monolithic one.

Studies show that the most serious effects of violence are not spread randomly. The people who are mostly affected are black, poor, male, and young (15 to 24 years old) (cf. Soares). The Evangelical churches in the urban periphery represent a large proportion of the black population. The data analysis (cf. IBGE Brasil Censo 2000; Barrera) leads to the conclusion that the Pentecostal churches have the highest share of black churchgoers, especially the Igreja Pentecostal Deus é Amor, the Igreja Universal do Reino de Deus, and the Assembléia de Deus respectively (cf. Barrera). Our field observations show that the share of black members in the Pentecostal churches in the periphery is higher than their share of the total population in the periphery.

8.   The Montanhão Neighborhood

This neighborhood is located on the left side of the Via Anchieta, the road that links São Paulo to Santos Harbor. Moreover, the Via Anchieta is the only way to reach this community. The first residential area is the Areião slum.

The 'slum' concept will be used here in the sense defined by Saraiva and Marques, reflecting the idea of 'under-average sectors' according to the Instituto Brasileiro de Geografia e Estatística (IBGE). The Areião residents have to walk about one kilometer in order to reach the Via Anchieta. The neighborhood started to grow in the late 1970s, over two decades after the inauguration of the highway (1947). On the left side of the Via Anchieta, the neighborhood closest to Billings Reservoir is located. Its residents walk up to two kilometers, especially on the weekends, to fish or to sunbathe. Therefore, the place known as 'Prainha' ["little beach"] is the only leisure area available. The data that follows was provided by São Bernardo do Campo city hall.

The annual geometrical growth rate (2.42%) is higher than that of São Paulo state (1.78%), São Paulo city, and the 'ABC region' (both 1.56%). Four decades ago, this difference used to be much higher when the 'ABC' rate was 9.52%. In 2005, the estimated population was 788,560, out of which 69.54% were Catholic, 16.49% Evangelicals, and 7.39% stated having no religion. Regarding race, 69.56% were white, 24.37% mixed races, and 3.44% black. Montanhão has the highest number of residents (116,773 in 2004) as well as the highest number of people per household in the city (3.84).

There are also subtle differences regarding economy and education. This neighborhood has the highest percentage of family leaders who receive only one minimum wage or less (6.87%) and have less than one year of education or none (11.11%). There is only one elementary school and one high school, with inhabitants having to walk two kilometers to get there. The latest IDEB (Basic Education Development Rate) evaluation showed that the school with the lowest score is the one in this region. In order to get medical care, the residents go to the health centers in Riacho Grande and São Bernardo do Campo. Regarding leisure opportunities, there is one unpaved soccer court.

It is worth pointing out that the residents of this neighborhood have a great capacity to organize and mobilize themselves, even though this happens only in special situations. In the beginning of 2006, the slum was flooded due to strong rains in the 'ABC region.' The lack of cleaning on the banks of a stream that flows along the neighborhood made the sewage flood the houses. As a way of protesting, the slum residents, mainly the ones who lived in the lower parts and were most dramatically affected, closed the Via Anchieta. The Pentecostal inhabitants participated as much in the protest as the other residents. Thus, this religious affiliation is not a factor that influences the practices of claiming basic citizen rights.

9.   Periphery and Identity in the Areião

In this part of the essay I would like to point out the most important features of the social identity of the residents of the slum being studied. One of the elements that makes up the social identity in the slum is the strong sense of belonging to 'the village,' which means more than just living in the Areião; this sense of belonging goes far beyond that. Usually the term 'slum' is not used; instead, the residents prefer 'the village,' obviously due to the strong social discrimination that the word 'slum' implies, although the interviews show that this is relative. When it comes to the founders of the community, they are proud to say "we built this slum." Another example are the people who managed to move from the slum in order to 'improve their lives'; there they were at least able to buy their own house, a car, cable TV, a phone, and even have some of their rooms rented, reasons why they state that "people live better in the slum." The third example shows a subtle semantic difference concerning the term 'slum' when used to refer to the 'slum culture.' In one of the interviews, a ten-year-old child was observed correcting verb agreement in the speech of her grandmother, Ms Tonha, who used the pronoun in the plural and the verb in the singular. It was clear that the grandchild neither lived nor studied in the slum; she was just visiting her grandmother. When the grandmother was corrected for the third time in front of the researcher, she responded annoyed that "that's the way people talk in the slum and there's nothing wrong about it."

Nevertheless, it is important to say that Ms Tonha was attending classes every night after work in a school for adult education, attempting to finish elementary school. Unfortunately, she ended up quitting since she had to leave home at 4 a.m. in order to get to the company where she worked as a cleaner at 6 a.m. Therefore it was too tiring to follow classes from 7:30 to 11:30 p.m., since she got home around 7 p.m. Her son Quico, a brick layer, had a similar experience. He tried several times to keep studying, but was not able to continue. He had recently bought his own house in the slum. His mother thought he would get married, but he rented the house and kept on living with the mother in the house he built together with his stepfather. Quico stated that "people live very well in the slum" and that he would never leave it.

The diversity of religious options, especially Pentecostal varieties, is the second important element regarding identity in the slum. The Pentecostal churches that are most successful are the old ones, the ones which had already been there through the years of massive migration to the territory which spawned the slum. These churches are a part of its landscape, since they have been there 'forever.' Most of them are small or medium-sized considering that nothing is big in the slum; the streets are narrow and crooked; there are many stairs to reach the highest parts of the land or the houses built on slopes; the houses and rooms are small, and there are small trades as well. So the Pentecostal churches fit in among the slum architecture. The new Pentecostal churches are not large either, and they do not fare as well as the old ones do. All of them, either new or old, offer a large variety of religious options; in addition, the churches are very close to each other. There are many religious options in the downtown area as well, and when the followers decide to change churches and it is noticed, it brings about recoil. In the slum, however, this happens frequently, and changing churches is not only a normal practice but also socially legitimate. The religious biographies of the people interviewed show many changes in religion. This scenario is interpreted here as evidence of unstable religious identities, since the people do not stick to one religion.

Another feature is that people in the slum are never part of more than one church simultaneously, though this phenomenon referred to as 'multiple religious belongings' has been witnessed downtown. This practice is neither usual nor acceptable in the slum. Usually, an individual who is simultaneously affiliated with different churches is stigmatized. A person is expected to join a church only after leaving another.[2] There is a remarkably strong sense of belonging in each group; however, there is no grudge if someone leaves the group. It is more acceptable to quit a group than to attend two.

The factor of frequent religious changes has led scholars to conclude that group identity frontiers have become weaker, just like the identity borders in the slums, if the same line of reasoning is followed. Surprisingly in fact, the slum religious groups have very clear identity frontiers. The reason why multiple belonging is not acceptable, while sequential belonging is indeed common, is probably to be found not least in the short distances between churches.

Recent research regarding the role of the churches in the periphery, more precisely in the slum context and its violent practices, has shown the capacity of Pentecostal churches to integrate 'the converted' into the 'community of brothers.' This effectiveness in the integration of the religious groups is a matter that has frequently been overlooked by researchers. It is known that the violent practices related to various crimes such as theft, robbery, and drug dealing that are performed outside the slum are facts of life in the slum.[3] Many Pentecostal churches in the slum are run or founded by

---

[2]   Thus, the researcher must carry out field research in one church at a time, since everybody knows when someone is attending more than one church. This also creates problems for the observer because it is difficult to form a complete picture.

[3]   Some unexpected events were witnessed during field observation, such as shooting by the police chasing a car that had been stolen; afterwards the car was left abandoned and the

former perpetrators. All of them are small churches that congregate in the pastor's house or in a rented room. One of the churches started in the house of a well-known drug dealer after a murder had taken place in the same location. I could not obtain information regarding the perpetrator or the victim, but the killing made the former criminal marry his partner and convert to the religion along with his wife, with whom the church is now run. There are also many former convicts who are faithful Pentecostal churchgoers in every church. One of the biggest differences between the Congregação Cristã no Brasil (CCB) and other Pentecostal churches is that in the former, the experience connected to crime is not part of the worship, whereas in the latter it is part of the sermons. These examples show that the Pentecostal churches are able to integrate these individuals into the community, and the reason why they stay is the great commitment the former perpetrators develop to the church. The churches are greatly respected by the leaders of organized crime, so are previous criminals who converted; however, the conversion of such people must be genuine; otherwise the leadership of organized crime will easily notice.

10. Sociability and Religious Identities in the Slum

In this last part I would like to discuss a theoretical issue in the analysis of peripheral identities and their link to social and religious practices. First of all, it is necessary to state that poverty in the slum is not enough to explain the prevalent social practices. Poverty is not solely to be defined as an economic issue; the reality of poverty concerns more. In the study of social identities in the periphery, it is very important to point out the analytical importance of informal social mechanisms of solidarity, one of them proposed by the initiative of religious groups. The associations for religious practices in the slum can be considered strategically important, because, although they seem to be spontaneous reactions to specific problems, the people who benefit from them clearly know the advantages they enjoy by being part of a religious group. These benefits are not only material but also social and affective, along with the possibility of sharing religious and non-religious activities with other members of the community.

Three factors should be taken into consideration when analyzing the construction of identities in the periphery: social associations, poverty, and religious practices. These factors are usually explicit in the discourse of the slum residents as the decisive elements for building group identities. The following figure attempts to illustrate the dynamic of these elements:

---

people inside ran away, hiding in the alleys and narrow streets of the slum. The police took the car minutes later and left. The residents stated that the police entered the slum to recover goods only when the victim paid them to do so. The occurrence did not catch the residents' attention. The incident happened on a Saturday night and nothing was mentioned either in the churches I attended on Sunday or in the ones visited later.

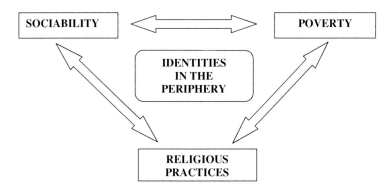

Fig. 2: 'Identity Triangle': Interplay of sociability, poverty, and religious practices in the construction of group identities in the periphery.

There is the Neighborhood Friends Association in the slum with the participation of Catholic, Spiritualist, and Evangelical people as well as people who state no religious affiliation. This association is a place for the articulation of two elements in our theoretical triangle: sociability and poverty. It is not a place for religious practices, so it could be described as a laic place. It is likely that the laicism comes from the fact that the people who organize the assisting activities are somehow linked to illegal practices.

On the other hand, the churches also organize social activities especially aiming at their followers. Some are very organized and permanent activities, while others are more circumstantial. However, both link elements of our theoretical triangle: poverty and religious practices. The spiritualist groups encourage participation by giving a basket filled with basic supplies to the people who will attend every meeting. The Congregação Cristã do Brasil (CCB) has a permanent group made up of women, called 'the Ministry of Mercy,' who assist the needy 'brothers.' These practices, more or less organized, allow us to claim that religious belonging soothes the exclusion from the labor market.

The different religious groups, especially the worship of the Pentecostal groups, are important spaces for sociability. The 'brothers' from different churches walk in groups going to or coming from their churches on Sunday nights and weeknights. The worship, the chats that happen afterwards, and the meetings in the houses for praying are social practices linking sociability and religious practices. Using this 'theoretical identity triangle' to show the three elements that determine the social practices or the elements that shape the people's identities allows for the identification of key elements which organize belonging to and differences among social groups inside the slum.

We also realize that the identity of the people in the slum is made up of several social nets: the family net, the net of migrants from the same region of the country, or professionals from the same field like the association of young bricklayers who joined forces to acquire a major contract for building outside the slum. This association is occasional and informal. There is no document that guarantees its existence or the members' rights. Everything is based on trust. Once the construction work is over, the association will no longer exist. A large group of Pentecostals who spend a great part of the day on the construction site forms part of this association of bricklayers. The different religious affiliations do not intervene in the labor relations since this association is professional rather than religious. Simultaneously, it is observed that the migrant net, for instance of *Cearenses* (people coming from Ceará in the northeast of Brazil), starts with family links because these families migrated together. Small associations that privilege people from the same church, the so-called 'believers,' are also common. The reason is the trust in the discipline, punctuality, and honor of the believers. Being a believer involves searching, spreading, and receiving effective 'mundane' benefits. Especially the CCB and the God Assembly temples provide a strong net that attracts people in vulnerable situations because of the reciprocal practices, usually performed by the Evangelicals who will help the 'brothers in faith.'

11. Conclusion: Social Religious Nets and Social Capital

One of the most interesting ideas of Pierre Bourdieu in *La Distinction* about the process of the construction of social capital and the development of a specific habitus concerns the importance of the permanent relations among the people in the social groups they belong to or intend to belong to. The efficiency of the social capital depends mostly on the capacity of taking part in a lasting network of relations. The biggest innovation of this hypothesis is that the possibility of accumulating or keeping social capital is not determined only by economic issues. Each person's position comprises a group of common practices, legitimate values, availability (more or less conscious), captured in the concept of habitus.

In the slum world, social groups are characterized by great instability and the overlaying of social nets. The social nets are not indeed firmly established groups. They are circumstantial ones and exist only while the circumstances demand the group activity. Nevertheless, in the slum, the different kinds of social nets (migrants from the northeast, family nets of the migrants blended with the children of migrants from Ceará or, for example, the young bricklayers etc.) produce group identities, plural identities in the sense of being made by people who consider themselves part of lasting groups such as the father family or a religious group. Ultimately, the most stable social groups are undoubtedly the religious ones, especially the classic Pentecostals, CCB, Assembly of God, and the Pentecostal God is Love. In conclusion, due to group instability, it is hard to distinguish the different social groups in the slum on the basis of their different habitus. We should ask if the analytical perspective of Bourdieu is more effective comparing groups and social practices in the slum to others in different social sectors. It is probably appropriate to think of a fairly homogeneous 'slum class habitus.' This would mean regarding the social and economic differences of the slum residents as minimal, although they exist. Members of CCB interviewed by us claim that there are no poor people in the congregation, and they live better than most of the people in the slum. Bearing this answer in mind, I asked whether the low prices of the slum real estate market—housing is cheap; construction costs are low; the work is usually done by the owners themselves or with the help of the community—and the availability of water, light, phone, and Internet along with the illegal market for CDs, DVDs, etc., also at very cheap prices, was the reason they 'live better.' Our interviewees agreed, stating that if they lived anywhere else, their lives would not be that easy.

Works Cited

Avritzer, Leonardo, ed. *Participação em São Paulo*. São Paulo: Unesp, 2004.

Baierl, Luzia. *Medo Social: Da violência visível ao invisível da violência*. São Paulo: Cortez, 2004.

Barrera, Dario Paulo Rivera. "Matrizes protestantes do pentecostalismo." *Movimentos do Espírito: Matrizes, afinidades e territórios*. Ed. João Décio Pasos. São Paulo: Paulinas, 2005. 213-47.

Caldeira Teresa Pires. *Cidade de muros: Crime, segregação e cidadania em São Paulo*. São Paulo: Editora 34 and EDUSP, 2000.

CELADE/CEPAL. *Boletín Demográfico* 66. Santiago, 2000.

IBGE. *Brasil Censo 2000*. <http://www.ibge.gov.br>.

Lavalle, Adrian, and Graziela Castello. "As benesses desse mundo: Associativismo religioso e inclusão socioeconômica." *Novos Estudos* 69 (2004): 73-93.

Leite, Márcia Pereira. "Novas relações entre identidade religiosa e participação política no Rio de Janeiro hoje: O caso do Movimento Popular de Favelas." *Religião e espaço público*. Ed. Patrícia Birman. São Paulo: Attar, CNPq, and Pronex, 2003. 63-95.

Machado, Maria das Dores. *Carismáticos e pentecostais: Adesão religiosa na esfera familiar*. Campinas: ANPOCs, 1996.

Marques, Eduardo. "Elementos conceituais da segregação, da pobreza urbana e da ação do estado." *São Paulo: Segregação, pobreza e desigualdades sociais*. Ed. Marques and Haroldo Torres. São Paulo: SENAC, 2005. 19-56.

———. "Espaço e grupos sociais na virada do século XXI." *São Paulo: Segregação, pobreza e desigualdades sociais*. Ed. Marques and Haroldo Torres. São Paulo: SENAC, 2005. 57-99.

———, and Sandra Bitar. "Grupos sociais e espaço." *Novos Estudos Cebrap* 64 (2002): 123-31.

Oliveira, Maria Coleta, ed. *Demografia da exclusão social*. Campinas, Unicamp: FAPESP, 2001.

Pochmann, Marcio, and Ricardo Amorin. *Atlas da exclusão social no Brasil*. São Paulo: Cortez, 2004.

Sampson, Robert, and W. Byron Groves. "Community Structure and Crime: Testing Social Disorganization Theory." *American Journal of Sociology* 94 (1989): 774-802.

Saraiva, Camila, and Eduardo Marques. "A dinâmica social dos habitantes de favelas da região metropolitana de São Paulo." *São Paulo: Segregação, pobreza e desigualdades sociais*. Ed. Marques and Haroldo Torres. São Paulo: SENAC, 2005. 143-68.

Seabra, Odette Carvalho. "São Paulo: A cidade, os bairros e a periferia." *Geografias de São Paulo: Representação e crise da metrópole*. Ed. Ana Carlos and Ariovaldo Oliveira. São Paulo: Contexto, 2004. 40-59.

Sento-Sé, João Trajano. *Prevenção da violência: O papel das cidades*. Rio de Janeiro: Civilização Brasileira, CESeC, and FAPERJ, 2005.

Silveira, Maria Laura. "São Paulo: Os dinamismos da pobreza." *Geografias de São Paulo: Representação e crise da metrópole*. Ed. Ana Carlos and Ariovaldo Oliveira. São Paulo: Contexto, 2004. 59-71.

Soares, Luis Eduardo. "Segurança municipal no Brasil: Sugestões para uma agenda mínima." *Prevenção da violência: O papel das cidades*. Ed. João Trajano Sento-Sé. São Paulo: Civilização Brasileira, 2006. 15-44.

Souza, Marcelo Lopes de. *Fobópole: O medo generalizado e a militarização da questão urbana*. Rio de Janeiro: Bertrand, 2008.

Torres, Haroldo. "A fronteira paulistana." *São Paulo: Segregação, pobreza e desigualdades sociais*. Ed. Eduardo Marques and Torres. São Paulo: SENAC, 2005. 101-20.

Valladares, Licia. *La favela d'un siècle à l'autre*. Paris: Maison des sciences de l'homme, 2006.

Whyte, William Foote. *Street Corner Society: The Social Structure of an Italian Slum*. Illinois: University of Chicago P, 1993.

Zaluar, Alba, and Marcos Alvito, eds. *Um século de favela*. Rio de Janeiro: FGV, 1998.

Addressing Urban Fear and Violence in Bogotá through the 'Culture of Citizenship': Scope and Challenges of a Unique Approach

YVONNE RIAÑO

Widespread violence and rising crime rates are one of the most challenging governance problems of many Latin American cities. Bogotá, the largest and most populous city in Colombia, has 7,259,597 inhabitants (cf. DANE 2009, *Colombia*). In 1995, Bogotá represented an extreme case of violence and insecurity in terms of numbers of homicides (3,657 per year), street robberies (13,027 per year), house robberies (1,301), bank assaults (382), and traffic accidents (cf. Camacho, "Ciudades" 5). Besides taking thousands of lives and producing thousands of handicapped people, this situation caused urban residents to live in an environment of fear, insecurity, and a permanent lack of confidence in their fellow citizens and in the city's institutions. Pérgolis summarized the then prevalent imaginary among the city's residents with the following words: "Bogotá of fear. Unliveable Bogotá. City of street robberies, beggars, armed pedestrians, never-ending traffic jams, uncollected rubbish. Bogotá of panic, intolerance, and hate" (30). A decade later, dramatic changes had taken place regarding the relationship of the citizens to their city. Some authors have even spoken of a "revolution": Residents are proud to live in Bogotá; they are willing to contribute to the city's finances; they are more inclined to respect traffic signals; their participation in development plans is steadily increasing (cf. Rojas). What is behind such a transformation? This paper addresses this question by examining the approaches to urban governance that have been implemented by the city's mayors since the early 1990s, when the mayors were first elected by popular vote. The paper focuses in particular on the 1995-2005 period when Mayor Antanas Mockus developed the 'culture of citizenship' approach.

This paper postulates that the urban governance approaches implemented by Bogotá's mayors during the 1995-2005 period are unique, for four main reasons. First of all, they are formulated with an intention different from the one prevalent in other cities of the continent, namely to prioritize social coexistence rather than economic profit. In recent years, many Latin American cities have been increasingly planned and governed according to the principles of a cultural economy which sees and uses culture and ethnicity as valuable marketing products. Thus, culture and ethnicity have become a means of creating a particular identity for the city in order to attract tourists and investors, thereby maximizing economic outcomes. In contrast to this stands the approach of *cultura ciudadana*, a term that has been translated as "culture of citizenship" (Rojas) or "cultural agency" (Sommer). This was conceived and implemented in the early 1990s by Antanas Mockus, when he was newly elected as mayor of Bogotá. The idea was to mobilize urban residents to adopt a set of shared habits, actions, and regulations that generate a sense of belonging and facilitate urban coexistence. Antanas Mockus saw the promotion of a 'culture of citizenship' as the key to counteracting social violence and insecurity. Second, and in contrast to other Latin American cities where the approach to tackling urban violence has often been repressive and defensive (i.e., creating gated communities and increasing the numbers of police and security guards), the mayors in Bogotá have emphasized that reducing crime and violence is not just a matter of repression but of education and culture as well. Thus, culture is equated with non-violence. Third, the approaches implemented in the city of Bogotá were embedded in a political process of decentralization dating back to the late 1980s, which made it possible to move away from patronage and clientelism and the general lack of citizen participation. Finally, the interventions of Bogotá's mayors during the period of study have been comprehensive—including reform of the police, the establishment of legal, educational, and cultural systems—and have been implemented within the framework of multi-sectoral partnerships.

This article is structured in three parts. The first briefly introduces Colombia's process of decentralization and describes in detail the urban governance approaches that were implemented by Bogotá's mayors during the 1995-2005 period. The second part reflects on the processes that have made Bogotá's transformation possible and discusses the long-term challenges of such approaches. Finally, the conclusion addresses the practical and theoretical lessons that can be drawn from the case of Bogotá with respect to the culture of citizenship.

1.   Political Decentralization and Urban Governance Approaches in Bogotá (1995-2005)

Decentralization processes started in Colombia in the 1980s in an effort to improve municipal finances and to devolve political power to local governments. An important characteristic of Colombia's decentralization process is that it was largely initiated as a response to the crisis of legitimacy of the national government and the traditional political parties (cf. Rojas; Angell/Lowden/Thorp). In 1986, a legislative act allowed municipalities to elect mayors. This was a significant step towards decentralization, since the President had formerly designated mayors. The constitutional reform of 1991 consolidated the decentralization process: One of its main emphases was to strengthen the levels of participation of citizens in decision-making processes. According to Article 2, the State has a constitutional mandate to ensure citizen participation in decisions related to the economic, political, administrative, and cultural aspects of the nation. To that effect, with the change of the Constitution, the mayor of the city of Bogotá was to be elected by the citizens. Thus, since 1991, five mayors have been democratically elected in the city of Bogotá: Jaime Castro (1992-1994), Antanas

Mockus (1995-1997 and 2001-2003), Enrique Peñalosa (1998-2000), Luis Eduardo Garzón (2004-2007), and Samuel Moreno Rojas (2008-2011). The election of mayors by city residents represented a notable break with traditional politics, which previously had been characterized by patronage, *clientelismo*, and *caudillismo*. Also, the previous designations of Bogotá's mayors were used by the political establishment to set up successors to the President of the Republic.

Bogotá's first democratically elected mayor was Jaime Castro (1992-1994), who is considered by some as the 'founding father' of Bogotá's transformation (cf. Ardila Gómez). Castro's main contribution to the city was to draft and enact a Charter for Bogotá, which modernized the city's tax code and created the instruments that allowed the city to markedly increase its revenues. The Charter also opened the door for civil society to participate in the city's decision-making processes. In 1995, Antanas Mockus, a mathematician (University of Burgundy, France), philosopher (National University of Colombia), and pedagogue, who had until then worked as rector of the National University, the country's largest university, was elected as Bogotá's mayor. The unique feature of his candidacy was that he did not belong to any political party. This represented a dramatic change in Colombia's political landscape, since Mockus was the first independent candidate to occupy one of Colombia's most important political jobs.

1.1. Mobilizing a Culture of Citizenship

When Mockus took office in 1995, he was faced with the challenge of tackling the severe problems of urban violence described above. However, he had a clear philosophy of how to address such problems. A central element of his philosophy, partly inspired by his readings of well-known academics such as Jon Elster, Jürgen Habermas, and Douglass North, is his firm belief that transforming the attitude of urban citizens towards their city was the key to the problem. Thus, he shaped the approach of *cultura ciudadana* ["culture of citizenship"], founded on the idea that urban violence is best combated by inducing citizens to be respectful of each other and thereby make peaceful interaction possible (cf. Mockus, *Cultura*). Mobilizing a culture of citizenship was considered to be a necessary first step before considering other measures, such as increasing the numbers of police officers and security guards, or improving urban infrastructure. Mockus argued that violence is rooted in a lack of shared values, in a lack of communication, and in mutual fear. The result is an absence of respect for other people's lives and disregard for the law. Acquisition of the values and attitudes of citizenship is central to his arguments. He argues that an 'individual is not born as a citizen but becomes one.' In his view, becoming a citizen implies being treated as a citizen, i.e., with respect, and learning to treat others as citizens (also in their relations with the state).

Overall, the culture of citizenship consists of a set of shared habits, actions, and regulations that generate a sense of belonging, facilitate urban coexistence, and lead to the respect and recognition of civic rights and duties. For Mockus, the task of city administrators is to mobilize the process of a shared culture of citizenship. Losing the fear of each other and being less prone to violence takes place via intensified communication. Since the city is above all a territory of communication and interaction, the task of administrators becomes one of helping citizens lose their fear by communicating more intensively. This raises the question of how to change people's behavior and induce them to be more respectful of each other. In Mockus's eyes, being able to mobilize a culture of citizenship first requires an understanding of the mechanisms that regulate people's actions and behavior in the public sphere. What are these mechanisms? Mockus's answer is that three different types of systems regulate the behavior of individuals: (a) self-regulation, (b) mutual regulation, and (c) legal regulation, as seen in table 1. Each one of these regulatory systems works on the basis of both 'negative' and 'positive' mechanisms. Negative mechanisms are generally associated with fear. For example, in the case of self-regulatory systems, individuals fear the guilt that they will experience when they behave in a way that is rejected by society. In the case of mutual regulatory systems, individuals fear social rejection and social shame. In the case of legal regulatory systems, individuals fear legal punishment. In contrast, positive mechanisms are associated with personal satisfaction, i.e., the satisfaction of obeying one's conscience (self-regulation systems), of obtaining social recognition (mutual regulation systems), and of obeying the law (legal regulation system). According to Mockus, the challenge of urban coexistence is the harmonization of these three types of regulation. Urban violence arises when the connection between these three regulatory systems is absent (cf. *Bogotá*).

Types of regulation	Negative mechanisms	Positive mechanisms
Self-regulation	Fear of guilt	Satisfaction of obeying one's conscience
Mutual regulation	Fear of social rejection/shame	Social recognition
Legal regulation	Fear of legal punishment	Satisfaction of obeying the law

Table 1: The behavior of individuals in the public sphere: three types of regulatory systems.

What is interesting about the culture of citizenship is that it goes beyond the commonly known concept of civic culture. Rojas, for example, argues that civic culture is a narrow term, restricted to attitudes and orientations of individuals toward political phenomena (cf. 293). In this conceptualization, attitudes and orientations are seen as given in some cultures. Thus, Almond and Verba conclude that civic culture has deep roots in the United Kingdom and United States, but that Mexico has almost no civic culture (cf. 323). Rojas values the culture of citizenship because it implies that culture is not something 'pre-existent,' but that it results from a process of regulation between individuals (cf. 293).

How to mobilize a culture of citizenship in practice? As explained above, the approach of Mockus was to harmonize the three regulatory systems displayed in table 1. In order to promote the ideas that the well-being of the collective is as important as that of the individual, and that people should voluntarily respect norms of coexistence, his administration developed a series of programs and actions, which are described below.

(a) Traffic Mimes and Behavior Cards: Respect for Others and Collective Well-Being

A large number of traffic violations, with the corresponding traffic accidents and rampant corruption among the traffic police, were a widespread problem in Bogotá. Rather than hiring more traffic officers, the Mockus administration hired 'traffic mimes' (mostly young actors and students of the dramatic arts), whose task was not to mete out fines to traffic offenders but to motivate citizens to behave in a more civic way. Initially, 20 traffic mimes shadowed pedestrians who did not follow road-crossing rules. A pedestrian who ran across the road instead of using a nearby pedestrian crossing would be tracked by a mime who mocked his every move. Later on, more than 400 traffic mimes stood at major street intersections and admonished, with extravagant gestures, any bus or car drivers who ran red lights, who failed to stop at pedestrian crossings, or parked on sidewalks. With time, many *Bogotanos* became terrified of being caught by a traffic mime because they did not want to experience social shame. In a further measure to tackle traffic violations, citizens were asked to put their social regulatory power to use with 350,000 'thumbs-up' and 'thumbs-down' cards that the Mayor's office distributed. The cards were to be displayed at the moment that a citizen approved or disapproved of another's behavior; it was a device that many people actively—and peacefully—used in the streets. The aim of these cards was a peaceful solution to law violations by invoking co-responsibility and self-regulation. Whereas the 'thumbs-up' cards awarded social recognition, the 'thumbs-down' card dispensed social shame.

Fig. 1: Traffic mimes were used by the Mockus administration to motivate traffic offenders to behave in a more civic way. Photograph © Danita Echeverry.

(b) 'Knights of the Zebra' and Road Stars: Social Recognition and Self-Regulation

Being robbed, abused, or kidnapped by a taxi driver used to be a serious security issue in Bogotá. The Mayor asked city residents to call his office if they found an honest taxi driver and provide his/her contact details. The Mayor's office organized a meeting with these taxi drivers, who were named by the Mayor "Knights of the Zebra" (for zebra crossing) and awarded a windshield sticker. Clients gave preference to taxi drivers who had such a windshield sticker. The intended effect of the 'Knight of the Zebra' measure was to raise consciousness among taxi drivers that taxi service is an instrument of collaboration between the drivers and their clients. A further measure adopted by the Mayor's office was to paint large yellow stars on the street spots where somebody had been killed in a road accident. By 1996, some five years later, 1500 such stars had been painted on Bogotá's streets. This measure clearly aimed at mobilizing the self-regulatory system: fear of guilt every time one sees a star and also the satisfaction of obeying one's own conscience when driving carefully.

(c) The 'Carrot Law' and the Women's Night:
Learning from Women and Protecting Life

Mockus's office proclaimed the 'Carrot Law,' from the Colombian slang for someone who is 'not cool,' by demanding that every bar and entertainment locale close at 1 a.m., with the goal of diminishing drinking, violence, and traffic accidents. Further, it proclaimed a 'Women's Night' program, which consisted of turning over the city's public spaces to its female residents. On specific Friday nights, women were encouraged to go out and take over the city's public spaces. Men were asked to voluntarily stay at home. Many women went out, flocking to free open-air concerts. They flooded into bars, pedestrian zones, and streets to celebrate their night. When they saw a man stay-ing at home or taking care of children they applauded. The idea of creating a Women's Night was based on statistical evidence that men are more likely than women to commit violence and that men are forty times more likely to be its victims. The Women's Night was intended as an opportunity for city residents to see what can be learned from women's forms of social organization and also to protect men from themselves. The program results showed that violence on Women's Nights was 40% lower than on ordinary Friday nights.

(d) Struggle against Police Corruption, Community Policing,
and Reduction of the Number of Guns

In his struggle against corruption, Mockus's administration closed down the traffic police because many of its 2,000 members were notoriously corrupt. Mayor Mockus reduced the corruption involved in policing the transit system by transferring this task from the police under the Secretary of Transit and Transport to the Metropolitan Police, which is directly subordinated to the National Police. At the same time, a system of community policing was created. The aim was to bring the community and the police closer together through the creation of Schools of Civic Security and local security fronts (cf. Camacho, "Reforma"). The creation of the schools and the fronts responded to the civic ideal of promoting community organization. A further measure was the 'Vaccine against Violence.' The Mayor's office mobilized city residents to protest against violence. They invented a 'Vaccine against Violence,' asking people to draw the faces of the people who had hurt them on balloons, and then purposefully to burst the balloons by inserting pins. About 50,000 people participated in this campaign. A further campaign started in 1995 with the aim of reducing the number of guns in the street by promoting voluntary disarmament. Industry owners and the international community supported the campaign through embassies that donated gift bonuses to the citizens who voluntarily handed over their guns. The 2,538 guns that the City Hall collected were melted, and the metal was used to produce spoons for children. The spoons bore the inscription "I was a gun." As will be explained in the following, these campaigns and measures, along with the other programs described above, contributed to strengthening awareness of violence and to significantly reducing the number of homicides.

(e) Fiscal Discipline and Reducing Water Consumption

Another aspect of building a culture of citizenship is what the Administration termed 'tributary culture.' In 2002, 63,000 individuals, households, and enterprises voluntarily paid 10% more taxes. The pedagogical objective was to link social policy as well as infrastructure development and maintenance to the taxes paid by citizens (cf. Mockus, "Advancing"). Further, during a drought, Mockus appeared in a television commercial taking a shower and asking citizens to turn off the water as they soaped. The aim of the campaign was to raise awareness of responsible use of water and how the individual can contribute to collective well-being. The campaign was followed by a 50% reduction in the use of drinking water.

(f) Culture at the Park

By the mid 1990s, there were few public festivities taking place in Bogotá's public spaces, mainly because of the citizen's fear of criminality and urban violence. Public spaces, however, were seen by Mockus's Administration as key sites for the mobilization of the culture of citizenship. Therefore, in 1995, the Institute for the Promotion of Culture and Tourism (IDCT) supported the initiative of a young group of *Bogotanos* to convene a rock festival involving several urban groups. The idea was to expand on the Youth Music Meetings held at the city's Planetarium in 1992. Thus, the first "Rock at the Park" festival took place in 1995. This festival initiative eventually became a wider policy known as "La cultura al parque" (cf. López Borbón). Parks and squares were upgraded to allow free public concerts in a variety of musical genres, such as jazz, salsa, opera, reggae, rap, and hip-hop. The festival takes place over three days at Bogotá's Simon Bolivar Park. The 'Culture at the Park' policy allowed people of different age groups and/or socio-economic levels to congregate in spaces where they share a common musical or artistic interest.

Fig. 2: Hip-hop at the park 2005 (Institute for the Promotion
of Culture and Tourism [IDCT], Bogotá).

*(g) Observatory of the Culture of Citizenship: Supporting and Monitoring
Policy Formulation*

Mockus's Administration identified the necessity of having well-founded studies on
Bogotá's urban violence problems, of supporting policy formulation, and of monitoring
the progress of the culture of citizenship programs. For that purpose, an Observatory of
the Culture of Citizenship was created in 1996. At the core of the Observatory was a
small group of qualified professionals who worked in close cooperation with university academics. The Observatory defined three priority research topics: violence and
crime, quality of urban life, and cultural supply and demand, which were jointly
investigated by members of the Observatory and of a variety of academic institutions.
The Observatory carried out more than 50 studies on the three priority topics, conducted several public opinion surveys on the Administration's actions and programs,
and published a newsletter (*Boletin de violencia y delincuencia*) disseminating
statistics on violence and criminality in Bogotá. This newsletter was the result of a
conscious effort between several public institutions to create the city's first information system providing periodic and reliable information on issues of urban violence
and criminality. This required cooperation between a network of government agencies,
such as the Attorney General's office, police, forensic medicine, hospitals, and public
health institutions. The periodic publication of crime statistics, followed by institutional efforts to involve the business community, led to an active participation of the
private sector in the solution to the problems. The Chamber of Commerce started

conducting periodic surveys of crime perceptions that were made public. The well-respected Fundación Corona and the Chamber of Commerce periodically reviewed results of the Administration in areas such as education, finances, and crime (Cámara de Comercio, *Bogotá*). Besides generating an information system, the Observatory also designed and applied a means to measure and thus to quantify the effects of the culture of citizenship programs.

Did the pedagogical efforts make a difference? Based on the information produced by the Observatory of the Culture of Citizenship, the Mayor's office undertook a study on the effects of the 'culture of citizenship' programs, which was published by the Interamerican Development Bank (cf. Mockus, *Cultura*). According to this study, before the beginning of the *cultura ciudadana* campaign, the homicide rate was 80 per 100,000 inhabitants (i.e., about 3,500 people killed each year). Less than a decade later, the rate had dropped to 22 per 100,000 inhabitants. Besides, a 20% reduction in the number of deaths caused by traffic accidents (from 25 to 20 per 100,000 inhabitants) was also achieved. The study showed that as a result of the campaign efforts, many drivers and pedestrians improved their civic behavior, showed more respect for others, and became more obedient to traffic rules. For example, before the campaign only 26% of drivers and pedestrians respected conventional traffic signs. In 1996 this percentage rose to 75%. The mimes program to promote respect for citizens using zebra crossings was highly effective: Citizens began asking others to use zebra crossings, and by 1996, 76% of drivers and 73% of pedestrians were systematically respecting and using such crossings. Overall, Bogotá's residents approved of the Administration's programs, giving them a rating of 7 out of 10 points. 61% said citizen education was the Administration's most important initiative, and 96% considered that these programs should continue (cf. Secretaría de Gobierno). Many of the measures towards reducing urban violence and promoting urban coexistence have been replicated in other cities of the country.

1.2. Building a Shared Image of the City: Public Space and Public Transport

Enrique Peñalosa, an economist (Duke University) and public administrator (International Institute of Public Administration, Paris), and also a politically independent candidate, was elected mayor in 1997. Public space and transport were the main priorities of his Administration. His approach to urban governance was based on the idea of an egalitarian city where all citizens enjoy equal access to public spaces, services, and facilities. Peñalosa believed that public spaces are one of the only environments where all citizens, regardless of income, can meet as equals:

> Parks, plazas, pedestrian streets are essential for social justice. High quality sidewalks are a most basic element for a democratic city. It is frequent that images of high-rises and highways are used to portray the advance of a city. In fact, in urban terms, a city is more civilized ... when a child on a tricycle is able to move about with ease and safety. (n.p.)

As he believed that the most essential roles of public spaces are to give citizens a sense of belonging and to create a more socially integrated community, he promoted a city model giving priority to children and restricting the use of private cars in public spaces.

Peñalosa inherited the city in a good financial state from the former two administrations (Castro's and Mockus's), and also benefited from significant proceeds from the privatization of the city's electrical power company. Thus, he was able to carry out massive investments in building sidewalks, bicycle pathways, pedestrian streets, greenways, parks, and public libraries. Up until the mid-1990s, sidewalks were practically unusable in many parts of the city, mostly because cars would park right up against storefronts, making it impossible for pedestrians to walk along the sidewalks. Many store-owners saw the sidewalks as parking spaces for their businesses. Mockus's Administration had already spotted the problem and interpreted it as a lack of a sense of citizenship, and initiated a program to restore the public character of sidewalks. This also became a main priority of Peñalosa's Administration, which installed thousands of physical barriers designed to stop cars from parking on the sidewalks. Store-owners reacted violently to the barriers and Mayor Peñalosa was almost impeached. The Defence of Public Space Office was created to recover space that had been illegally occupied, and space for pedestrians was substantially renovated through improvements in sidewalks, traffic signals, lighting, and the planting of trees. Furthermore, *ciclovías* were also implemented, consisting of the temporary closing of some main streets for cars (Sundays and holidays from 7 a.m. to 2 p.m.) in order for runners, skaters, and bicyclists to take over car lanes (cf. fig. 3).

Fig. 3: *Ciclovías* allow runners, skaters, and bicyclists to take over car lanes on Sundays. Photograph © Mike Ceaser.

Bogotá's weekly *ciclovías* are used by 30% of the citizens on over 120 km of car-free streets (cf. Hernández). The joint efforts of Peñalosa's and Mockus's Administrations

tions bore fruit, as it is now common to see people strolling down sidewalks and using pedestrian crossings in an orderly fashion (cf. Concha-Eastman).

Perhaps the best-known project of Peñalosa's Administration is the building of TransMilenio, a modern bus network including fixed bus stops (a novelty to Bogotá) and road lanes designated exclusively for public transport. Modeled on the successful schemes in Quito, Ecuador, and Curitiba, Brazil, it opened to the public in December 2000 and now moves 1.4 million people daily (cf. Hidalgo). Before TransMilenio, Bogotá's mass-transport system consisted of thousands of independently operated and uncoordinated buses that used all available lanes and stopped to pick up or let off passengers at any point they desired, even in the middle lanes of busy roads. Traffic chaos was the result. Private owners operated old buses that emitted enormous amounts of exhaust gas, thus significantly polluting the air. The goal of the TransMilenio transit system was to provide a well-organized, efficient, and more ecological means of public transport. New TransMilenio lines have been added gradually over the years, and today 9 lines run throughout the city, a length of 84 kilometers, linking with subway and bicycle paths. Overall the TransMilenio system has reduced commuting times by 32% (cf. Hidalgo), and it is widely regarded as a vast improvement over Bogotá's previous public transit system.

Another of Mayor Peñalosa's priorities was to reduce the number of automobiles on the road and thereby to reduce air pollution. For this purpose, he introduced the *'pico y placa'* program (*pico* refers to peak traffic hours and *placa* to license plate number), whereby private cars are prohibited from driving at rush hour on two days of the week, according to the last digit in their license plates.

Fig. 4: TransMilenio: Bogotá's mass transport system.
Photograph © Peter Danielsson, World Resources Institute.

This scheme has considerably reduced congestion at peak times and lowered private automobile use (cf. Montezuma). In addition to this measure, the Peñalosa Administration invited Bogotá's residents to imagine how the city would be without cars. On 29 February, 2000, Bogotá held its first (and the world's largest) Car-Free Day. It proved to be so popular that citizens voted in a citywide referendum to make it an annual event. In addition, Peñalosa convinced the City Council to increase the tax on gasoline. Half of the revenues generated by the increase were then invested in the TransMilenio bus system. Further activities by Peñalosa's Administration included the creation of the Urban Land Reform Institute, the building of more than a hundred nurseries for children under five, and the installation of computers in all public schools, including connections to the Internet and three large new libraries.

2. Scope and Challenges of Governance Approaches in Bogotá (1995-2005)

What were the main achievements of the Mockus and Peñalosa Administrations? Besides the specific achievements described above, there are two main areas that can be considered especially innovative regarding urban governance in a Latin American context. First of all, the governance policies were based on the idea that tackling urban problems requires a comprehensive approach. Thus, reforms were carried out in the police, legal, educational, and cultural systems. These programs and reforms were conducted through intense inter-institutional cooperation and partnerships between several public agencies, thus ensuring the effectiveness of their implementation. Second, and most importantly, changes were made to the political sphere. Owing to the fact that Mockus and Peñalosa did not represent any of the traditional parties, they were able to produce profound changes in the way of conducting politics in urban areas in Colombia: moving away from patronage and *clientelismo* and the virtual absence of citizen participation. By breaking the traditional clientelistic relationship that existed in Bogotá between the mayor and the members of the City Council, they were able to introduce a model of urban governance based on citizen participation and to render processes of planning and decision-making more transparent. Also, they were able to choose the best-qualified professionals as members of their staff rather than appointing individuals for political reasons. This resulted in a more professional style of urban governance, which in turn reduced corruption, increased staff efficiency, and improved surveillance of contracts awarded to the private sector.

Although at the end of the two Administrations much remained to be done regarding participatory governance, the following two Administrations of Luis Eduardo Garzón (2004-2007) and Samuel Moreno Rojas (2008-2011) were able to build on their predecessors' approaches. Nevertheless, several challenges remain. Bogotá is a large and complex city characterized by great socio-economic disparity among its residents. Although Bogotá is one of the largest industrial centers in Latin America, the unemployment rate reached 11.3% in 2008, and 33% of the population were affected by underemployment (cf. Cámara de Comercio de Bogotá, "Comportamiento"). The National Department of Statistics (DANE 2009, "Encuesta") estimates that the income of a third of Bogotá's households is insufficient to cover their basic needs and that nearly two thirds of the city's households earn barely enough to cover their basic needs. The World Bank estimates that Bogotá has over 1400 low-income *barrios* housing 22% of its population (cf. Fainboim). The population of the *barrios* continues to increase owing to the influx of people fleeing poverty and violence in rural areas of the country. According to the Foundation National Forum for Colombia (2006), in the period 1999-2005 more than 260,000 people migrated to Bogotá as a result of displacement, about 3.8% of the total population of Bogotá. The need to improve the lot of Bogotá's low-income population was the clear message that city residents conveyed when they elected the past two mayors, Luis Eduardo Garzón and Samuel Moreno, both belonging to the left-leaning Alternative Democratic Pole party. Moreno and Rojas had a clear agenda of addressing the social issues of poverty and social exclusion and have strived over the past five years to improve the living conditions in Bogotá's most deprived areas. However, this understandable emphasis has meant that programs to continue promoting a culture of citizenship have been somewhat neglected. At the same time, Mayor Samuel Moreno is increasingly facing criticism owing to his lack of results in terms of urban security and traffic improvement as well as on accusations of corruption when contracting public works. The Attorney General's office has started an investigation on these allegations. Finally, it needs to be taken into account that the future of Bogotá depends not only on the policies of its mayors and on local dynamics, but also on the general situation and political dynamics of a country affected by problems of fiscal crisis, economic recession, unemployment, organized crime as well as guerrilla and paramilitary warfare.

At this point, it is worthwhile to reflect on the factors that made Bogotá's transformation possible. Clearly, any city is embedded in its national context, and changes taking place at the local level may reflect wider changes. Thus, Bogotá's transformation was possible owing to a combination of national and local factors. At the national level, the process of decentralization that took place in Colombia in the 1990s made it possible to elect candidates who were politically independent and thus to introduce innovations in the way that cities were governed. Without this political development at the national level, local changes in Bogotá would not have been possible. However, it is interesting to note that, although politically independent mayors were elected in other Colombian cities and many innovative measures were implemented, the scope of local transformations was more limited than that achieved in Bogotá. This is for example the case with the city of Cali, where Rodrigo Guerrero was elected mayor in 1992. At the time, the city was in the midst of a wave of mafia-related violence. Guerrero, a physician and epidemiologist (Harvard University, U.S.A.) and also a university professor, argued that social disintegration was a main reason for the large murder rate. His DESEPAZ program—*Desarrollo, seguridad y paz* ["Development, Security, and Peace"]—followed a public health approach aimed at reducing crime by controlling risk factors in the city. The program was successful in reducing the number of murders in Cali, thus inspiring candidates who were then running for the position of mayors elsewhere, such as Antanas Mockus in Bogotá. Unfortunately, Cali's DESEPAZ program was abandoned after Guerrero left office. Thus, although Cali and Bogotá had similar policies to counteract urban violence, Bogotá was able to maintain the policies for a longer period of time than Cali. Also, the reduction of murders observable in Bogotá was of a greater magnitude than reductions in Cali or other major capital cities (cf. Guerrero). According to Mayor Guerrero himself, the explanation for Cali's inability to maintain the policies over a longer period of time is due to the lack of political will of the municipal authorities. At this point, it also needs to be recalled that the characteristics of Cali's and Bogotá's urban violence were very different. Whereas in Cali the problem of urban violence was to a large extent characterized by the violent activities of mafia cartel criminality, no such cartels existed in Bogotá, and violence was a social problem largely resulting from the negative relationship of citizens to their city and from their poverty. Possibly, Bogotá's type of violence was less challenging for city administrators to tackle than mafia violence.

Finally, another important factor in Bogotá's case is the continuity and complementarity that existed between the urban governance approaches of the three Administrations (Castro, Mockus, and Peñalosa) in office during the 1992-2003 period. Jaime Castro's Administration created the instruments that allowed the city to increase its revenues and to open the door for civil society to participate in the city's decision-making processes. Mockus continued Castro's policies and educated the citizens to become more respectful of each other and to view culture as non-violence. Building on the fiscal savings of the two former Administrations and the education programs led by Mockus, Peñalosa was able to move a step further and carry out significant investments in mass transportation, restricting private car use and improving public space. Clearly, long-term continuity is an essential factor in sustainable urban governance.

3. Conclusion

The city of Bogotá has experienced a dramatic transformation in recent years regarding its quality of life and the relationship of the citizens to their city. While in the 1990s residents viewed their city as a place characterized by panic, intolerance, and hate, a decade later residents were proud to live in Bogotá, and they were more inclined to respect each other and participate in development plans. Quality of life had significantly improved as urban violence had decreased. An efficient public transportation system had been created and public space and cultural activities had been expanded.

Bogotá's transformation between 1995 and 2005 yields important practical and theoretical lessons. At the practical level of implementation, several cities have tried to replicate Bogotá's model. This paper has argued that the urban governance approaches implemented by Bogotá's mayors during the 1995-2005 period are unique, for four main reasons. First of all, they are formulated from a perspective that prioritizes social coexistence rather than economic profit. In contrast, other Latin American cities have been governed according to the principles of a cultural economy that see and use culture and ethnicity as valuable marketing products. Second, rather than tackling urban violence from a repressive perspective, the mayors in Bogotá have emphasized that reducing crime and violence is also a matter of education and culture. Third, the approaches implemented in the city of Bogotá were embedded in a political process of decentralization, which made it possible to move away from clientelism and the general lack of citizen participation. Finally, the interventions of Bogotá's mayors during the period of study have been comprehensive, including reform of the police, establishment of legal, educational, and cultural systems, and they have been implemented within the framework of multi-sectoral partnerships. However, in spite of its many successes, the city of Bogotá still faces many challenges particularly in the area of poverty and social exclusion. Thus, the election of the last two mayors in the past five years reflects a consensus regarding the importance of fighting poverty. Evaluations of their programs to combat poverty are urgently needed. It is also imperative to carefully analyze and attempt to explain current developments at the Mayor's office.

The case of Bogotá's transformation during the 1995-2005 period is also important at the theoretical level because it reveals issues that still need attention regarding the concepts of culture and citizenship. As Rojas argues, the concept of the culture of citizenship developed by Mockus has the strength that it treats culture not as something 'given,' but as something resulting from a process of regulation between individuals. What is also interesting about this concept is that it allows culture to be understood not as customs inherited from the past but as practices in the making. Further, it demonstrates that citizenship is a quality that needs to be learned. Such a pedagogical perspective allows us to expand current notions of social citizenship, which are confined around discussions on rights and political struggle (cf. Marshall; Yuval-Davies/Werbner). Further theoretical reflections on issues of culture, citizenship, and the city are a promising avenue for future research.

Works Cited

Almond, Gabriel, and Sidney Verba. *The Civic Culture: Political Attitudes and Democracy in Five Nations*. Princeton: Princeton UP, 1963.

Angell, Alan, Pamela Lowden, and Rosemary Thorp. *Decentralizing Development: The Political Economy of Institutional Change in Colombia and Chile*. Oxford: Oxford UP, 2001.

Ardila Gómez, Arturo. "Bogotá." *Cityscapes: Latin America and Beyond*. Special issue of *ReVista: Harvard Review of Latin America*. David Rockefeller Center for Latin American Studies, 2003. <http://www.drclas.harvard.edu/revista/articles/view/561>.

Camacho, Alvaro. "Ciudades sin ciudadanos." *Lecturas Dominicales El Tiempo*. Bogotá, 15 July 1996.

———. "Reforma de la policía: Realidades inmediatas y objetivos estratégicos." *Análisis Político* 19 (1999): 3-20.

Cámara de Comercio de Bogotá. *Bogotá, cómo vamos: Cambios en la calidad de vida de la ciudad 2000-2002*. Fundación Corona. Bogotá: Casa Editorial El Tiempo, 2003.

———. "Comportamiento del mercado de trabajo en Bogotá." *Observatorio Mercado de Trabajo* 22 (2008). Bogotá: Dirección de Estudios e Investigaciones de la Vicepresidencia de Gestión Cívica y Social, 2008.

Concha-Eastman, Alberto. "Ten Years of Successful Violence Reduction Program in Bogotá, Colombia." *Preventing Violence: From Global Perspectives to National Action*. Ed. Clare McVeigh, Karen Hughes, Clare Lushey, and Mark A. Bellis. Liverpool: Centre for Public Health, Liverpool John Moores University, 2005. 13-18.

DANE. *Colombia: Proyecciones de población departamentales por area*. Bogotá: Departamento Administrativo Nacional de Estadística, 2009.

———. *Encuesta de calidad de vida 2008: Resultados generales por regiones*. Bogotá: Departamento Administrativo Nacional de Estadística, 2009.

Fainboim, Israel. *Colombia Urban Services Projects*. World Bank Report. Washington, D.C., 2004.

Foundation National Forum for Colombia. "Pobreza y exclusión social en Bogotá, Medellin y Cali." *Foro Debates* 5. Bogotá: Fundación Foro Nacional por Colombia, 2006.

Guerrero, Rodrigo. "Violence Prevention through Multi-Sectoral Partnerships: The Cases of Cali and Bogotá, Colombia." *African Safety Promotion* 4.2 (2006): 88-98.

Hernandez, Javier C. "Car-Free Streets, a Colombian Export, Inspire Debate." *The New York Times* 24 June 2008.

Hidalgo, Darío. "Why is Transmilenio Still so Special?" *The City Fix: Sustainable Urban Mobility*. 2008. <http://thecityfix.com/why-is-transmilenio-still-so-special>.

López Borbón, Liliana. "Políticas culturales orientadas al plano de la vida cotidiana: Evaluación de las estrategias de comunicación del programa de Cultura Ciudadana (Bogotá, 1995-1997)." 2001. <http://bibliotecavirtual.clacso.org.ar/ar/libros/becas/2000/lopez.pdf>.

Marshall, Thomas Humphrey. *Citizenship and Social Class, and Other Essays*. Cambridge: Cambridge UP, 1950.

Mockus, Antanas. *Cultura ciudadana, programa contra la violencia en Santa Fé de Bogotá, Colombia, 1995-1997: Estudio Técnico*. Inter-American Development Bank SOC-127. Washington, D.C.: Inter-American Development Bank, 2001.

———. "Bogotá: ¿cohesión social vía innovación? Cultura ciudadana y espacio público: Motivaciones y regulaciones." Paper presented at the *Encuentro de representantes de gobiernos sub-nacionales de la Unión Europea y de América Latina: Lecciones y experiencias del programa URB-AL*. Rosario, Argentina, 2007.

———. "Advancing against Violence in Bogotá: Creating Civic Agency and 'Cultural Change': The Case of Bogotá." 2004. <http://www.paho.org/English%5CAD%5CFCH %5CCA/BogotaViolence.pdf>.

Montezuma, Ricardo. "The Transformation of Bogotá, Colombia 1995-2000: Investing in Citizenship and Urban Mobility." *Global Urban Development* 1.1 (2005): 1-10.

Peñalosa, Enrique. "Social and Environmental Sustainability in Cities." *International Mayors Forum, China.* 2004. <http://www.efchina.org/csepupfiles/workshop/2006102695218836. 5224720074849.pdf/Penalosa-Sustainable_Cities-EN.pdf>.

Pérgolis, J.C. *Bogotá fragmentada: Cultura y espacio urbano a fines del siglo XX.* Bogotá: TM Editores and Universidad Piloto de Colombia, 1998.

Rojas, Cristina. "Decentralization and the Culture of Citizenship in Bogotá, Colombia." *Citizens in Charge: Managing Local Budgets in East Asia and Latin America.* Ed. Isabel Licha. Washington, D.C.: Inter-American Development Bank, 2004. 291-328.

Secretaría de Gobierno. *Seguridad y convivencia en Bogotá: Cómo se logró disminuir la violencia y la delincuencia, 1995-2001.* Bogotá: Secretaría de Gobierno, 2002.

Sommer, Doris. "Introduction: Wiggle Room." *Cultural Agency in the Americas.* Ed. Sommer. Durham and London: Duke UP, 2006. 1-28.

Yuval-Davis, Nira, and Pnina Werbner, eds. *Women, Citizenship and Difference.* London and New York: Zed Books, 1999.

Film Analysis as Cultural Analysis: The Construction of Ethnic Identities in *Amores Perros*

RAINER WINTER AND SEBASTIAN NESTLER

1. The Practices of Films

Since the 1980s, Cultural Studies has helped to transform the academic study of film by linking textual analysis with the observation of various forms of reception and also with ethnographic audience research. The conception of deriving the viewer's positions from the structure of the media texts gives way to a qualitative treatment of the 'real' audience. It is thus from their experiences and practices that the affective and meaningful potentials of the media text can unfold (cf. Winter, *Filmsoziologie*; *Das Kino der Gesellschaft*). In so doing, Cultural Studies deals with films as they are embedded within the larger cultural and historical contexts in which they have an impact on the world.

On the one hand, film is a product of cultural and social processes; on the other, it plays an active role in these very processes (cf. Gunning 186). A constitutive characteristic of Cultural Studies approaches is their common starting point: social practices, social relationships and constructions. It is in these practices, relationships and constructions that objects, events, and experiences gain their social relevance and significance in the first place. The Cartesian subject-object paradigm, which characterizes some approaches in film studies, postulates an abstract, hypothetical viewer who is intended to be representative of all viewers. This, however, is decisively called into question and ultimately dismissed. Accordingly, the focus of analysis is shifted to the practices of film, i.e., all practices within the context of film as well as their interactions with other cultural, economic, and social practices. Essentialist opinions, the dominant aspect in some parts of film theory, are thus surrendered and interest shifts towards the history and sociology of changing film practices. These practices are understood as dynamic processes of production and performance, as relations, or as "verbs" (cf. Denzin, "Ein Schritt"). In the theory of practice, we speak of "culture in action" (cf. Hörning/Reuter). Relating to film, this means that it is not considered as an isolated text—as in some parts of semiotics—or, correspondingly, as a cognitive mentality—as in neo-formalistic film theory. Rather, we are concerned here with the normal uses and regular practices dealing with film texts. Practices as distinguished and schooled forms of acting and speaking routinely draw on existing stocks of knowledge, not only unfolding them but also starting new processes of interpretation and configuration through the competent use of knowledge (cf. Hörning, "Kulturelle

Kollisionen"). In this way, films present a social reality which is created interactively in the action, in the field of production, circulation, reception, and appropriation. The textual characteristics of genre films, for instance, which make them recognizable and predictable, are the result and the medium of 'doing genre' by various agents in various contexts (cf. Tudor; Winter, *Filmsoziologie*).

For film analysis, this means that cultural, political, and sociological contexts define the production as well as the experience of films. The focus of analysis is thus not—at least not in the first place—on the individual subject who receives a film, but rather on the culturally attuned, repeating practices dealing with the film and the social results of interpretation (cf. Winter, *Der produktive Zuschauer*; Staiger; Mikos), e.g., the influences of viewing within a group in a certain place, reviews in newspapers, online fan discourses, or even discussions after viewing in a circle of friends or in a classroom. Just by speaking about a film, certain meanings can become central while others can be pushed into the background. Thus, shared interpretations develop, which may help to solve puzzling elements or ambiguities of the film's plot. An essential characteristic of these practices is that they recur. However, they can never reproduce the past identically, but are bound to "reproduction of a situation in another context under another signature" (Hörning, "Soziale Praxis" 34, our translation). The repeated viewing of a film, for instance, produces differences in perception and in experience. If this process is enjoyed over and over again, a film can become a cult film.

Against this backdrop, as Tom Gunning (cf. 192) suggests, a film can be understood as a palimpsest into which the traces of varied and versatile film practices have been written. Even if the viewing is already anticipated in the production process, the processes of viewing and appropriation are complex, contradictory, varied, and often unpredictable.[1] This is because the post-modern subject has different socially constructed and performed identities (cf. Denzin, *Symbolic Interactionism* viii; Zima), which are constituted in various cultural practices. Categories like class, ethnicity, age, or gender account for practices of production and performance in which differences are articulated while forms of social and cultural inequality are reproduced as well as discussed.

A film can thus be interpreted in different ways by the same person in various contexts, depending on whichever aspect of their identity is being staged. By watching a film, viewers can change their perspectives and so the framing of the film. Likewise, different subject positions concerning, for example, gender or ethnic issues can be addressed. This is in line with a conclusion drawn by Georg Seesslen: "The postmodern work of art is a type of schizophrenia machine, which can address very different people with different expectations as well as one person at the same time in very different ways" (138, our translation). In the course of interacting with films,

---

[1] The studies by Richard Maltby show that this is why the film practices in Hollywood do not aim at a definite interpretation of a film text, but rather aim at a variety of interpretations in various (local) contexts.

subjectivity is constructed. This, however, is irrevocably linked to medial representations.

Next, we would like to consider these processes of contextualization more closely and investigate the film analysis of Cultural Studies more deeply, which is pursued mainly in the framework of critical media pedagogy, which aims at reading films for their possible political meaning, thus deriving from them a set of pedagogical interventions. Incorporating these theoretical impulses, we will then contextualize and analyze the film *Amores Perros* from an ethnic perspective.

2.   Film Analysis as Cultural Intervention: Cultural Studies and Critical Pedagogy

Critical media pedagogy, which was primarily developed in the U.S.A. (cf. Winter, "Kultur"; Wimmer), regards films as cultural practices and events in which political debates and social conflicts are expressed. Thus, their analysis allows access to cultural, social, and historical contexts which are already written into the practices or are produced by them. In this way, we can show how forms of cultural policy and arrangements of social representation are expressed in everyday life, how they are maintained through (hegemonic) patterns of meaning, and how they can be discussed and transformed by (pedagogical) interventions in the shape of analyses, interpretations, and conversations about films.

The medium film not only serves the purpose of entertainment, but can also educate, as Henry A. Giroux (cf. 3) asserts. By expressing political ideologies and cultural values, films become matters of public discussion. In terms of pedagogical processes it can also be shown how films, understood as social practices, shape everyday life by allocating, for example, certain subject positions or by reflecting and staging the post-modern subject in audio-visual, dramaturgical representations (cf. Denzin, *Images* viii). New, alternative interpretations can intervene in these processes, question them, and broaden the space for self-formation. This applies in particular to the fields of gender and ethnic belonging. Representations of gender or ethnic identity should be scrutinized in (complementary) analyses. This can demonstrate that identities are never 'naturally' given but can be transformed in everyday practice. Popular films can be understood as a form of public pedagogy which, according to Douglas Kellner (*Cinema Wars*), creates the opportunity to question and challenge current politics of representation and to look for social alternatives. Deconstructive analysis should read films against the grain in order to reveal their polysemic structure and the possibilities of rearticulation in reception and appropriation (cf. Winter, "Filmanalyse"). We react to the public pedagogy of Hollywood with committed analysis and discussions with young people, students, and addressed groups, by means of which possible, everyday versions of films should be identified, alternatives developed, and counter-narratives initiated. Giroux as well as Kellner thus highlight that film analysis should not isolate individual aspects; they should rather, according to Fredric Jameson, be regarded as social and political allegories, which do not gain their meaning as separate texts but in the network of social practices, of cultural debates, and of institutional formations. One of critical pedagogy's concerns is thus to examine how films relate to cultural and social transformations and communicate with them, how they express fears, apprehensions, sexism, and political doubt as well as hope and utopia. Moreover, the analysis of popular films from a critical media pedagogy's point of view also offers the chance to partake in society's dialogue with itself and, according to John Dewey, to put democracy further into action. Discussing films creates or broadens public spaces in which enjoyment, reflection, and the ability to act can enter a fruitful synthesis. As Henry Giroux points out, film offers room for discussions which can connect questions of personal experience, politics, and public life with those of greater social impact.

A pedagogically orientated film analysis tries to understand social conflicts and discourse to which the audience should be sensitized. The educational intention of a critical media pedagogy aims at the teaching of skills through the deconstruction of cultural texts with the intention of raising the viewer's ability to act (cf. Kellner, *Media Culture*; Winter, *Medienkultur*). Thereby, any analysis of film is partially and perspectively constructed and can be revised or questioned at any time (cf. Giroux 13).

One analysis we carried out was that of *V for Vendetta*, which showed the potential that cultural analysis of popular films carries within it as a method of critical pedagogy (cf. Nestler/Winter). In this film, current social discourses of surveillance and control society, of media spectacles, and of terrorism appear in transcoded form (cf. Kellner, *Media Culture*; *Media Spectacle*). The film articulates risks, dangers, and fears but also refers to social discourses of hope, change, and transcendence as they are expressed, for example, at the beginning of the 21st century in the course of social movements for global justice.

Thus, *V for Vendetta* shows aspects of utopia. By staging themes like difference, the telling of infamous stories, or the unmasking of power, it visualizes the possibility of forms of resistance in totalitarian regimes. Thereby, it broaches the issue of deviance from socially defined normality, be it another religion, a different sexual orientation, or diverse political and cultural thinking: In the film, the totalitarian regime vigorously opposes all these forms, because they express a resistant potential of difference. Therefore, communication is controlled and censored in as many areas of life as possible or even cut off in the first place. These mechanisms of control, however, prove increasingly less successful because the main figure V understands that criticism of power must take place within the field of power itself. He takes advantage of the communication strategies of the system and circumvents them by means of his subversive tactics.

The double metaphor of the mask plays a central role here. By masking himself, V does not only hide his true identity, meaning that he cannot be found and therefore escapes his arrest. He furthermore succeeds in unmasking as false the established truth, namely the ideology of the current system. V uses his mask against the mask of the system. At the end of the film, thousands of equally disguised people remove their masks and are unveiled as different individuals. This illustrates the victory of diversity over leveling. Finally, by referring to the notion of 'multitude' in the sense of Michael Hardt and Toni Negri, it shows the victory of 'love,' the affective communitization, which is the engine of utopia, over the paranoid controlling ideology of the regime.

Our analysis of *V for Vendetta* thus reveals the perspectives of a pedagogically motivated film analysis which allows for discussions of social and cultural contexts that would otherwise be difficult to initiate. By means of this method, we also manage to preserve the notion of utopia, the imagination of another world, to chart a differentiated image of it, and to put to use its potential of hope for democratic practices as well as for an alternative future of society. In our analysis, which itself is a form of 'doing cinema,' we have considered the popular film reflexively. Unlike positivistic methods, we are no longer distant and indifferent researchers, i.e., the subject facing the object of examination, but we are rather observers who are taking part, experiencing, and who are also able to change in the course of observation and the subsequent discussion because the dominant description of the work is unstable and fluid. The reflexive analysis of this particular film opens the space of a utopia because it reveals alternatives to the establishment and, at least in the realm of the recipient's imagination, it creates a palpable chance of realizing these alternatives. It also makes evident that the meaning of a film is an embattled terrain on which cultural and social debates, which are neither determined in the direction of utopia nor in the direction of the dominant ideology, never cease.

In this way, popular films with their polysemic representations, which are given meaning to in the processual interaction with the viewer, can give insight into social and cultural dimensions, which otherwise would scarcely be possible (cf. Denzin, "Reading Film" 426). Norman Denzin thus declares: "Films are cultural and symbolic forms and can be used to discover and reveal important characteristics of social life" ("Reading Film" 428). Film analysis becomes cultural analysis, which also offers pedagogic opportunities for intervention and, as demonstrated by Douglas Kellner in his analysis of American films (cf. *Media Culture*; *Cinema Wars*), can run into a diagnostic criticism of social ideologies. The narratives of films can be linked with one's own stories and experiences as well as with qualitative-ethnographic investigations with the aim of grasping, understanding, and possibly breaking the spell of those all-embracing cultural narrations which shape our lives (cf. Denzin, *Images* 157).

3.   Film Analysis as Cultural Analysis:
The Construction of Ethnicity in *Amores Perros*

In the following, we will analyze *Amores Perros* whose (commercial) success is attributed to its complexity, intricate narrative structure, and visual persuasiveness. When we analyze this film with a view on the representation of ethnic identities, we place a perspective at the center which touches an important theme of the film, namely the question of Mexican identity. What does it mean to be a Mexican in Mexico City, in a polycentric megacity full of contrast and conflict, social and ethnic differences, in which life becomes an "anthropological experiment" as director Iñárritu said in Cannes in 2000 (qtd. in Smith 14)? It is precisely this question of *mexicanidad* which is given central significance in the artistic, intellectual, and political life of Mexico, because the experience of national identity is shaped by the tension between its European roots in the Old World and its establishment in the New World, which places it in a permanent crisis of identity (cf. Berg). One can thus understand our analysis as an offer to reflect on the construction of subjectivity in social and cultural practices and to understand ethnicity as a social field of staging and performance. In this way, the film can be experienced as a social practice which articulates current political, social, and cultural conflicts. Our interpretation is thus a practice in the context of this film, which can be connected with other practices of a political, social, and cultural nature. With our interpretation we thus encroach upon the space of self-formation and hope to open up new spaces of contemplation and discussion. This is an intervention in the sense of a critical media pedagogy, which can in this case initiate scrutiny and review of essentialist concepts of ethnic identity. These processes can of course also occur without pedagogical assistance in the everyday interaction during and after the viewing of the film.

Here, we understand *Amores Perros* as an analytical instrument, which can reveal to us something about certain social configurations, processes, and movements like the construction of ethnic identities and their increasingly fragmented character in the process of globalization. In the film itself, however, this questioning is subordinate to the aim of telling a story as excitingly and effectively as possible. A deconstructive reading, however, turns to the margins, subtexts, and other subordinated elements in order to be able to reveal opportunities of rearticulation and of change, of resistance, transition, and empowerment.

For us, an important theoretical starting point is the notion of 'polycentric multiculturalism,' a term coined by Ella Shohat and Robert Stam. They develop it in contrast to liberal multiculturalism in order to stress how cultural identities are embedded in relations of power. Shohat's and Stam's sympathy applies to the disenfranchised and marginalized, whose voices were or still are oppressed in the media. Against this backdrop, we are interested in whether the film succeeds in crossing dominant representations and if it is able to scrutinize Eurocentric ethnic stereotypes, prejudices, and clichés in their 'naturalness' through their re-enactment understood as performative subversions in the sense of Judith Butler. Finally, we would like to find out if the film can possibly initiate a rethinking of those stereotypes, prejudices, and clichés.

The notion of polycentrism also opposes that of Eurocentrism. This is done along an axis of contrasts, namely those of East/West and North/South, whereby the West and the North occupy privileged positions in contrast to the East and the South. Admittedly, this axis is determined arbitrarily, but nevertheless it is very powerful, because it leads to an essentialization of (ethnic) identities. However, it cannot be assumed that Europe is 'the West' because Europe itself exhibits a synthesis of different cultures. This applies all the more in the context of globalization, which reveals every essentialist conception of culture as a delusion (cf. Shohat/Stam 14f.; Hall, "The Question"). As a consequence, a strategy of the construction of identities (or communities) is to represent them as stable units and to suppress difference. In contrast, polycentric multiculturalism considers identities as historically and socially situated, as diverse and modifiable, as products of differentiated and complex processes of identification.

Furthermore, Eurocentrism is closely linked to colonialism and to racist doctrines. When it comes to normalizing and naturalizing racism, everyday practices of implicit racism, such as language use and media production, are of particular significance (cf. Hall,"The Whites"; Shohat/Stam 18). In line with the findings of Shohat and Stam, who claim that it can sometimes be more revealing to deconstruct the stereotyper rather than the stereotypes (cf. 21), we will investigate to what extent the staging of certain ethnic identities can be regarded as a form of performative subversions. Therefore, we understand *Amores Perros* as a film of the 'Third Cinema,' a form of cinema which, in a sensual-carnivalesque way, negotiates the conception of the western-dominant (Hollywood) cinema (cf. Shohat/Stam 27-30). Seen in this light, the film appears as a subversive pleasure (cf. Stam), which does not allow for an essentialist reading but rather plays with the hybridity and the tension between cultural homogenization and heterogenization inherent within it. This pleasure always keeps an eye on the contest for power from the perspective of the social periphery and marginalization. It can thus empower by deconstructing and rejecting essentialist and oppressing forms of identity as well as by opening spaces of dialogue and of cultural exchange, in which identity is newly negotiated and viewed as transformable.

Amores Perros provides us with a view into a microcosm of conflictive ethnic identities, through which the film, by using Mexico City as a stage, also highlights dramaturgically the contrasts between the different personal destinies in this anonymous urban world. Above all, it tells the story of three individual destinies: that of Octavio, who, along with his friend Jorge, engages in dogfights trying to earn enough money in order to change his life. While not exactly poor, he is relatively underprivileged and willing to risk a new beginning in another town. He would like to lead his new life with Susana, the current wife of his brother, Ramiro. It is even Ramiro's dog, Cofi, whom Octavio (ab)uses, trying to earn money. These circumstances alone provide enough cause for conflict. But the situation becomes even more intense, since all three live with Octavio and Ramiro's very religious mother.[2] Moreover, Octavio and Jorge tangle with their opponents at the dogfights to such an extent that they make attempts on their lives. We see that these characters belong to an underprivileged social class. They have minimal financial means at their disposal and only a basic education, which prevents them from extensively analyzing and decisively changing their lives.[3] More-

---

[2] In the family flat there is a portrait of Pope John Paul II, next to the ubiquitous icons of Mary as indicators of the religiousness of the mother. Furthermore, she is shown as deeply conservative in terms of family values and a gender-specific division of roles.

[3] Susana is an exception to this. Although she must care for her child and her husband, Ramiro, she also attends secondary school in order to be able to lead a life which offers her

over, they are defined through ethnic aspects. By representing them as dark-skinned Mexicans, Iñárritu produces a link between marginalization and ethnic identity.

In contrast to this, the film presents a wealthy 'white' family: Daniel, Julieta, and their two children. Iñárritu thus plays with primordial elements, such as skin color, and physiognomy, and places these in direct relation to social symbols of wealth like, for example, a luxury car, expensive clothes or a large flat. As we learn in the course of the film, Daniel has an extramarital affair with a model, Valeria, whose family has links with Spain. Even here, the connection between a privileged life and Europe as well as a white skin color is established. Their 'colorlessness' makes them the normative starting point for the definition of a hierarchy of ethnic groups (cf. Dyer). In order to live with Valeria, Daniel ultimately leaves his family.

Finally, we meet El Chivo, who occupies a special role. He lives on the streets with a pack of dogs as, in fact, he is not without means. On a regular basis he takes on a contract as a professional killer, but his apparent homelessness helps him to conceal his identity and to avoid arrest. In earlier times, El Chivo led a bourgeois life: he lived with a wife and daughter, until he decided to give up this existence and henceforth to fight as a left-wing guerrilla. He then got arrested, spent 20 years in jail, and, after his release, opted for his current way of life. El Chivo appears quite dark-skinned. However, towards the end of the film, he decides to once more begin a new life and to carry out another transformation of his identity.

All these extremely different worlds exist basically alongside one another in regularized daily normality, and it is not until a fateful car accident that these worlds collide. Octavio and Jorge are on the run, pursued wildly by their dogfight opponents, while Valeria is driving through town in order to go shopping. At a crossroads their two cars ultimately crash into each other and El Chivo witnesses the accident. This accident tears all those involved from what until now has been their normality: Octavio survives seriously injured, while his friend Jorge dies. Valeria's leg is so seriously injured that it has to be amputated later on, which puts an end to her model career. This, in turn, puts tension on her relationship with Daniel who, in a few moments, fluctuates between his wife Julieta and Valeria. El Chivo changes from a mere witness to a participant when he saves Cofi, the dog, from Octavio's car and accepts him into his 'dog family.' This, however, will plunge him into a crisis as well: Having been raised as a fighting dog, Cofi, after recovering from the crash, kills all the other dogs of the pack. The accident confronts all the characters, who are also linked by the fact that they are all dog owners, with the problem of reflecting on and redefining their own—not only ethnic—identities.

Yet, except for El Chivo, they do not, or rather only to a very limited extent, succeed at re-defining their lives. Octavio, badly marked by the accident, has to

---

more alternatives. This is even more difficult for her, as she gets no support from her family: her mother is an alcoholic and there is no father (figure) presented in the film. Additionally, she must defend herself against accusations from her mother-in-law that she does not sufficiently care for her child and husband.

abandon his plans of beginning a new life with Susana. Not only have Susana and her husband Ramiro plundered Octavio's hidden stash of money, but Ramiro is also shot dead by a guard in a bank robbery. In the end, Susana does not want to leave with Octavio anymore. The life of Daniel and Valeria also continues less happily than expected. Valeria loses her leg and with it her carefree existence as a model, which makes her tense and aggressive. When, to make matters worse, her dog, Richie, becomes the trigger for a serious fight, Daniel and Valeria's relationship is on the brink. The film, however, does not provide a clue as to whether they stay together or not. El Chivo is the only one who understands how to handle his identity crisis, by reinventing himself once more. Cofi almost gets killed by El Chivo for having annihilated his dog pack. Yet, El Chivo decides to spare Cofi's life and to give up his existence as a professional killer. He renames Cofi to Blackie and starts a new life. Consequently, he also changes his appearance significantly. He cuts his hair and his fingernails; he shaves and starts wearing his glasses again. By doing so, he no longer appears as 'dark,' but rather as an upper-class businessman. The film ends with El Chivo and Cofi/Blackie heading off into the sunset with a bag full of money—El Chivo's 'income' and his money from the sale of the cars of two potential victims, whom he, in the end, did not kill. But even though El Chivo now seems almost bourgeois again, it is clear to him that he cannot continue his earlier life as a family father.

We can thus say that El Chivo, at least as far as the film tells us, is indeed the only one who successfully weathers his identity crisis and manages to create a new identity. A decisive reason for this may be that he actively created new identities throughout his whole life and does not see any single one as guaranteed and unchangeable: from the bourgeois family man to the guerrilla, from the prisoner to the professional killer, and now on to something new, whatever this will be. Octavio and Valeria, on the other hand, seem scarcely able to handle the crisis. Most notably, Valeria seems to struggle with the new situation. This is particularly tragic because she has fallen the furthest from her mostly privileged previous life. She must accept that her European background, symbolized by her skin color and her Spanish accent, cannot guarantee her any existential security.

In this way, *Amores Perros* successfully shows that we have to submit Eurocentrism, and with it all essentialist identity concepts, to a far-reaching criticism. Because neither are ethnic identities so one-dimensional and essential as Eurocentrism suggests, nor can it guarantee a socially, politically, and culturally privileged position. The film's use of ethnic stereotypes in this case is therefore a performative subversion of current ethnic clichés, because it confuses rather than confirms certain ideas of ethnicity. It is clear that there is no pre-existing identity (cf. Butler 141), which can define which ethnic identity is true or false. Thus, the film debunks "the boundaries of the body as the limits of the socially hegemonic" (Butler 131)—as the limits of a strategy whose aim it is to immunize the vulnerable periphery of each identity against disruptions which challenge the hegemony. Precisely this challenge reveals that the hegemony is not the 'natural' order but rather a construct—and at times a very fragile one. Its challenge therefore also shifts the meaning and need of its order, which is always concerned with coherence, in order to hide discontinuations, which are the actual normality (cf. Butler 133-34). Otherwise, the regulating ideal would reveal itself as norm and fiction (cf. Butler 135-36).

Amores Perros demonstrates the performances through which (ethnic) identity is produced, whereby the illusion of an inner core organizing an identity (cf. Butler 135-36) is revealed. Our ideas of the 'true essence' of a certain identity are thus unmasked "as the truth effects of a discourse of primary and stable identity" (Butler 136), which allows us to finally recognize that there is no 'truth' in identity, no ahistorical core that would define it. Rather identity must be understood as personal/cultural history of assumed meanings (cf. Butler 138). Even when the relationships between single moments of an identity are arbitrary in the end, they are in no way free from balances of power, but are always embedded into systems of constraint. This shows us, once again, that identity is indeed negotiable, and that these negotiations of identity signify a struggle for power—which can also be lost. In this sense, Iñárritu brings his characters to and sometimes beyond their limits, which they experience painfully.

Finally, in regard to the cultural dimensions of identity, the car accident in *Amores Perros* can be understood as a metaphor for globalization. Globalization questions all securely held identities and challenges us to actively and creatively form new ones, which escape essentialist concepts. In this sense, those involved in the accident no longer appear as autonomous subjects who have full sovereignty over their identity. Rather, they each become what Stuart Hall describes as 'a decentred subject', i.e., a dispersal of the subject over a series of breaches in the discourses of modern knowledge (cf. "The Question"), which brings with it a variety of paradoxes and ambivalences. This dispersal also has effects on national and ethnical identities, which can no longer be seen as 'natural' but rather as imagined and constructed (cf. "The Question").

Thus, all those involved in the accident are torn out of their previous identities. Here they learn, for example, that a particular ethnic background, in this case Valeria's European roots, cannot guarantee a privileged position in society. This certainty is nothing more than an illusion. Similarly, as the discourses of modern knowledge disperse the autonomy of the subject, Valeria is torn from her securely held existence by Octavio. Read metaphorically, the West here loses its sole hegemony and defining power, so it is no longer in the position of presenting itself as consistent and homogenous. By staging the dialectical interplay between the various ethnic identities, *Amores Perros* confirms what Hall had predicted for globalization, namely that globalization would prove itself as a part of the slow and uneven but perpetual story of the decentralization of the West, although in many ways it first gained its power from the West (cf. "The Question").

4. Conclusion

The starting point of our deliberations was a plea for the sociological consideration of film, which, like historical analysis, questions abstract and universal conceptions of the viewer. As we have tried to show, it should start from the social context of 'doing cinema.' Thus, not only the processes of production but also those of reception and acquisition must be considered as practices which are in no way passive. In them, the images and sounds of a film are (newly) created and the meanings of the film text are actively produced. The interest of a film analysis inspired by Cultural Studies should be directed to the social practices and relationships of 'doing cinema' which in no way excludes differentiated analyses of films and their potential meanings.

Cultural Studies show that, first and foremost, popular films can be socially relevant, as we have shown in the example of *Amores Perros*. By means of our contextualization, we were able to demonstrate that this film, regarding ethnic identities, not only criticizes the hegemonic position of the West, as it is expressed in the concept of Eurocentrism, but simultaneously deconstructs it in the sense of the concept of polycentrism. *Amores Perros* stages certain stereotypical preconceptions about certain ethnicities in Mexican society, but does not confirm them by doing so. Instead, the film scrutinizes them critically. In *Amores Perros* (ethnic) identities are displayed not as essential facts but rather as discussable and negotiable, if nonetheless powerful cultural, social, and political constructions.

Popular films and their analysis can thus have interventionist effects. In the sense of Cultural Studies, they allow people to approach knowledge, even if they are not bound in the circle of academic knowledge production. Films come with the potential of making complex issues easily accessible as well as understandable through images and their montage, without bereaving them of their ambivalence, their ambiguity, and their inner contradictions (cf. Nestler, "Die Dezentrierung"). In films, the complexity of social and cultural debates can be expressed in a transcoded form. From this perspective, Sam Fuller's statement in Jean-Luc Godard's *Pierrot le Fou* has been proven true: "Film is a battleground."

Works Cited

Berg, Charles Ramirez. *Cinema of Solitude: A Critical Study of Mexican Film 1967-1983.* Austin: U of Texas P, 1992.

Butler, Judith. *Gender Trouble: Feminism and the Subversion of Identity.* New York: Routledge, 1990.

Denzin, Norman K. *Images of Postmodern Society: Social Theory and Contemporary Cinema.* London: Sage, 1991.

———. *Symbolic Interactionism and Cultural Studies: The Politics of Interpretation.* Oxford: Blackwell, 1992.

————. "Ein Schritt voran mit den Cultural Studies." *Widerspenstige Kulturen: Cultural Studies als Herausforderung.* Ed. Karl H. Hörning and Rainer Winter. Frankfurt/M.: Suhrkamp, 1999. 116-45.

————. "Reading Film: Filme und Videos als sozialwissenschaftliches Erfahrungsmaterial." *Qualitative Forschung: Ein Handbuch.* Ed. Uwe Flick. Reinbek: Rowohlt, 2000. 416-28.

Dyer, Richard. *White.* London: Routledge, 1997.

Giroux, Henry A. *Breaking in to the Movies: Film and the Culture of Politics.* Malden: Blackwell, 2002.

Gunning, Tom. "Film Studies." *The Sage Handbook of Cultural Analysis.* Ed. Tony Bennett and John Frow. London: Sage, 2008. 185-205.

Hall, Stuart. "The Whites of Their Eyes: Racist Ideologies and the Media." *Silver Linings: Some Strategies for the Eighties: Contribution to the Communist University of London.* Ed. George Bridges and Rosalind Brunt. London: Lawrence and Wishart, 1981. 28-52.

————. "The Question of Identity." *Modernity and Its Futures.* Ed. Hall, David Held, and Tony McGrew. Milton Keynes: Polity P and The Open University, 1992. 273-316.

Hardt, Michael, and Antonio Negri. *Multitude: War and Democracy in the Age of Empire.* New York: Penguin, 2004.

Hörning, Karl H. "Kulturelle Kollisionen: Die Soziologie vor neuen Aufgaben." *Widerspenstige Kulturen: Cultural Studies als Herausforderung.* Ed. Hörning and Rainer Winter. Frankfurt/M.: Suhrkamp, 1999. 84-115.

————. "Soziale Praxis zwischen Beharrung und Neuschöpfung: Ein Erkenntnis- und Theorieproblem." *Doing Culture: Neue Positionen zum Verhältnis von Kultur und sozialer Praxis.* Ed. Hörning and Julia Reuter. Bielefeld: transcript, 2004. 19-39.

————, and Julia Reuter. "Doing Culture: Kultur als Praxis." *Doing Culture: Neue Positionen zum Verhältnis von Kultur und sozialer Praxis.* Ed. Hörning and Reuter. Bielefeld: transcript, 2004. 9-15.

Jameson, Fredric. *The Geopolitical Aesthetic: Cinema and Space in the World System.* Bloomington: Indiana UP, 1992.

Kellner, Douglas. *Media Culture: Cultural Studies, Identity, and Politics Between the Modern and the Postmodern.* London: Routledge, 1995.

————. *Media Spectacle and the Crisis of Democracy: Terrorism, War, and Election Battles.* Boulder: Paradigm, 2005.

————. *Cinema Wars: Hollywood Film and Politics in the Bush-Cheney Era.* Oxford: Blackwell, 2010.

Mai, Manfred, and Rainer Winter, eds. *Das Kino der Gesellschaft—die Gesellschaft des Kinos: Interdisziplinäre Positionen, Analysen und Zugän*ge. Köln: Herbert von Halem, 2006.

Maltby, Richard. *Hollywood Cinema: An Introduction.* Oxford: Blackwell, 1996.

Mikos, Lothar. "Film und Fankulturen." *Das Kino der Gesellschaft—die Gesellschaft des Kinos: Interdisziplinäre Positionen, Analysen und Zugänge.* Ed. Manfred Mai and Rainer Winter. Köln: Herbert von Halem, 2006. 95-116.

Nestler, Sebastian. "Die Dezentrierung des Weste(r)ns: Zum Begriff fragmentierter Iden-
titäten in Jim Jarmuschs *Dead Man*." *Das Kino der Gesellschaft—die Gesellschaft des
Kinos: Interdisziplinäre Positionen, Analysen und Zugänge*. Ed. Manfred Mai and Rainer
Winter. Köln: Herbert von Halem, 2006. 289-306.

————, and Rainer Winter. "Utopie im Film—*V for Vendetta*." *Gesellschaft im Film*. Ed.
Markus Schroer. Konstanz: UVK, 2008. 309-332.

Seesslen, Georg. *David Lynch und seine Filme*. Marburg: Schüren, 1994.

Shohat, Ella, and Robert Stam. *Unthinking Eurocentrism: Multiculturalism and the Media*.
London: Routledge, 1994.

Smith, Paul Julian. *Amores Perros*. London: BFI, 2003.

Staiger, Janet. *Perverse Spectators: The Practices of Film Reception*. New York: New York
UP, 2000.

Stam, Robert. *Subversive Pleasures: Bakhtin, Cultural Criticism and Film*. Baltimore: Johns
Hopkins UP, 1989.

Tudor, Andrew. *Monsters and Mad Scientist: A Cultural History of the Horror Movie*.
Oxford: Blackwell, 1989.

Wimmer, Jeffrey. "Henry A. Giroux: Kritische Medienpädagogik und Medienaktivismus."
Schlüsselwerke der Cultural Studies. Ed. Andreas Hepp, Friedrich Krotz, and Tanja
Thomas. Wiesbaden: VS Verlag, 2009. 189-99.

Winter, Rainer. *Filmsoziologie: Eine Einführung in das Verhältnis von Film, Kultur und
Gesellschaft*. München: Quintessenz, 1992.

————. *Der produktive Zuschauer: Medienaneignung als kultureller und ästhetischer Prozess*.
München: Quintessenz, 1995.

————. *Die Kunst des Eigensinns: Cultural Studies als Kritik der Macht*. Weilerswist: Vel-
brück Wissenschaft, 2001.

————. "Filmanalyse in der Perspektive der Cultural Studies." *Film- und Photoanalyse in der
Erziehungswissenschaft*. Ed. Yvonne Ehrenspeck and Burkhard Schäffer. Opladen: Leske
& Budrich, 2003. 151-64.

————. "Die Filmtheorie und die Herausforderung durch den 'perversen Zuschauer':
Kontexte, Dekonstruktionen und Interpretationen." *Das Kino der Gesellschaft—die Gesellschaft des Kinos*. Ed. Manfred Mai and Winter. Köln: Herbert von Halem, 2006. 79-
84.

————, ed. *Medienkultur, Kritik und Demokratie: Der Douglas Kellner Reader*. Köln:
Herbert von Halem, 2005.

————. "Kultur, Reflexivität und das Projekt einer kritischen Pädagogik." *Cultural Studies
und Pädagogik: Kritische Interventionen*. Ed. Paul Mecheril and Monika Witsch. Bielefeld: transcript, 2006. 21-50.

Zima, Peter V. *Theorie des Subjekts: Subjektivität und Identität zwischen Moderne und Post-
moderne*. Tübingen: Francke, 2000.

Filmography

Amores Perros. Dir. Alejandro González Iñárritu. Lions Gate, 2000.

Pierrot le Fou. Dir. Jean-Luc Godard. Société Nouvelle de Cinématographie, 1965.

V for Vendetta. Dir. James McTeigue. Warner Bros., 2005.

Globalization and Transnational Place Identity along the U.S.-Mexico Border

LAWRENCE A. HERZOG

The U.S.-Mexico border represents a regional laboratory in which to study the processes of culture clash and ethnic intersection in an era of globalization. One way of understanding these processes of globally-driven cultural integration is by exploring place identity. In this essay, I explore some of the dimensions of what I term 'transnational place identity' in the bi-cultural setting of the United States-Mexico border region. This 2000-mile zone along the border between northern Mexico and the southwestern United States is a vibrant place that is constantly being reinvented. I will argue that the place identity of this region is best understood by analyzing slices of the 'transfrontier metropolis,' a prototype for the bifurcated urbanized culture regions that have formed along this giant international frontier.[1]

It is generally accepted that a critical driver of global change is economic. If regions are able to develop economies that can compete in the global economic system, those regions will prosper. But, in a globalizing world, economic space is dramatically shifting, changing the entire landscape. Along the border, those shifts have to do with the injection of specific kinds of border space (commerce, tourism, etc.) into the global economy.

Seen from above, the U.S.-Mexico border evokes a hard landscape of arid desert, mountains, canyons, and plateaus, suddenly interrupted by two distinct cultures that have slowly imposed their will on the natural environment.

The border is a study in contrast—a place that for centuries was what one historian called the "land of sunshine, adobe and silence" (Lummis 3), yet suddenly in the modern age, this border became a zone of attraction, growth, industry, and cities. This rapid transformation, in some ways, serves as a defining measure of the border's identity—a place of change, experimentation, and hybridization.[2] These changes express themselves continually across a range of measures—art, music, literature, architecture, and the informal or vernacular landscape. In fact, one distinguishing feature of

---

[1] The concept of the 'transfrontier metropolis' was first introduced in my 1990 book *Where North Meets South.*

[2] The idea of U.S.-Mexico border hybridity is developed in Dear/LeClerc.

the U.S.-Mexico border is the prodigious outpouring of creative expressions of its meaning as a place.[3]

The border is, above all, a life space; it is not merely a transition zone between two nations whose center lies somewhere else; the border has become its own center—of production, trade, and the formation of cities. The border has its own unique culture.

One feature of the transnational border landscape lies in the different ways in which urban space and territory are created north and south of the border. On one side (south), the periphery is a social landscape largely defined by uncertainty, inequality, spontaneity, and lack of formal government intervention. Across the border to the north, the landscape is more formal, orderly, framed by laws and codes and planning permits, a far less spontaneous place, a product of modernist urban planning. The quality of place north of the border is mediated by privilege, and tends to be dominated by private interests. The quality of place south of the border is defined by struggle and chaos. North of the border, the periphery tends to house the upper end of the social ladder. South of the border, the opposite is true—the periphery is where the poor, marginalized residents live in spontaneous squatter conditions.

These differences also define the place identity of the U.S.-Mexico frontier region. However, despite different socio-economic conditions, culture and politics overlap here. The global economy has increasingly brought North and South together into a single daily urban system. To grasp the essence of this global transnational space, I will argue that we need to view the border region through the lens of a set of 'ecologies' that increasingly define it as a place and increasingly also define its fluid, constantly changing landscape. Several of these ecologies are explored below.

1.   Ecology of the Global Factory

The idea of a global factory—or export processing zone—dates back to the 1960s, but its legacy along the U.S.-Mexico border took hold in the 1970s, 1980s, and 1990s. In many ways, the global factory is a metaphor of sorts—for the idea of a region inherently shaped by outside forces—industrial investors or national governments negotiating treaties, deals, and tax breaks. As a whole, they form a kind of exogenous decision making that would remake the lives of millions. This inherent dependence on outside forces is a legacy of the border. Historically, the border has been a place shaped by outsiders—from its early transformation by outside investors, later by immigrants, and then by a variety of global economic forces in the modern era. This has also made the U.S.-Mexico border region a place in a constant state of flux—and subject to cycles of change and new forces, which, like the *maquila* ["assembly plant"]

---

[3]   For example, numerous art exhibitions have highlighted the U.S.-Mexico border region. They include a project called "InSite" along the California-Mexico border. A huge array of films has been made about this region.

can take shape, adjust, reinvent themselves and move on. This makes the border region an inherently malleable if not protean place.

For more than a century, however, the border region remained distant from the political and economic centers of power in the U.S. and Mexico, and thus was viewed as a somewhat marginal region, a risky place for investment. But, by the second half of the 20th century, new global actors legitimized the region as a place for serious investment.

It has been argued that assembly plants forever changed the region's image as the 'red light district' on the edge of the U.S. Perhaps. But *maquilas* are a risky strategy to build a region's economy around, since they are tied to the global economy and to the whim of investors. They also depend heavily on lightly regulated labor and environmental laws, which are part of the attraction to outsiders. The recession of the late 2000s demonstrates the fragility of the border region's export-based economy. With massive unemployment on the U.S. side, and less industrial inventory being produced by U.S. companies, the attractions of cheap labor enclaves in Mexico have diminished for now. The border economy once again struggles.

But one has to acknowledge that the 'global factory' is one of the great global shifts of late 20th-century world capitalism. As labor costs impinged on profits among multi-national firms in the 1950s and 1960s, the idea of global cheap labor enclaves emerged. Firms discovered they could simply move the factory floor to a less developed nation. 'Third-World' countries suddenly loomed as the new industrial labor pools for global industrial giants. Thus was born the global factory.

Mexico quickly became a key player through the so-called 'twin plant' or *maquiladora* project. In the 1960s, Mexico's government hatched a new federal office to promote border economic expansion—it was known as PRONAF, the National Frontier Program. The biggest plank in the PRONAF development strategy was reduction of unemployment through industrial growth. In 1965, the Border Industrial Program (BIP) was introduced. It built on the emerging 'off shore' production concepts that U.S. manufacturers had already started in places like Hong Kong or Taiwan. The BIP project envisioned foreign-owned (mainly American) factories relocating their labor-intensive assembly operations to the Mexican border.

Since the first *maquilas* sprung up on the border around 1970, their numbers grew exponentially—from about 160 (with 20,000 workers) to an estimated 2,400 assembly plants in Mexico, employing nearly three quarter million workers 25 years later. By the 1990s, the *maquila* sector contributed between three and four billion dollars per year to Mexico's economy. The plants were foreign-owned; the big new global actors came mainly from the U.S., Japan, South Korea, Canada and Germany.

These assembly plant complexes created a huge growth catalyst that anchored the already powerful demographic boom of the U.S.-Mexico border in the last four decades of the 20th century. *Maquila* parks generated growth poles around which huge new suburban developments dramatically transformed the geography of border zones. Along with new roads, sewers, and other infrastructure, global factories produced larger multiplier effects, which brought office complexes, shopping centers, multi- and single family housing subdivisions to employ millions who would work in the factories or other sectors (real estate, finance, insurance, schools, etc.) that grew as a result. More migrants arrived, fueled both by the hope for jobs north of the border, or the fallback option of a job in a global factory.

The factory complexes also changed the cultural landscape of border towns. They added a more pristine, 'modern' and manicured look to the previously spontaneous, unplanned geography of border cities. They were not unlike industrial parks north of the border—drawing from textbook industrial design features such as uniform lot sizes, street setbacks, and controlled landscaping. They added other 'modern' features—including high tech security and sprawling parking lots. Often surrounded by poor *colonias*, the new industrial parks typify the continued social polarization of border cities between affluent and poor.

2.   Spaces of Consumerism

The border's history is defined by consumerism, dating back to its liberation in the 1920s as an outlet for American consumers seeking a place where the morality laws north of the border from that era could be avoided. The result in Mexico was the proliferation of bars, brothels, and distilleries in the 1920s, and the eventual birth of a border commerce economy. One can say that the border's role as an edge between two cultures historically generated a certain buzz in defining comparative advantages for products and services across those distinct cultures. Over time, this 'edge' has also pushed entrepreneurs to experiment with different kinds of marketing strategies, leading to innovation.

But the border's intense focus on consumerism also has a down side. As sociologists have pointed out, giant corporations (fast food, coffee, soft drinks, etc.) benefit from building a "culture ideology of consumerism" (Sklair 129), in which, through advertising, safe, homogenous products are sold all over the planet. Part of the success in marketing these commodities globally can be traced to corporate strategies to homogenize consumer tastes. By constructing globally uniform consumer behavior (through advertising and construction of recognizable images), multinational corporations can better control the marketing of their products.

However, it is now clear that this ideology is not merely product-driven, but place-driven as well. Along the border, this place-driven, consumerist ideology has threatened to obliterate the local and to replace the border landscape with corporate spaces controlled from beyond the region. Place-based homogeneity can be seen in the form of border shopping malls, fast food restaurants, hotels, resorts, and other urban spaces.

Shopping malls in China, Ireland, Peru, or Mexico tend to have identical designs. Malls have a standardized site plan and design concept, which includes 'anchor' stores, public areas for walking and sitting, food courts, movie theaters, and restaurants. Further, there is a growing trend in renting space to global chain stores that sell clothing, electronics, and other consumer goods. Hotels and resorts often use standardized designs as well. Indeed, many corporate hotel chains believe that travelers like the predictable, familiar designs of hotel chains in the United States and Western Europe, and thus seek to replicate those designs in other cultural settings.

These designs are not merely limited to buildings. The new public spaces of the 21st century are generic designs reproduced along the border—privatized streets, festival marketplaces, or giant mall complexes. Increasingly, these consumer spaces seek to replace the traditional downtown as the primary pedestrian-scale gathering place for post-modern city dwellers.

Along the international border, the dominance of a U.S.-driven culture of consumerism has been intensified by the 'free trade culture' of the 1990s. Following the signing of the North American Free Trade Agreement (NAFTA) around that time, a surge of new fast food outlets arrived, virtually overnight. In the span of just a few years, all of the global fast food chains—McDonald's, Carl's Jr., Burger King, Domino's Pizza, etc.—burst onto the urban landscape. Meanwhile, fueled by NAFTA boosterism and a climate of investment, an array of commercial centers of different sizes sprung up in most border cities. From Tijuana to Mexicali, Nogales and Nuevo Laredo, these mini-malls began to challenge the original pedestrian scale of border communities, since the new commercial buildings were set back from the sidewalk, while parking lots stood in front.

The regional shopping mall also found its way into border towns, were none had existed. Mexican consumers proved to be as loyal to the 'mall world' as citizens north of the border. Indeed, it could be argued that captive Mexican audiences were influenced by either U.S. advertising itself along the border, or U.S.-style advertising, which is copied across the planet, and certainly in nearby Mexico. For decades, Mexican buyers have 'learned' to consume through the U.S.-controlled media, American movies, television, magazines, and, now, websites. As a result, Mexicans living along the border have proven to be highly motivated customers on the U.S. side. In southern California, for example, research shows that Mexican consumers get the same or better information about products, and often know the markets north of the border better than California residents (cf. Herzog, *Aztec*).

Border cities display what landscape writer J.B. Jackson once called "other-directed space," that is, places that are constructed not for local city dwellers but as stage sets for outsiders (visitors). Border commercial streets are set up to create an ambience American tourists expect to find a place where they can let their imagination run loose about what Mexico might mean to them. This stage set is purposefully artificial as a way of playfully creating an open canvas for outsiders.

Universal Studios in Los Angeles has packaged this idea of 'commodified streets' into a giant prototype of the future—a new fake mall called City Walk, literally a shopping center disguised as a series of real streets. However, this kind of artificiality does not end at the border—even the sacred colonial, historic centers of Mexico are no longer free from global commerce. Mexico City's historic center and its surrounding neighborhoods are also filled with examples of global consumerism—illustrated by the post-NAFTA boom of Blockbusters, 7-11s and other globally owned franchises.

3. Tourism Enclaves

Tourism poses an important global ecology in the border region. It is a force that inherently implies the creation of separate enclaves, theatrical spaces of consumption that are defined, not always by the real identity of the place, but by an imagined identity that is manufactured and marketed by global advertising firms to pull in the largest market of consumers.

A central premise of tourism design is the manipulation of visitors' experience of place to maximize profit. Global tourism investors and corporate decision makers tend to view regions as stage sets for generating profit, rather than as genuine places whose identity should be protected. Thus the 'sense of place' produced by architecture for the visitor industry tends toward what one writer calls the 'tourist gaze,' in effect, a landscape socially constructed for a targeted population (cf. Urry).[4]

Tourism developers tend to build homogenous, recognizable, easily consumed built environment experiences for their client populations. Controlled resort structures with familiar designs (oceanfront boardwalks, small clustered shopping and restaurant complexes, hotels, fast food outlets, global boutiques) have become the central pillars of tourism landscape design. The value of tourist space is measured by its marketability for short-term tourism visits, rather than by its cultural uniqueness or environmental purity.

As with product marketing, global companies want to standardize the tourism experience. Large-scale tourism resort developments, based on uniform design criteria, are not crafted with the local environment in mind, which is why they are often not sustainable.[5] The tourism industry, controlled from international headquarters in wealthy nations, tends to promote distorted images of 'Third-World' nations like Mexico, the main destinations of their clients. Global tourism firms have little interest in portraying nations as they really are. In most cases, social conditions like poverty are downplayed, and many local customs and practices are not designed into the tourist experience, unless they are profitable in some way.

Along the U.S.-Mexico border, the rich cultural integration of Mexico and the U.S. is compromised by the corporatized control exerted over tourism development. In Tijuana, Mexico, for example, the main commercial street in the old downtown tourism

---

[4] The 'tourist gaze' has been compared to Foucault's 'medical gaze,' a strategy of controlled design aimed at a different economic interest group—consumers of medical services and facilities (cf. Urry).

[5] Proponents of sustainable development point out that 'bioregionalism'—the relationship between settlement formation and nature—must be one of the anchors of economic growth (cf., e.g., Pena).

district—Revolution Avenue—is a striking example of a manipulated, commodified space. Revolution Avenue is to Tijuana what Main Street, U.S.A. is to Disneyland—an artificial promenade that sets the mood for a carefully choreographed experience. In Disneyland, visitors park their car and walk across the parking lot, through the entrance gates, and onto Main Street, a theatrical stage set, built at 4/5 scale, and lined with costumed characters, from Mickey Mouse to a Barbershop Quartet. In Tijuana, tourists park their cars in vast lots just north of the border, cross the pedestrian entrance into Mexico, and move along a path that leads them into Revolution Avenue.

Mexicans laugh at the choreography and scenography of this electronic corridor of tourist destinations. In boom times, it was crowded and hyperactive. In post-9/11 borderlands, it has struggled. At the edge of Revolution Ave. sits an abandoned theme park, Mexitlan, perhaps a victim of border entrepreneurialism that was out of control. Mexitlan was a theme park created to celebrate Mexico in miniature—its architecture, history, and culture. It did not last. Some have wondered why it failed as a business. Perhaps the border experience led Americans to arrive in border towns, seeking, not a theme park of real Mexican culture, but a place to create their own fantasy of what Mexico is or of what the border is, and not be given a map or a guide by someone else. When it opened, the entrance fee was close to 20 dollars, then lowered to 10, 8, 5 dollars, and finally it shut down completely after only a few years of existence.

Tourism breeds 'enclavism,' the creation of isolated zones for visitors, buffered from the everyday city, to allow the outsider's fantasy of the place to remain distinct from its reality, which is usually less exotic. Along the beachfront, just south of Tijuana lies an excellent example of an enclave: the village of Puerto Popotla, near the town of Rosarito. Popotla was once a small fishing village of less than 100 residents. The Hollywood film company Twentieth Century Fox leased land adjacent to the village to build a major studio—Fox Baja Studios—for film production in the mid-1990s. The first film was *Titanic*; its enormous global success has had ripple effects on this zone of Baja California. The *Titanic* facilities consisted of imposing, massive, ugly gray metal warehouses, and a giant concrete wall surrounding the site, which townspeople have dubbed 'the Berlin wall.' The film production facilities completely dwarf the fishing village and evoke the feeling of a prison: security around the site is extremely tight, with high walls and a guardhouse.

Here 'enclavism' takes an interesting form: a 'movie maquiladora,' or an 'assembly plant for film making.'[6] This enclave has also brought environmental degradation to the Tijuana/Baja coastline. During construction, underwater explosives may have been used to grade the beach area and to build several giant pools for the *Titanic* filming, causing destruction of marine life for kilometers around the site. Further, according to some observers, during filming the company dumped chlorine into the pool and emptied its tanks in the ocean, allowing the chlorine to seep into the kelp beds and nearby ecology.

---

[6]   This idea is explored in the documentary *Factory of Dreams*.

4.   Post-NAFTA Social Geography

The traditional social geography of Mexican border towns reveals an inverse model of the U.S. pattern. In Mexico, wealthy residents cluster in older established neighborhoods adjacent to downtown, or along a commercial corridor leading out of the central business district. Middle-class, working-class, and poor neighborhoods are arrayed concentrically around the core, with the poorest residents living farthest from the center.

Globalization has both continued the pattern of social polarization, while altering its form. New residential enclaves were built for and by transnational investors and visitors. In Tijuana, the valuable coastline just beyond the city offered comparatively inexpensive real estate for U.S. residents, either in the form of second homes, or permanent dwellings for retirees. Some 25,000 Americans reside in the coastal corridor between Tijuana and Ensenada, and that number is expected to grow, though the late 2000s recession has brought it to a complete halt.[7] Still, before the recession, global real estate projects were aiming to produce golf resorts, beachfront condo complexes and luxury marina housing enclaves for foreign residents. These high-paying land users routinely outbid Mexicans for coastal properties; the result is that the social ecology of the coastal strip is increasingly dominated by foreign interests.

And values from north of the border are sweeping south. One former border architect spoke of his frustration with people who, despite incredibly limited incomes, refused to live in houses that could be technically designed to fit their budgets:

> My clients don't want to live in a house designed with recycled metal or junk parts, even if it is excellently constructed. They want a California tract house, with a picture window and a garage. A lot of people can't afford to buy a house in the United States, but they buy the magazines, and then they find a photograph of a house they like. They bring it to the architect in Tijuana, and they say "I want a house like this." (Jorge Ozorno, qtd. in Herzog, *Aztec* 206)

Some worker housing has been dispersed around the *maquila* zones. But most migrants to Tijuana continue to live on the edges of the city, near or beyond the zone of *maquila* workers, in squatter communities of sub-standard housing, known locally as *colonias populares*. This class of marginal, disenfranchised urban poor may not ultimately benefit greatly from globalization, but they respond to its seductive pull. The struggle of the urban poor to survive in booming, globalizing cities constitutes a key debate underlying the globalization protest movements around the globe.

---

[7]   Mexican property law does not allow foreigners to own land; however, post-NAFTA legislation makes it possible for foreigners to lease land through a trust or *fideicomiso* arrangement for up to 60 years.

5.   A Return to the 19th Century?

> "Si el de Berlin cayó, el de Tijuana porqué no?"
> ["If the one in Berlin fell, why not the one in Tijuana?"]
> —graffiti on the international boundary fence
> at Tijuana-San Diego

For more than a century, the existence of Mexican border cities was defined by their link to the physical boundary. Their existence was schizophrenic in that they struggled to balance their economic ties to the United States with cultural loyalty toward their ethnic home—Mexico. The physical boundary—the wall, the fence—stood as a constant reminder of this double identity.

Today, in a post-9/11 world, globalization along the border raises new issues for transnational citizens living and working around it. Specifically, is the border's future going to continue to be defined by old symbols of exclusion—such as national security, sovereignty, defense against the threat of international terrorism—, or will the border region map out a way of life that transcends the 19th-century boundary?

This theme shapes an underlying tension embedded in the built environment of border cities, a tension that is manifest by the conflicted landscapes of the immediate boundary zone where the two nations meet. The most famous icon of traditional 'militarized boundaries' is the Berlin Wall. It conjures images of barbed wire, concrete barriers, and soldiers in watchtowers. Before its destruction, it had 66 miles of twelve-foot high concrete block, 35 miles of wire and mesh fencing, and over two hundred watchtowers.

The U.S.-Mexico border has its share of 'Berlin Wall'-like infrastructure: corrugated metal walls, made from recycled landing mats from the Persian Gulf War, wire fences, and 18-foot high concrete 'bollard' pilings topped with tilted metal mesh screens put up by the U.S. Army Corps of Engineers (cf. fig. 1).

Fig. 1: Concrete bollard fence along U.S.-Mexico border.
Note older fence in background. Photograph © Lawrence A. Herzog.

For more than a decade, landscapes along the Mexico-U.S. boundary have communicated messages of danger and conflict. The border has been defined as a war zone, a place controlled by national governments and their police forces. Signage on fences and along the line reinforces an underlying theme—that only the governments can decide who enters and who crosses. An example lies in the 1994 Operation Gatekeeper project, described by one official as an operation that would "restore the rule of law to the California-Baja California border."[8] This general theme of militarization along the border has remained as part of the landscape, always threatening to move to the forefront each time a crisis looms. The September 11, 2001 terrorist event in the U.S. had the immediate effect of resurrecting the policing, enforcement-oriented functions of the international border.

But this landscape is not sustainable. For one, it is challenged by the forces of global markets. Despite a recession in the 2000s, global capital has arrived here in the form of NAFTA and all its future possibility. Along the California-Mexico border, eight million inhabitants share an economy with the potential for 10 billion dollars in annual trade. Some have said that this corner of North America could be a great global boom area like Hong Kong. But there are also new dangers here—such as those involved in cross-border narcotic smuggling. Thus, the boundary remains well guarded, and sovereignty is alive and well. The wall will not disappear just yet.

6.   Finding Community in a Transnational Border Space

The creation of community spaces and places near international borders runs counter to nearly two centuries of history, where cities were organized as physical entities that lie territorially within the boundaries of one sovereign nation. This is no longer the case today. In a number of global boundary zones, most notably Western Europe and North America, we find community spaces that sprawl across international boundaries.[9]

Today, global actors explore ways to bring citizens across either side of the U.S.-Mexico boundary; in an ideal world, old differences would be set aside as urban neighbors become part of a common transnational living and working space. The building blocks of these new transnational communities lie in the social and physical linkages that connect settlements across the boundary. Such linkages include inter-

---

[8]   Alan D. Bersin, U.S. Attorney, San Diego, qtd. in Nevins 159.

[9]   Important European transfrontier urban agglomerations, with populations ranging between 300,000 and one million inhabitants, include Basel-Mulhouse-Freiburg (Swiss-French-German border), Maastricht-Aachen-Liège (Dutch-German-Belgian border), the Geneva metropolitan area (Swiss-French border) and the Strasbourg metropolitan area (French-German border). In North America, one finds transfrontier urban regions housing between 250,000 and four million people along the Canadian-U.S. border at Vancouver-Victoria-Seattle, Detroit-Windsor and Toronto-Hamilton-Buffalo, and on the Mexico-U.S. border at Tijuana-San Diego, Ciudad Juarez-El Paso, Mexicali-Calexico/El Centro, Nuevo Laredo-Laredo, Reynosa-McAllen and Matamoros-Brownsville.

national commuters, transnational consumers, global factories, cross-border land and housing markets and transnational architecture.

Nearly 300,000 workers legally travel across the border, from the Mexican to the U.S. side of a transfrontier metropolis, to work in the United States on a daily or weekly basis. Countless thousands of others cross illegally with a border resident card (which permits Mexican border residents to cross into the U.S. for non-work purposes, but which is frequently used illegally to get to work). Billions of dollars in cross-border commercial transactions take place annually. Several hundred million border crossings also occur each year, primarily between the partners that form the trans-national metropolis. Consumers constitute the most active group of legal border crossers and are perhaps the primary population that ties together the two sides of the U.S.-Mexico transfrontier metropolis. Collectively they form a complex regional network of flows north and south across the border. The existence of this volume of flows is leading to the emergence of what we might term 'transnational citizens,' people who exist on both sides of the border.

Of course, transnational citizenship remains a work in progress. Cross-border drug smuggling and associated violence, as well as the threat of terrorism, continues to cast a shadow over any long-term transformation of the U.S.-Mexico border as a more socially, culturally and economically integrated place.

In a globalizing world, the border zone's best prospect for the future may be to reinvent itself as more than just a 'pass through' space. It could become a connector for the regional economy, and even an important destination in its own right. Thousands of transnational citizens utilize this space each day. Trade and tourism flourish here.

This zone is ripe for an 'invented connection' that links people and begins to build a truly cross-border community. Initial attempts at inventing connections have often come from global investors or entrepreneurs. Before the recession of the late 2000s, large-scale privately funded development projects at boundary crossings were in various stages of completion along the entire two-thousand-mile boundary. These projects envisioned a number of different types of developments, mostly mixed-use, and medium-density. Many were private development spaces, with partnerships maintained with relevant public border-monitoring agencies.

On the San Diego-Tijuana border, adjacent to the San Ysidro crossing, a private firm purchased large tracts of land, and, with the Redevelopment Authority of the City of San Diego government, put together a new, large-scale project called "Las Americas." Their initial idea was to create a complex of mixed uses, a public plaza, a landmark pedestrian bridge linked to a new pedestrian crossing, a World Trade Center, a market facility, and links to the existing trolley, as well as across the border to Revolution Ave (cf. LandGrant Development). The investment plan imagined a new future for Mexico's boundary—an integration of pedestrian walkways, gardens, and plazas with private retail, entertainment, hotel and office buildings. What was novel about this vision is its recognition of the boundary itself as a space of community life rather than a space of instability, conflict, and smuggling.

This vision sought to transform the boundary zone at Tijuana/San Ysidro into a destination where more tourists and local residents would simply come to the border, and not necessarily even cross it. To the north, San Ysidro and the surrounding "South Bay" region would become a surrogate for a 'Mexican'/border cultural experience, where consumers would feel comfortable coming to the border without having to deal with the perceived inconveniences of crossing into Tijuana. If pedestrian bridges and other new infrastructure make it easier to cross back and forth into Tijuana, the invented 'border urban village' would benefit the economies of both sides. However, this vision has not yet been realized. The original developer did not stay long; the project was sold to another investor. Many of the most visionary elements of the project have not been built—to date, it is simply a shopping mall with a lot of lost intentions.

7. Conclusion

In this essay, I have sought to explore the changing place identity of the U.S.-Mexico border. I have argued that this region offers a metaphor for the process of ethnic and cultural integration, disintegration, and reintegration that may be occurring in North America. The border zone offers some interesting lessons about the dynamics of U.S. and Mexican cultural mixing in a globalizing era.

One idea that has been floated along the border is the theme of cultural hybridity, the notion that the border creates an unusual, locally based form of integration. I would argue that the hybridity of the U.S.-Mexico border is one based on different forms of creative expression, both those that speak to the region's changing identity, and those that speak to inequity and struggle. These creative, hybrid forms were significantly interrupted by eight years of an American political approach (the Bush presidency, 2000-2008) to the boundary in which the old divisions and defensive notions of 19th-century borders were resurrected, and the border was reconstituted as a place of danger and fear.

But, in the end, that legacy cannot hold. Markets cross the border, people cross, and creative flows cross, and it is this idea of globalization that has the strongest future. This represents the new foreign policy outlook of the Obama presidency in the U.S. A new era of transnational cooperation was publicly announced by the presidents of the U.S. and Mexico in the spring of 2009.

Some years ago, in the border city of Tijuana, there was a call for artists and architects to design a new symbol of the city's future, which had, for a long time, been associated with negative images—prostitution, gambling, drug smuggling, and illegality. Many residents complained that the money might be better spent on infrastructure badly needed. But city leaders argued the image of the city was vital to its future, and this vision won out. In the end, an arch was constructed—and was seen as a symbol of reaching out, the endless curve that stretched toward the north and toward the west, the two futures of Mexico in a global era (cf. fig. 2).

Fig. 2: Arch in Tijuana symbolizes future of U.S.-Mexico border region.
Photograph © Lawrence A. Herzog.

Border identity may be encapsulated by the story of this arching ellipse, which transcends the moment and reaches toward the sky and toward the future, one of unity across borders in a global age. But, of course, the story does not exactly end there. Border place identity, like the larger discourse of globalization, is a dance between two realities, often contradictory—one old (the defended borders, walls, fences, and separated nation states), the other new (the end of walls and a new era of transnational identity and cross-border societies), one modern, the other post-modern, one planned, the other spontaneous, one rich, the other poor.

This is a useful point to conclude upon. U.S.-Mexico border cultural identity symbolizes a slice of the future in globalization discourse—a struggle with the virtues of transcending borders, while, at the same time, forces that seek to obliterate that project, and return to a world of national insularity, rigid boundaries, segregated spaces, and boxed-in thinking.

Works Cited

Dear, Michael, and Gustavo Leclerc, eds. *Postborder City: Cultural Spaces of Bajalta California*. New York and London: Routledge, 2003.

Herzog, Lawrence A. *Where North Meets South: Cities, Space, and Politics on the United States-Mexico Border*. Austin: U of Texas P/CMAS, 1990.

————. *From Aztec to High Tech: Architecture and Landscape across the Mexico-United States Border*. Baltimore: Johns Hopkins UP, 1999.

Jackson, John B. "Other-Directed Houses." *Landscapes: The Selected Writings of J.B. Jackson*. Ed. Ervin H. Zube. Amherst: U of Massachusetts P, 1970. 55-72.

LandGrant Development. *International Gateway of the Americas*. Project Proposal. San Diego, 1997.

Lummis, Charles. *The Land of Poco Tiempo*. New York: Charles Scribner & Sons, 1925.

Nevins, Joseph. *Operation Gatekeeper and Beyond*. New York: Routledge, 2010.

Peña, Devon G. *The Terror of the Machine: Technology, Work, Gender, and Ecology on the U.S.-Mexico Border*. Austin: CMAS Books/U of Texas P, 1997.

Sklair, Leslie. *Sociology of the Global System*. Baltimore: Johns Hopkins UP, 1991.

Urry, John. *The Tourist Gaze*. London: Sage, 1990.

Filmography

Factory of Dreams. Dir. Paul Espinosa. KPBS-TV, 1999.

Contributors

Cerstin Bauer-Funke is Professor of French and Spanish literature and culture at the University of Duisburg-Essen. She has published and co-edited numerous books and articles on French, Spanish, and Mexican literature from the 17th to the 20th century. Most recently, she has published articles on Sor Juana Inés de la Cruz, Juan José Arreola, Ignacio Padilla, Esther Tusquets, Yasmina Reza, and Frédéric Beigbeder. Her latest monographs are *Spanische Literatur des 20. Jahrhunderts* [*Spanish Literature of the 20th Century*], 2006, and *Die 'Generación Realista': Studien zur Poetik des Oppositionstheaters während der Franco-Diktatur* [*The 'Generación Realista': Studies on the Poetics of the Theater of the Opposition during Franco's Dictatorship*], 2007.

Paulo Barrera Rivera studied at the Institute for Latin-American Studies at Heredia University. He received his doctorate in Social Sciences and Religion from the Methodist University of São Paulo for his thesis *Tradição, transmissão e emoção religiosa: Sociologia do Protestantismo Contemporâneo na América Latina* (Olho d'Água, 2001). During his doctoral studies (1997-1998) he did research at the École des Hautes Études en Sciences Sociales in Paris. His post-doctoral research was on *Reinventing Traditions in Brazilian Protestantism* (USP, 2005). He is Professor of Social Sciences and Religion at the Methodist University of São Paulo. His research interests include Protestantism and Pentecostalism in Latin America, religion, and secularization. More specifically, he works on contemporary problems linking religions and urban periphery. He is co-editor of *Estudos de religião* and director of the Research Group *Religion and Periphery in Latin America (REPAL)*.

Axel Borsdorf is a geographer and Full Professor at the University of Innsbruck and Head of the Institute for Mountain Research of the Austrian Academy of Science, of which he is a full member. He is Vice President of the Austrian Institute for Latin America and has been visiting professor in Santiago de Chile (PUC und UdCh), Tamaulipas/Mexico, Bangkok, Eugene/Oregon and Berne. He is the author of numerous books and journal publications on Latin America.

Martin Butler is Junior Professor of American Literature and Culture at Carl von Ossietzky University in Oldenburg. His main areas of research include the study of popular culture, particularly focusing on (the history of) political songs and on urban cultures. His publications include *Voices of the Down and Out: The Dust Bowl Migration and the Great Depression in the Songs of Woody Guthrie* (Heidelberg: Winter, 2007), a volume on protest songs (*Da habt Ihr es, das Argument der Straße: Kulturwissenschaftliche Studien zum politischen Lied*, co-ed., Trier: WVT, 2007), *Hybrid Americas: Contacts, Contrasts and Confluences in New World Literatures and Cultures* (co-ed., Münster and Tempe: LIT and Bilingual P, 2008) and *Sound Fabrics: Studies on the Intermedial and Institutional Dimensions of Popular Music* (co-ed., Trier: WVT, 2009).

Alexandra Ganser holds an MA in English and American Studies and History from the University of Vienna and a PhD in American Studies from the University of Erlangen-Nuremberg, where she works as an Assistant Professor of American literary and cultural studies. Her dissertation has been published as *Roads of Her Own: Gendered Space and Mobility in American Women's Road Narratives, 1970-2000* with Rodopi (2009). She is a Fulbright Alumna (2003-04) and has co-edited a volume on gender and popular culture (*Screening Gender: Geschlechterszenarien im gegenwärtigen US-amerikanischen Film und Fernsehen*, 2007, with Heike Paul). Her current book project examines the textual representations of piracy and is tentatively titled *The Transatlantic Spectacle of Piracy: Discourses of Crisis and Legitimacy from the Late 17th Century to the Civil War*. In the context of this project, she has been Christoph-Daniel-Ebeling fellow at the American Antiquarian Society (2009) and European Fellow 2009-10 at the Bruce Centre for American Studies, Keele University, Great Britain.

Aloisia Gómez Segovia has a degree in Theoretical Applied Geography from the University of Vienna, where she focused on urban geography, cartography, and geomorphology. She wrote her diploma thesis on *Peruvian Immigration to Santiago de Chile*. In 2009 she spent six months at the Anton Melik Geographical Institute in Ljubljana, the scientific research center of the Slovenian Academy of Science and Art. She is currently on leave.

Jens Martin Gurr is Professor of British and Anglophone Literature and Culture at the University of Duisburg-Essen. He studied English and German at the University of Mannheim and received his doctorate from the University of Duisburg for his thesis *Tristram Shandy and the Dialectic of Enlightenment* (Heidelberg: Winter, 1999). His post-doctoral thesis *The Human Soul as Battleground: Variations on Dualism and the Self in English Literature* was published in 2003 (Heidelberg: Winter). His research interests include urban cultural studies, contemporary Anglophone fiction, literary and cultural theory, the politics of identity in the Americas, film and film theory, literary and cultural history, 18th-century British literature and British Romanticism. He is director of "Urban Systems," one of the main research areas of the University of Duisburg-Essen.

Lawrence A. Herzog is Professor and Chair of the Graduate Program in City Planning, School of Public Affairs, San Diego State University, San Diego, California. He specializes in urban/environmental design and planning and comparative urbanization in the Mexico-United States border region, as well as Latin America. He has written or edited seven books, including *Global Crossroads: Planning and Infrastructure for the California-Baja California Border Region* (Trans-border Institute, 2009); *Return to the Center: Culture, Public Space and City Building in a Global Age* (University of Texas Press, 2006); *From Aztec to High Tech* (Johns Hopkins University Press, 1999); and *Where North Meets South* (CMAS/University of Texas Press, 1990). He has been a Fulbright Scholar in Peru and the U.K., as well as urban/regional planning consultant to the U.S. Agency for International Development (in Peru and Bolivia), the U.S. Embassy (Mexico City), and other agencies, and a visiting scholar/professor at the Autonomous University of Madrid, Spain (Department of Geography); the National University of Engineering, Peru (Lima Planning Institute); the National Autonomous University of Mexico, Mexico City (School of Architecture); the Tec de Monterrey (ITESM, School of Architecture); and the Federal University of Rio de Janeiro (UFRJ, School of Architecture and Urbanism).

Karin Höpker is Assistant Professor of North American Studies at Friedrich-Alexander University Erlangen-Nuremberg, Germany. Her book *No Maps for These Territories: Cities, Spaces, and Archaeologies of the Future in William Gibson* is forthcoming with Rodopi in 2011. She is currently working on a project on risk, reason, and fiction in 19th-century American literature.

Walter Alejandro Imilan studied Social Anthropology at Universidad de Chile and completed a Master's degree in Urban Studies in Santiago de Chile. He wrote his doctoral thesis at the Habitat Unit of Technische Universität Berlin on urban ethnification in Latin America with a focus on Mapuche society. Since 2010 he has been working at the Instituto de la Vivienda (INVI) of Universidad de Chile and the Department of Anthropology at Universidad Alberto Hurtado, both in Santiago, focusing on urban identity-building processes and social exclusion. He has recently published *Latein-amerikanische Städte im Wandel: Zwischen lokaler Stadtgesellschaft und globalem Einfluss* (2011, edited with Paola Alfaro d'Aléncon and Lina María Sánchez) and *Warriache—Urban Indigenous: Mapuche Migration and Ethnicity in Santiago de Chile* (2010).

Olaf Kaltmeier is Junior Professor of Transnational History of the Americas at Bielefeld University, Germany. He is co-organizer of the Research Group "E Pluribus Unum? Ethnic Identities in Transnational Integration Processes in the Americas" at the Center for Interdisciplinary Research, where he coordinated the working phase on urban studies. He has recently published *Los Andes en movimiento: Identidad y poder en el nuevo paisaje político* (2009, with Pablo Ospina and Christian Büschges) and *Selling EthniCity: Urban Cultural Politics in the Americas* (2011).

Rüdiger Kunow is Full Professor and Chair of the American Studies program at Potsdam University, Germany. He has taught at the Universities of Würzburg, Erlangen-Nuremberg, Freiburg, Hanover, and Magdeburg. Furthermore, he was a Research Fellow at the University of California, Santa Cruz and Visiting Professor at the University of Texas at Austin, the State University of New Mexico, Albuquerque, and the State University of New York at Albany. Until very recently, he served as Director and Co-ordinator of the interdisciplinary research project and Graduate School "Cultures in/of Mobility" at Potsdam University. His major research interests include cultural constructions of illness and ageing, transnational American Studies, and the South Asian diaspora in the U.S. He is editor, with Wilfried Raussert, of *Cultural Memory and Multiple Identities* (2008), with Alfred Hornung, of *Representation and Decoration in a Postmodern Age* (2007), with Renate Brosch, of *Transgressions: Cultural Interventions in the Global Manifold* (2005), and with Liselotte Glage, of *Decolonizing Pen: Cultural Diversity and the Transnational Imaginary in Rushdie's Fiction* (2001), and author of *Das Klischee: Reproduzierte Wirklichkeiten in der englischen und amerikanischen Literatur* (1994). Until 2008 he held the position of the President of the German Association for American Studies.

Eva Marsch studied English and German language and literature at the University of Duisburg-Essen and at the University of Limerick, Ireland. She wrote her final thesis (Staatsarbeit) on *Conceptualizing Street Art as Critical Meta-Discourse and Imaginative Counter-Discourse in Urban Environments* in 2009. She is currently working on a PhD thesis on contemporary German literature and teaches in the German Department of the University of Duisburg-Essen.

Christoph Marx studied History and Musicology at the University of Freiburg, where he received his doctorate in history in 1987. His 1996 habilitation thesis was published in an English translation in 2008 as *Oxwagon Sentinel: Radical Afrikaner Nationalism and the History of the Ossewabrandwag* (Münster/Pretoria: LIT/Unisa Press 2008). He has taught at the universities of Freiburg, Basel, and Zurich. Since 2002, he has been Professor of Extra-European History at the University of Duisburg-Essen. His books include *Geschichte Afrikas: Von 1800 bis zur Gegenwart* (Paderborn: Schöningh UTB 2004) and *Pelze, Gold und Weihwasser: Handel und Mission in Afrika und Amerika* (Darmstadt: Primusverlag 2008). His research interests include the history of apartheid in South Africa, comparative history of the frontier, settler colonies and racism as well as the Indian and Chinese diaspora in South Africa.

Sebastian Nestler is assistant to Rainer Winter at the Department of Media and Communication at Klagenfurt University, Austria. His work focuses on cultural and media studies as well as critical media pedagogy. Here, he uses film analysis as a method of social analysis. This approach is also the subject of his dissertation project, which will demonstrate the importance of Michel Foucault's and Judith Butler's writings to film analysis as diagnostic critique.

Yvonne Riaño studied Architecture at Javeriana University, Colombia and Environmental Protection and Urban and Regional Planning at the Swiss Federal Institutes of Technology in Lausanne (EPFL) and Zurich (ETH), Switzerland. She received her PhD in 1996 from the University of Ottawa, Canada for her thesis on *The Geography of Social Networks in Popular Barrios of Quito: Creating and Maintaining Spaces of Social Participation.* She is currently a Senior Lecturer at the Department of Geography of the University of Berne and a Research Project Leader at the University of Neuchâtel

(MAPS). Her research interests include governance in Latin American cities, Latin American migration to Europe, transnational social networks, and social inequality. Currently she is leading a research project on how migrants living in Switzerland create transnational social spaces between Colombian, Ecuadorian, Spanish, and Swiss cities through their everyday social, economic, and cultural exchanges with members of their cross-border networks. Yvonne Riaño has published extensively in edited books and in international journals such as *Environment and Planning A, International Journal of Migration and Integration*, and *Nouvelles Questions Féministes*.

Marc Simon Rodriguez is Assistant Professor of History, Law, and American Studies at the University of Notre Dame, where he is also a fellow of the Institute for Latino Studies. He is the founder of the Newberry Seminar on Latino and Borderlands Studies based in Chicago, and is the author of *Tejano Diaspora: Mexican Americanism and Ethnic Politics in Texas and Wisconsin* (Chapel Hill: University of North Carolina Press, 2011) and editor of *Repositioning North American Migration History* (2004) as well as *Migration and History* (2007; co-edited with Anthony Grafton), both published by the University of Rochester Press. He is currently writing a history of the Chicano Movement for Routledge Press.

Juliana Ströbele-Gregor is a cultural and social anthropologist and an educationalist. She received her doctorate from the Free University of Berlin for her thesis *Dialektik der Gegenaufklärung: Zur Problematik fundamentalistischer und evangelikaler Missionierung bei den urbanen Aymara in La Paz*. Having taught at the Latin American Institute, Free University Berlin, at the universities of Frankfurt/Main, Costa Rica, and Cuenca, Ecuador and forming part of the research group *E Pluribus Unum? Ethnic Identities in Transnational Integration Processes in the Americas* at Bielefeld University, she is now an Associated Researcher at the Latin American Institute of the Free University Berlin. She currently participates in the international research program "desigualdades net" as a fellow at the Ibero-American Institute Berlin, working on inequalities and lithium mining in Bolivia. Her research interests include indigenous movements and identity politics; human rights, indigenous law, citizenship, and gender; intercultural education; religious movements, especially evangelical fundamentalism. Her regional focus is Latin America, mainly the Andean Region and Guatemala.

Rainer Winter is Professor of Media and Cultural Theory, Media and Cultural Studies at the Department of Media and Communication at Klagenfurt University, Austria. His works include research on film and television audiences as well as theoretical contributions on cultural studies' sociological and philosophical aspects. Recently, he has been making notable efforts in connecting the European and American tradition of cultural studies with cultural studies in China, where some of his work has been translated into Chinese, too.